Witness to Barbarism

Liberation at Dachau, April 28–29, 1945.

Witness to Barbarism

Horace R. Hansen

Thousand Pinetree Press • St. Paul • 2002

On the front cover and frontispiece: Three from a series of photos taken upon the liberation at Dachau, April 28–29, 1945.

Illustration credits: The author's personal photographs: pp. 6, 18, 21, 42, 44–45, 58, 61–63, 65–66, 68–70, 72, 74, 78, 81 right, 82, 85, 89–90, 110, 113–15, 117, 120, 138, 155–56, 178, 190, 210, 264, 269, 272 top and middle, 300, 302, 316, 325, and 335.

Other illustrations are from the personal collection of the author, whose attempts to gain permissions were mostly frustrated by the demise of organizations or lack of information about which organizations or individuals owned the rights, if any. Because of the time passed since their origination, such photos most likely are now in the public domain. Permissions were obtained from those credited and still in existence.

The author's collection includes postcards (pp. 25, 80, 81 left, 126, 292 bottom); personal and U.S. Army documents (pp. 49, 57, 196, 306); clippings (pp. 76, 87–88, 93–94, 96, 98, 180 top, 196, 198, 216, 272 bottom, 290, 306); SS photos (pp. 151, 236, 241, 322–23); photos courtesy of the Seventh Army, 45th Division Signal Corps (cover, frontispiece, and pp. 168, 171–72, 177, 244, 247–48, 331–32); materials obtained from Hitler's military-conference recorders (pp. 100, 103, 105); miscellaneous images (pp. 63, 83, 116, 185, 271); National Archives (p. 30). Jean Hansen Doth took the photos of artifacts from her father's collection (pp. 180 bottom, 329).

The following images of key World War II figures, apparently in the public domain, are available on World War II internet sites: pp. 38, 131, 158–59, 163, 219–20, 226, 229, 234, 239, 250, 259, 274, 282, 287, 292 top, 296–97.

Cover design: Gail Tromburg, St. Paul
Map of author's route: Patricia Isaacs, Parrot Graphics, Stillwater
Editing, text design, production: Ellen Green, E. B. Green Editorial, St. Paul
Indexing: Patricia Green, Homer, Alaska
Printing & Binding: Sexton Printing and Muscle Bound Bindery

Contents

Foreword

My father, Horace R. Hansen, dedicated many years to preparing the manuscript for this book before his death in 1995. His work as chief prosecuting attorney at the trial for Nazi war crimes at the Dachau prison camp, Germany, and his relationship with Hitler's chief stenographers, or recorders, provide its solid foundation. Other primary sources include his letters home and photos taken as he moved through Europe with U.S. replacement troops during World War II. Horace used his legal expertise to present this firsthand view of his experience of crimes against Jews, gypsies, political and military prisoners, and others who did not fit the Nazis idea of a master race.

Horace hoped to publish his story so that it would not be forgotten. This book is the culmination of his family and editor's work to fulfill that wish.

—Jean Hansen Doth, 2002

Acknowledgments

M any persons provided valuable help in the making of this book. I owe more than I can ever repay to Ludwig Krieger, Ewald Reynitz, Hans Jonuschat, Heinz Buchholz, and Karl Thoet, the recorders of Hitler's military-situation conferences who shared with me their personal knowledge of Hitler when they served on my staff as translators during the trials at Dachau. Ewald Reynitz confirmed and added to that information during my two visits with him in Germany in 1984 and 1985.

George R. Allen, the counterintelligence agent of the 101st Airborne Division who cleared the recorders at Berchtesgaden, Germany, in May 1945 (and now a rare book dealer in Philadelphia), shared much information by letter and telephone and critiqued my manuscript with great skill. A man who speaks excellent German, he provided the statement he took from Col. Erick Kempka, special adjutant to Hitler, telling of Hitler's last days in Berlin. Allen also wrote the foreword to Felix Gilbert's book *Hitler Directs His War* (New York: Award Books, 1950, and subsequent reprints) based on the unburned records of Hitler's war conferences (about 1 percent of the total) found by Allen at Hintersee, Bavaria, after the war. While Gilbert extensively edited the translations of these papers, Ewald Reynitz assured me his book is a fair representation of Hitler's conferences.

Col. William D. Denson, chief trial judge advocate for the prosecution of the Dachau concentration-camp case, gave generously of his time for an interview in his New York law office in 1984.

The National Archives in Washington, D.C., gave me leads to the whereabouts of the English transcripts of interrogation of the recorders and their photographs, and of the half-burned documents of Hitler's minutes. This eventually led me to the photo of Heinz Buchholz. The members of Writers Unlimited, a 26-year-old writers' club to which I have belonged more than three years, and especially its spokesperson, Jean Barnum, who has taught creative writing at the college level for more than 30 years, gave me excellent critiques, enabling me to change the style of my writing.

Charles Knox, my neighbor, friend, and author of three published works, persistently encouraged me to write this one. Ellen B. Green, a free-lance editor in St. Paul, helped prepare my manuscript for publication [and later designed the text]. We edited and repunctuated my notes and recorded conversations to minimize repetition and increase clarity while maintaining their tone and content.

My loving wife, Ruth, and daughter Jean Hansen Doth spent many hours at the computer, typing my manuscript. [Daughter Gail Tromburg later designed the cover.] Along with my son, John Christian Hansen, they supported me in my research and writing in ways beyond counting.

—Horace R. Hansen, 1995

Introduction

Look at the universe, the planets and stars millions of light years away, moving in exact orbits. What is man compared to that? Nothing but a louse . . . You can smash it.

—Adolf Hitler, at a wartime military conference

Fifty years after Hitler lost his bid to rule the world, we struggle to understand his contempt for all human life, even for his own people. That he could run two wars at once—for the conquest of territory and the genocide of the Jews—without noticing that the efforts mutually limited each other—is difficult to fathom. But he gave plenty of warning about his intent. In his early writing and on an almost daily basis at his wartime conferences, he revealed deep-seated nihilism in speeches like the one above, again and again. No wonder the military losses (his own and others'), the concentration camp deaths, and the extermination of millions of Jews, Gypsies, Communists, intellectuals, homosexuals, labor leaders, and others didn't bother him.

While we would prefer to forget about the suffering inflicted by this man and his deputies, we cannot. For even in the face of international memory—made vivid through the opening of the Holocaust

Museum in Washington, D.C., the debut of Steven Spielberg's film *Schindler's List,* and the 50th anniversary of the end of World War II—Neo-Nazis and others claim the Holocaust never occurred.

Now we are beginning to hear, on a grand scale, the stories of the thousands, representing silenced millions more, who suffered in the face of Hitler's insanity. Finally, many who had been silent have decided they must give testimony before it is too late. Finally, in Willmar, Minnesota, for example, eyewitnesses gather at the request of history teacher William F. Borth for "A Night of Remembrance" before an audience packed into a local auditorium.

Here Dachau slave laborer Monsignor Stanislaus Grabrowski says, "What is hunger? It's not appetite. Hunger you feel with every fiber of your mind and body. There is such an emptiness. It is difficult to think. We prayed that our skin and bones would be saved and that somehow we would be filled in.

"There is no way to really describe it. If you ever try to talk to a blind person about colors describing the beauty of nature, the blind person would not understand because he never saw it. It was a daily struggle to survive and a daily danger of being killed. There were over 2,000 priests taken to Dachau. When the Americans liberated us, we were 860."

And concentration-camp prisoner Fred Baron describes his journey by train to Auschwitz: "The guards drove us with clubs, dogs, and weapons until each car was filled to capacity—then they closed the sliding doors. I found myself in pitch black darkness . . . There was no food, no water, and, worst, no sanitary facilities . . . It took us several hours before we devised a method whereby half of us in the car would keep standing while the other half would squat in each other's lap, to be able to rest our bones. The trip took us three days and three nights. There were men, women, old and young, and children. In our car, people died and went insane."

There are others here as elsewhere: William Landgren, formerly a U.S. Infantry company commander, describes the bodies piled by the crematory at Dachau when the American troops liberated the camp in April 1945. I am here, too, to recount discoveries made during the prosecution of Nazi war criminals at the Dachau trials and during my interviews with five of the stenographers who recorded Hitler's military conferences.

But I realize that *saying* what I know is not enough. This evening's program is a response to hate mail and newsletters denying the Holocaust, demanding the resignation of Bill Borth, and threatening his family because he teaches high-school seniors a course (in its 12th year as I write this) on Hitler's quest for territory and extermination of the Jews. Without our stories—told again and again—and without an easily accessible record of the things we have seen and heard, our young people will find it too easy to believe the disbelievers and rest content that such evil could never happen anywhere, much less here. (See appendix.)

Too often we have been content to let others do our thinking, to be uninvolved in controversy. Such complacency—evidenced by poor voting records, for example—could leave us ripe for a government and Holocaust like Hitler's. Leading a flock of sheep is, after all, easier than controlling a lot of strays. Without knowledge of the past, ourselves, and human nature, and with economic depression, street riots, and a strong president, we could permit a dictatorship by default. (See appendix.)

And so I bear witness along with others now gone, who have told their stories to me. A bit of background seems in order: Born Horace Russell Hansen on February 20, 1910, I am the son of Richard and Dagny Elizabeth Hammer Hansen of St. Paul, Minnesota. My father was a tailor, my mother a homemaker, and I the first of their four children. I grew up on Marshall Avenue, attending Richard Gordon School and Central High School.

After preparatory classes at the University of Minnesota, I entered the St. Paul College of Law (William Mitchell College of Law) in the fall that the Great Depression started with a crash—1929. Four years later, just after I was admitted to the bar, a family friend who was head of the Minnesota Industrial Commission, called me:

"How would you like to be an attorney in the Workers' Compensation Division? It pays $175 a month."

"Wow," I thought. "Big bucks in hard times!"

Representing injured workers before a referee became my primary task, and I soon found the work to require knowledge of more than the law. So I began to take courses in anatomy and physiology at the University of Minnesota School of Medicine—two evening hours twice a week for two years. What I learned took the mystique out of doctors' testimony and gave me an edge in court.

During that time, I also represented the State of Minnesota in U.S. District Court in plans for reorganization of insolvent insurance companies so that workers compensation awards (after trial) would be fully paid. My contention, that the awards should be treated as unpaid wages entitled to priority, prevailed.

In 1936, I joined the staff of the Office of the Ramsey County Attorney, for which I handled arraignments and tried felony jury cases.

After six years in that office and shortly after Japan attacked the United States at Pearl Harbor, I decided to join the army.

After personal training to the position of a second lieutenant, I trained others in Alabama and Mississippi, then was sent to England in May 1944. I traveled with the army across northern Europe—France, Belgium, Holland, and Germany—as the Allied forces defeated Germany, sending home monthly records of what I saw.

Assigned to war-crimes investigation in January 1945, I arrived at the Dachau concentration camp on October 1, 1945, and was named chief prosecutor (chief of staff) at the trial facilities there. Mine was the decision as to which of 32,000 camp administrators and workers should stand trial for war crimes. In addition to gathering pretrial evidence, I attended and heard most of the testimony at the trials. Again, I took copious notes; these have been verified by the official record of the trials, presented in part in the latter portion of this volume.

On my staff of 65 at Dachau were five of the eight recorders who took down verbatim Hitler's military-situation conferences. Unable to reach their families in Berlin because of Russian advances at the end of the war, they offered to act as translators at war-crimes trials. During off-hours I questioned these highly educated men (three had doctorates), recording their answers in speedwriting. The five non-Nazi recorders gave me insight into and information (some of it never reported elsewhere) about how Hitler rose to power, established dictatorship, and directed his war.

My story comprises an eyewitness report (including personal photos) of my journey across Europe with the liberating forces, the testimony of trial witnesses heard firsthand, and personal interviews with intimate observers of Hitler in action. I tell it as here and now.

Clockwise from top right: The author, Horace R. Hansen, upon applying for officer's training in fall 1942; training troops at Camp Van Dorn, Mississippi, a year later; and on leave in St. Paul, before going overseas in May 1944.

Chapter 1

Single, 32, and subject to the draft, I decide to enlist in the Volunteer Officers' Training Corps at Fort Snelling in Minneapolis. There I'm ushered into a room full of civilian men. When my turn comes, I'm referred to a sergeant major.

"What branch of the service are you thinking about?"

"I've been practicing law for more than ten years, the last six as a felony prosecutor. I think the Judge Advocate General's Department [JAGD] should be right for me."

"You can't serve an injunction on Hitler." He turns in his swivel chair and types out a form. "I'm sending you to Camp Roberts in California. You'll be in basic training in the infantry."

He doesn't like lawyers. Disappointed, I swallow hard and take the paper. At Camp Roberts, I deliberately stand at the front of a squad of 12 GIs (literally "government issue," the common name for privates) and do everything I can to show that I want to get ahead. At the end of boot camp, a few of us who have completed officers' training make corporal. Along with the mayor of Carmel, California, and an opera singer from Philadelphia, I am by April 1943 on a train to Georgia.

Fort Benning is even tougher than Camp Roberts, but I work hard at everything and make second lieutenant at the end of the three-month course. My first assignment is to train rookies in Alabama and Mississippi—for eight months. Then the army sends me to England.

Spring/Summer1944

On June 6, D-Day, the Allied invasion of France is in progress. I have been sitting in a tent in a cow pasture near Yeovil, England, for almost a month. Finally, a sergeant tells me, "The colonel wants to see you at three o'clock sharp."

The colonel has my personnel file in front of him. "Hansen, I see that you are 34 years of age and have six years of experience as a felony prosecutor. You are too old to lead men 14 years younger on the front lines. I'll recommend that you be assigned to the JAGD. Meanwhile, I'm sending you to France to serve in a replacement company."

So, at 2:00 A.M. on July 7, I am suddenly awakened and told to get ready for inspection in an hour. We ride on trucks to Southampton, then on a "tugboat" across the English Channel. After a rough trip, we transfer to a landing craft, then disembark at Utah Beach, an American invasion site in Normandy. A temporary pier has been damaged by German artillery, so we wade in about 200 feet.

The beach is a mess of half-sunken ships and barges, about 75 of them, the aftermath of D-Day, during which nine of every ten

Allied troops were killed or injured. No wonder—the flat landing beach extends 300 feet to an almost sheer cliff that was covered by German artillery and machine guns. Bomb craters, barbed wire, smashed life preservers, and equipment piled in makeshift heaps litter the beach. At the top of the cliff are hastily dug mass graves.

––––––––––––

On D-Day plus 31, I assemble my 20 men, some rookies, and others just out of the hospital, including officers of all ranks. In a column of twos, we march inland with others down a trail marked by American mine markers. The first casualty I see is a fresh one—a soldier walked off the marked path to urinate and stepped on a bounding-type mine. It exploded about waist high, killing him and injuring 14 others. Nauseated, I look away.

We pass through two small villages. The natives who bother to look our way seem tired; a few give faint smiles and halfhearted "V" signs. No one looks enthusiastic. I can't blame them—they are watching just another section of the big parade, and why should they think we can win? All are ragged, and most wear wooden shoes. They seem well nourished, but this is farming country. I wonder about their poor clothing.

Our first bivouac area, near Sainte-Mère-Église, leaves much to be desired, and when a heavy tank outfit moves into the field, we move our troops out in trucks to another one. From there we move south, passing through several villages and two larger towns, all severely damaged. The Germans are still close to one of the towns near Carentan, where a major battle has occurred. As our convoy reaches the town, we hear two terrific explosions behind us. I learn later that the Germans are trying to knock out the bridge there.

As we wait near the rear of the front line to replace the battle casualties of the 29th Division, I talk with wounded officers and men who return every day from the front. They say it's impossible to crawl through the terrain here. At the edge of each two-acre field is a ditch about a yard deep and a yard wide. A pileup of dirt six feet wide—overgrown with thorny brush, trees, vines, and weeds—separates the ditch for one field from the ditch for another, forming what is called a hedgerow. Each hedgerow provides a drainage ditch, an effective fence, and a permanent land boundary. But the arrangement also gives an enemy standing on one side of the hedgerow an excellent camouflaged view—he can see us, but we can't see him.

The Germans burrow themselves into the hedgerows in L-shaped foxholes, below the root system. They have machine-gun emplacements concealed in the corners, where there is a good field of fire. We need artillery to blast them out. They also string land-mine trip wires through the hedgerows in this perfect setup for defense. Later, American tanks with long, two-inch steel rods on either side will poke holes through the hedgerows, so sticks of dynamite can blast large holes, permitting tanks to get through. But this ingenious plan is too late to do much good. Given the landing site and the hedgerows, I think Gen. Dwight Eisenhower picked a poor spot for the invasion.

(Four decades later we learn of an even more ill-conceived secret, pre-D-Day, test invasion on April 27, 1944, on the southern coast of Devon. Two German torpedo boats sank two unarmed landing barges, killing at least 749 Americans. Some shot at each other. Misinstructed by inexperienced officers, many drowned in life jackets worn about the waist. The families learned of this 43 months later.)

Today is Bastille Day, July 14, commemorating the French people's victory over tyranny in 1789 and similar to our Fourth of July. The chaplain scrapes up a band and invites the natives to hear it. The band plays "La Marseillaise," and the Frenchmen sing—timidly at first. After reassuring themselves that there will be no reprisals, they really let loose. Wearing broad smiles and flinging their arms, they throw their berets in the air and sing like mad. The artillery crew sometimes beats time in the wrong place, but the band is a howling success.

I've been in France only a week, but so much has happened, it seems like a month. We've been sending replacements to Gen. Charles Gerhardt, commander of the 29th, in record numbers, as his troops, in hand-to-hand combat, try to take the city of Saint Lô. After that we'll be done with the hedgerows.

On July 20, I hear on the British Broadcasting Corporation (BBC) station the report of a bombing at Hitler's headquarters. Will the war soon be over? Then there is complete radio silence. Four days later, propaganda minister Joseph Goebbels announces that Hitler is conducting the war as usual.

Finally, on July 25, the static front (both sides dug in) at Saint Lô is broken by the bombing of 3,000 American sorties. A few days later I see the bombed area near Saint Lô. It's completely churned up. I count up to 50 wrecked enemy tanks, some almost buried. Dead German soldiers and cattle are scattered everywhere. The breakthrough has come so fast there's no time for cleanup. There are some bizarre sights—a tank balanced on one end, the carcass of a cow hanging in a tree, and a headless German soldier sitting against a tree. The town of 12,000 has been bombed previously. Now it's completely gone, not one whole building left.

We are besieged by rain, but when it stops, Gen. George Patton's armored forces fan out in a wide area, southward, then eastward toward the Seine River.

I take advantage of lulls in the action to talk—with my pidgin English and standard-issue phrasebook—to French civilians in the area. When the Germans first invaded, they came with "requisitions" for crops and cattle, paying small prices with counterfeit money. If they liked a house, they just took it. Later they took anything they wanted, without formality, including all good clothing, which they sent home to Germany. If they saw a woman they wanted, they took her, too.

One local woman tells me that the French Red Cross collected shoes and clothing for destitute refugees. In a remarkable act of generosity and with hardly any clothing themselves, the workers took the goods to a church to give to the refugees. "The Germans took the clothing and shoes and shipped them home," she says grimly.

Normandy is a region of plentiful grain, vegetable, fruit, and dairy products, with a climate similar to that of the American Midwest. With the Germans gone and no market for their surplus, the natives now have plenty to eat. On some farms, the potatoes aren't dug up, fruit is left on the trees, and the grain is not cut. I ask a farmer, "What are you going to do with all this food?"

"Nobody asks us for it," he answers. "Your troops are moving too fast, and they seem to have enough food of their own."

While waiting to move on, Lieutenant MacDougal (Mac) and I stumble upon a beautiful chateau in a valley near the camp. Large and isolated, it houses the elderly Vicomtesse de Puthod, her son, and three daughters, all in their teens and early twenties. A Cambridge graduate, short and thin, the vicomtesse is genuinely cordial and speaks fluent English. She invites us to dinner and tells us her story.

"My husband is an architect in Paris, and this is our summer home," she says. "When the Germans started to occupy this area in 1940, we agreed I should take the children from Paris because food is plentiful here. I moved in, and we housed 35 refugees.

"I got here just before the Germans, who eventually demanded use of the place. My adamancy and the fact that we housed refugees got me by, and I was able to remain. The refugees eventually left, but like others in our situation, I kept my family here. I trained the children to lie flat on the floor when shells came close, and we all escaped injury."

"What was it like before the invasion?" I ask.

"Before the American invasion, British agents (dressed as peasants) did an excellent job of harassing the Germans," she says. "The snipers were mostly German women who had lived in France before the war. Reprisals for killing Germans reached as high as 50 to 100 French people for each dead German. Most of the killings have been the Free French of the Interior (FFI), the members of the French Resistance commonly called *maquis*.

"There would be no French Resistance if it weren't for [Charles] de Gaulle," she continues. "People of all political persuasions feel he has the best chance to lead France. He is regarded as a hero.

"General de Gaulle wanted to occupy France, stating that four years of Nazi occupation was enough. We heard that General Eisenhower felt there were too many Communists in France and that occupation by de Gaulle was too risky. I think de Gaulle should take over now. The people went wild when he spoke here recently."

"What happens to those who have collaborated with the Nazis?"

"Lists of collaborators are kept for the day of reckoning when we get our own government," she says sternly. "We choose to do this properly and legally."

As the evening draws to a close, the vicomtesse hands me a piece of paper. "My greatest concern now is my inability to communicate with my husband, to tell him we are safe," she says. "If you get to Paris, please give him this message. It tells him what has happened here during the occupation."

We leave our bivouac in good order as we move south. Another officer and I stop momentarily in a small town and just start up the Jeep again when two German officers pop out of nowhere. One says, "We surrender to American soldiers." We turn them over to the maquis, to be taken to the camp for prisoners of war (POWs). The Germans protest, and I can't blame them. The maquis don't have any means of taking care of prisoners and often shoot them, saying, "They were trying to escape." But we have no means of holding them. We are moving too fast.

The Germans are right to be afraid of the *maquis*, a word referring to Corsican bandits. They are a big help to us, relieving us of prisoners, sweeping the woods, cleaning out bypassed towns, providing information about the enemy, and guarding roads and bridges. They dress in civilian clothes and arm themselves with anything they can capture or steal from the Germans. Their only identification is the red, white, and blue band worn with the Cross of Lorraine on the upper left arm. They have no personal ID.

Ten men are in each maquis "cell," each with one leader, the only one who knows the leader above or below. The arrangement ensures that no one can betray more than ten men. During the occupation, the maquis have carried on raids and sabotage against the Germans, operating mostly from the woods. Many say they join to escape Germany's labor draft. This isn't easy; every person in France must carry an identification card to obtain food from the German occupation. The danger of exposure by paid collaborators is always real. So the maquis go into hiding. Some tell us frankly that they have joined simply because all good Communists do.

The maquis tell me of many instances of Nazi brutality during the occupation. In a recent incident, the German SS (Schutzstaffel, a shooting detachment) left a town after hearing of approaching Allied armored vehicles. As a parting shot, an SS man sprayed the street with submachine-gun bullets from the back of a truck, killing and wounding women and children.

Driving farther south near Laval, we see farmer refugees drifting back. They have been through trying times—fire, lack of food and shelter, and searching interrogation, even at the hands of their rescuers. I ask one of them about being strafed by American planes and shelled by our artillery.

One man says, "I was scared stiff, and I was almost killed along with the Germans. I ran a lot and got some shelter under bridges and behind buildings. It was hell." The Germans, anxious for their own lives, simply abandoned the farmers.

In walking northward, the farmers set their wooden shoes and sore feet on free territory. Despite their suffering and the expectation of finding their homes in ruin, none fails to grin and wave at every passing truckload of Americans. Now they are sure of our winning.

Another man says, "We are tired and hungry. Do you have any food?" We give them all we can spare and say, "Best of luck."

When we turn east toward the Seine River, we find the people's spirits riding high on a wave of victory. Enthusiasm is unbounded. Work is practically abandoned. People line the roads, yelling themselves hoarse. Women throw kisses. Homemade tricolors of red, white, and blue hang everywhere. We are just past Le Mans.

In the towns, where homes and stores squeeze tight against the narrow sidewalks, people protrude from almost every door and window in a mass of smiling faces and waving arms. We can hear the cheers above the roar of our trucks. When a traffic jam stops us, a woman runs up to me with a bottle of wine and one of cognac and kisses me on both cheeks. Touched by her sacrifice, I almost cry.

Closer to the Seine, General de Gaulle speaks to the people, announcing the liberation of the capital. To the natives, Paris means France, and the floodgates of emotion open. The French people lose themselves in a tide of hysterical joy. The people come up to us and thank us no end. Again, I feel moved to tears.

One old woman in a second-story window spots a convoy of trucks loaded with German prisoners. It passes us, going the opposite direction, as we halt. The woman thumbs her nose as each truckload passes, on the way to POW camps in the American rear.

In another town, we meet some maquis who have armored vehicles and are American-equipped, even to their uniforms. Their only distinction is the bright red color of their caps and their tricolor armbands. They are off their vehicles, drinking cognac and kissing women. One well-oiled motorcycle rider wobbles uncertainly and falls slowly to the ground, out cold on the cobblestones.

Welcome signs are plastered everywhere. One says, "Welcome at our liberty." A woman pokes her arm into the cab and hands me two eggs, "Merci beaucoup," she says with sincerity. Others along the way give me apples, tomatoes, peaches, and pears. The GIs in the trucks toss cigarettes, rations, candy, and gum all the way.

In the evening, we still must dig foxholes. There is no compact line between us and the enemy. Armored spearheads lead the way, but the Germans are all around us. Instead of hedgerows, there are open fields and occasional patches of woods for bivouacs. Scattered bands of Germans use them for hiding places—we find them in or near every place we camp. We disarm them, and if there are no maquis, we assign GIs to lead them to the nearest POW camp.

As we begin to move eastward, I say to Mac, "I'm delighted to be moving, even if it's a damned nuisance to dig all those foxholes."

"I don't mind the foxholes, so long as we're getting near Paris," he tells me.

Author with Lt. Joe "Mike" (right) at Arc de Triomphe, August 28, 1944.

Chapter 2

All units are almost out of gasoline as we reach the Seine. General Eisenhower orders all units to halt until they are resupplied. Finally, our outfit stops in a green valley with a pristine creek, near Billancourt, 18 miles southwest of Paris. After determining that we won't move out soon, Chaplain Brown walks to our tent. "Hi, fellas," he smiles. "How would you like to go to Paris for a day?"

"We're almost out of gas," I say.

"Let me worry about that." He is quite sure of himself.

"I'm taking you three officers along to help me track down the bishop of the Episcopal church. I want to know where he's been during four years of German occupation, whether the church was open for worship during that time. We'll work in pairs and try to find out. Captain Faris will go with me. Lieutenants Michael and Hansen will be the other pair. Are you with me?"

On the way, the chaplain pulls off on a shoulder on a high hill. "There it is," he says. The Eiffel Tower gleams tall and stately amidst our breathtaking view of the city. I reach for the chaplain's camera and walk ahead to a vantage point, then feel a tug on my sleeve.

"I honor you. God bless you!" a Frenchman says excitedly. "Got any cigarettes?"

"Do you know Paris?" I ask, then make a quick deal. For five packs of cigarettes ($3.00 a pack) he becomes our willing guide and interpreter. There is so much to see. I will not remember it all.

De Gaulle was here three days earlier, on August 25, and the city is still flush with excitement. As we near the Arc de Triomphe, the profusion of color is dazzling—red, white, and blue bunting on the buildings, many shades of dresses, hats, shoes, and bicycles. Red-and-white awnings flank sidewalk cafes opening for the first time in four years.

A French soldier, appearing to be no older than 17, tells us in English: "The fighting is over except for a little sniping at night by Germans who apparently haven't been told of the evacuation. The people are wearing their best clothes just to test the feel of it. They kept the clothes in hiding for the four years of German occupation."

This is a good time for a visit to Paris. The city is off limits to troops, except for anti-aircraft (AA) guns and a few MPs and other small units. We enjoy more prominence with our letters of introduction than is deserving for an American group. Our MPs are not here in force, and the city is run by the maquis, who just can't do enough for us.

We park the truck near the Arc de Triomphe to see the Tomb of the Unknown Soldier. The flame burning at its center has been alive through the years of occupation. Men walking by it remove their hats; we remove our helmets. A French gentleman, Maurice Cochet, obligingly takes snapshots of us, writes down our addresses, and plans to mail the prints to our homes. I give him a cigar.

In good English, he says, "I was an engineer for Westinghouse Electric Company before the war. When the war started, I wasn't permitted to leave."

"What happened to your family?"

"My two sons were taken by Germans, apparently for forced labor. My wife is living and well. I saved my automobile from seizure by hiding the wheels. I told the 'pigs' that they were stolen."

We walk down the main street—Les Champs Elysées. The wide street is filled with bicycles, about three abreast, riding in both directions. The riders, mostly women, pedal gracefully. Imagine a model, fresh out of Lord and Taylor's, riding a chrome, light blue, or lavender bicycle. Imagine many such women, each quite thin, probably for lack of food. Together they form a floating, billowy mass of color and tinkling bells. Some of the women in short skirts are prostitutes, I think.

Crossing the street is a major task. I can't take my eyes off the women, and their bicycles almost hit us. Three of the riders proposition us. The sidewalk is as wide as the street. It has two auto-park strips divided by two pedestrian walks. Joe and I find a vacant table at a sidewalk cafe and order two glasses of wine.

"What do you think of this?" I ask.

"Beats hell out of the army. Can't think of anything better."

We agree on the beauty of the Parisian women and try to analyze it. Joe says, "They have the right combination of complementary colors, short dresses, and a flattering shape to their hats. They never overdo their makeup. A homely woman can be made to look beautiful." But it isn't all eyewash. They are subtly, completely feminine, have a free, vivacious air and a fetching way of being absorbed in their male escorts, of which there are not many. The shortage of men is due to the newly formed French army, to the forced labor in Germany, and to membership in the maquis.

We notice too, in the stylish parade, a sprinkling of fancy, barbered pooches on leashes. The shops are showplaces, with the French taste for color and design evident. Red, pink, yellow, and blue are most prominent. The Germans have not touched the stores, which show a fair amount of women's clothing, almost nothing for men. Shoes are made mostly from cloth, with jointed-wood or rope soles. Toiletry and perfume shops are everywhere. The artistic displays are fascinating. Everything is expensive.

Everyone we ask says there are no worship services anywhere in the city except in Catholic churches, which have a concordat with the Nazis. When we all meet again, Captain Faris wants to find a gift for his wife. After trying three places, we find a store on a side street that looks like a millionaire's home. Circular marble stairways, statuary, paintings, exquisite rugs, drapes, chandeliers, and graceful furniture enhance the establishment. No merchandise is on display. A gracious woman with a cultured English voice greets and seats us, saying, "May I help you?"

"I'm looking for a black negligé for my wife," Faris stammers.

"Certainly. One moment please." She goes to a back room, and in a few minutes, the parade begins—five gorgeous creatures dripping with silk and lace. Poor Faris! He is shown the nightclothes in detail, inside and out, at close range. The models are lightly clad, to say the least. He picks a black negligé trimmed with white lace (or, perhaps, the dream wearing it). The price is 12,000 francs ($240.00). Joe asks, "Does the price include the blonde?" Faris is alarmed but pays the price. I guess the show is worth something, too.

A few things for sale tempt me but aren't worth the price. If we had American dollars instead of the army's print of francs, we would get four times the current rate of exchange—100 francs for two dollars. The Allies make their own francs as the Germans have counterfeited every kind of paper money. The French people had to turn in all their francs at one time. They can draw out a modest sum of the new print money each month. This is the only legal tender.

———————

Reluctantly we return to Billancourt. The chaplain has another thought on the way there. "Maybe the religions went underground and have quiet services at places other than the church. I think it's worth asking about, " he says. Now I know he wants to see more of Paris. We determine that our outfit will not be moving soon, and the next visit is longer—three days and two nights.

After quite a few inquiries about the church, we again devote our time to sightseeing. Outside the Arc de Triomphe, we are impressed by the Cathedral of Notre Dame, especially its architecture. Inside, it is dark and dreary. We also see Opéra Garnier (on Place de l'Opéra), where we learn the Germans poured gasoline and set the seats afire in retaliation for sniping. We visit Les Invalides, where Napoleon is buried, and the Grand Palais, a magnificent structure.

"This is something to see. I didn't know Napoleon was buried here," Joe says. "They sure do everything with elegance."

"Amen," says Chaplain Brown.

"I understand that no building can be higher than the monuments," Captain Faris says, looking all around.

"Now that you mention it, I haven't seen a building higher than those monuments. The tallest is eight stories," I remark.

There are also beautiful circles, like Place de la Concorde, with the Egyptian Obelisk of Luxor at its center. Some hotels are as luxurious as castles, with marble floors and walks, winding stairways, and crystal chandeliers. On every windowsill is a box with magnificent, many-colored flowers.

We see modern buildings, too, such as the Palais de Chaillot Hotel, which has an underground theater. It is neat and clean. A doorman with a colorful uniform stands in front. I wish I could stay at such an elegant hotel. Graceful statuary, lots of neatly cropped trees and shrubbery, and artistic bridges over the winding

Opéra Garnier on Place de l'Opéra.

Obelisk of Luxor on Place de la Concorde.

Seine River put the finishing touches on this most beautiful city. The place gives me a feeling of luxury. Only one thing mars the view. All the buildings are dirty on the outside, and they have a look of neglect.

But the more I see the French people, the more I admire them. Their zest, easy laughter, open emotions, and childlike curiosity are always evident. As we look at the statues around the outside of L'Opera, three young girls approach to hand us their calling cards for autographs. This starts a crowd that soon reaches into the street. Some insist on our addresses, and we will probably receive mail at our homes someday from people we won't remember. My indulgence of their wish for a kiss with each autograph doesn't hold the crowd down and apparently provides some entertainment. Our faces are red. This crowd is a beaner.

As we walk along, three girls wave at us from a corner window. We go inside and introduce ourselves. One has a pretty smile, and I ask her out for dinner. She is excited and wants to accept but says she'll have to go home first and get her parents for chaperones. I say I can't wait. She looks disappointed.

Later, at one end of a bridge over the Seine, we see two GIs sitting at a big AA gun, encircled by a pile of sandbags and a lot of people. Their eyes are glued to the one using the telephone. To a French civilian, he probably looks important, even heroic, with that big gun and the telephone. I stop and catch part of the bull session he shares with a buddy on the line, probably at another gun!

"I got a mob of Frogs [French civilians] round here gawking at me. Geez, don't those babes on the bikes drive ya nuts? I see one who has bare legs and a short dress. I bet she doesn't have panties on." The incongruity of those serious faces makes it all the more ridiculous.

While we are having a Martell cognac at a sidewalk cafe, a silver-headed doctor accompanied by an attractive young woman leans toward us, states he has gasoline, and volunteers to drive us around. "I admire you Americans," he says. "All you need to do is motion to a girl, and she will come to you, even my wife here." His wife, who is smiling at us, gives him a sharp elbow in the ribs. We pile into his blue Citroen for a whirlwind tour.

———————

Returning again to Billancourt, we check that the outfit will not be moving and then return to Paris, ostensibly to find some trace of the bishop. "I can't believe he has just disappeared," says the chaplain as he picks up the three of us. We are happy to go back, especially because the maquis have arranged a hotel for us.

The next day Chaplain Brown, Captain Faris, Lt. Joe Michael, and I make inquiries, then decide to go pursue our individual interests and meet later in the day. As I wander along the tree-lined Champs Elysées, my thoughts turn to the Vicomtesse de Puthod and her concern for her husband in Paris. I pat my pocket containing the letter and his address—55 Rue de Bellechasse—and try to find the place on foot.

After some wandering, I find the poorly marked street. The square brick building stands at the end of a cul-de-sac. In the lobby I find the vicomte's name on the directory. He is on the second floor. I go up the steps and knock on the door. A woman, rather short, neatly dressed in gingham, lightly perfumed, and with her brown-gray hair pulled straight back in a bun, opens the door and asks me who I am.

I tell her, "I have a message for Vicomte de Puthod from his wife in Normandy." Eyebrows raised, she smiles, steps aside, and motions me to an elderly gentleman sitting in a wingback chair by the window. He is thin and casually dressed in a sweater, baggy trousers, and slippers. When I tell him his family is safe and well in Normandy, his eyes became moist and he grasps my hand, too overcome to speak. He turns to the woman, who is his sister, and quietly asks her in English to bring us tea. The air in the room is stale, and it smells old.

When he is satisfied that I have given him all the news, he says, "Will you write an account of all you have told me in your own words?" He gets out of his chair, shuffles over to a hard-cover guest book, and opens it for me. When I finish writing, he goes back to his chair, and I sit across from him. He lets me in on a secret.

"I have been in the Underground since the first day of the occupation," he says, running his fingers through his sparse gray hair. "One of the things I did was to print anti-Nazi slogans on small slips of paper that others secretly distributed and posted all over Paris. They must have been effective. The distributors constantly asked for more."

"How did you print them?"

"I did it with blocks of wood about three by eight inches, to which I glued slogans cut out from auto inner-tubes." He rises and asks me to follow him to another room, where he shows me his collection of print blocks. Entry to the small room is gained through a swiveling bookcase. I wonder, then reason that he *is* an architect. This room smells even more musty, probably for lack of windows.

He gives me two of the blocks dated September 1941 and a piece of white paper. "Go ahead. Stamp," he says, handing me an inkpad. I press the first stamp down. Translated it reads: "Collaboration Equals Treason. Death to Traitors." The other depicts a spiked club, marked USA, smashing a swastika: "Germany Shall Be Crushed."

"Didn't you put your neck out pretty far?"

"It was such a little thing," he replies.

"Tell me, how did you and your wife become separated?"

"We agreed that she and the children would take care of our summer chateau near Saint Lô, where it was relatively safe and food still plentiful, while I watch our properties here in Paris. We also agreed we would do all we could in the Underground. I didn't realize that the Germans would cut telephone and postal service."

The vicomte's sister refills our cups with tea. "Our worst suffering," she says, "has been lack of fuel last winter. German planes knocked out our electric plants and took almost all the coal in late August but left the rest of the city alone. Old Louise, our housekeeper, who has been with us for 70 years, stayed in bed most of the winter to keep warm, and *we* waited on *her.*"

"My sister, who lives in Paris, wants to return to America. We are so proud of her. She taught French history at Wellesley College for a short time." She quietly sips her tea.

It is time to meet my army companions but hard to leave these new friends. I add their names to my well-worn address book.

As I walk away on the narrow, quiet street, a short, plump girl runs up to me. She hesitates a moment, then slips her arms around me, stands on her tiptoes, and places a kiss squarely on my mouth. "Merci beaucoup," she says again and again. I look at my watch, finally release myself from her grasp, and walk away. As I glance back, she smiles and waves.

The French Resistance parades "collaborators" with shaven heads through a French town on Bastille Day. The author witnesses a similar scene at Arronville.

Chapter 3

September-October 1944

Gasoline and food are constant problems, primarily because General Patton's armored vehicles are moving so fast. Ammunition is also critical. Our First Army is advancing, as are other Allied armies to the south. We are a little north of Patton's Third Army. We must keep up with him to form a front.

Flexible underground pipelines, six inches in diameter, channel fuel from England to the landing beaches in France, where American pipes are filled. Our plastic pipe, also about six inches in diameter, is mounted on wooden crosses to keep it off the ground. The crosses are two pieces of wood, about a-foot-and-a-half long, nailed together. The upper part of the cross holds the pipe. There are pumping stations for uphill stretches. Jeeps ride the pipeline to see that it is working properly. I talk with one of the drivers.

snare drum. A few people shout hateful remarks at them. I feel loathing for the women, too. Later, I visit the barnyard where 18 such women are kept. Their bare heads seem too small for their bodies. The swastikas on their foreheads add an evil look to their drab, worried faces. They walk in a circle, led by a man, apparently for exercise. I ask a Frenchman what will happen to them, but he doesn't answer.

"Where are the male collaborators?" I ask.

"The men don't need protective custody. Instead, they must report to the *mairie* (city hall) at a certain hour each day. If they fail, the maquis hunt them down as fugitives. The collaborators who fail to report are soon dead."

———

It is easy to tell we are crossing into Belgium. In the border town are mobs of noisy well-wishers, cheering us on. Almost everything is covered with the black, yellow, and red flags of the pre-Hitler kingdom.

At first, nothing seems different from France but the flags. As we move in farther, we see that the buildings and houses are of brick rather than concrete or stucco, and they are more trim and clean than in France. The sidewalks and streets in Namur are washed every morning. People dress a little better than in France.

Belgium seems the most densely populated place in Europe. You hardly leave one town when you are in the next. Some automobiles are on the streets, most of them adapted to use charcoal burners mounted at the rear. Methane gas, produced by the burners, serves as fuel for the engines. This is the first place I see dogs pulling carts. In Liege, I find excellent bottled beer—and ice cream.

After we've set up camp, a Belgian priest visits. We share my mess kit at lunch. He sits on a pail, eats C ration, and tells this story:

"Belgium got off on the right foot when King Leopold capitulated early, and since then the organized Resistance has been slight," he says. "Most people have been able to keep cars, bicycles, and radios. Enemy programs are forbidden."

"So the Nazis have compassion?"

"Rarely." The priest is outspoken on the inhuman treatment of Jews. "I have seen old men and women beaten by German soldiers on the street for failing to wear a six-pointed star or for talking to a Christian. I have seen small children kicked viciously for no reason."

"All able-bodied Jews have been taken to Poland, apparently for slave labor or death," recalls the priest. "Those who remained in Belgium have had a hard time getting food. They couldn't personally go into a Christian store and often had their ration cards confiscated for insignificant reasons. The Belgians in the Catholic Church, including nuns in convents, have helped these unfortunate people hide themselves. They have given them food and clothing. Some Belgians have been shot or imprisoned for doing this."

The maid of another bivouac neighbor, an intelligent Jewish girl of 19, speaks English. "My sister and I were herded on the train marked for Poland at Mons with other Jews. When the train was going slowly through a switchyard on the edge of the city, both of us leaped off. A Nazi guard on the train fired a submachine gun at us, missing me but wounding my sister in the leg. She was in the hospital for about three months, then found shelter and has been hiding with this Belgian family, who treat her like a daughter. My parents, if alive, are in Poland," she says.

Howard Triest, our 19-year-old water-tender, is also Jewish. He got away to America from Munich in 1937.

"I had a special pass to see my aunt in Brussels," he says. "My aunt was hard to find because she has been hiding in seven different places for the last three years. With no address registered, it took me two days to trace her. She has lost 90 pounds and is quite ill. My parents, who fled to Marseilles, France, were 'schnappen' [snatched] there a year ago, and there is no news of them."

We have learned firsthand of many incidents like these. A Jewish man tells me, "My pregnant wife was taken away over two years ago with no word from her since."

But the Germans abandoned Belgium in a hurry, apparently in fair order. We have a light time of it for about a week, running into little fire on the ground and not much from the air.

———————

Holland (Netherlands) is a different story. We're on the back doorstep of Germany, where armament is always ready. The weather is bad for flying, so the Germans have a chance to man their forts and make more. German airdromes are closer. We Americans are getting more V-1 robot planes and V-2 rocket bombs—anytime day or night.

My favorite bivouac neighbor here is Jannis Bernardus de Hullu, a retired Dutch schoolmaster. He evacuated from Zeeland when the Germans flooded that part of northern Holland. A London University graduate, he is a keen observer and good host.

"Any collaborators here?" I ask.

"Holland has had more than its share," he says. "They are mostly the riffraff who never made good or who had criminal records. The burgomaster [mayor] of a nearby town was ousted for corruption but recovered his job when the Nazis came. All collaborators were paid, given double rations, and could keep a radio.

"The collaborators reported their neighbors to the Gestapo. They selected the hostages and put some people on the slave labor lists. On the mere whim of one of those rats, a peaceful citizen might find himself in jail. Once he was in jail, it would take months for charges to be brought. Sometimes a citizen would be set free with no explanation of his arrest in the first place. If it came to trial, the burden was on him to prove his innocence."

"How about the Underground?" I ask.

"The Underground, called the *Onderduiker* [under diver], was so secret that I never knew positively of any person who was in it. They operated at night, distributing propaganda."

"How did they get food?"

"They took cattle, grain, and vegetables from wealthy farmers without their knowledge, leaving an itemized receipt. Dutch farmers have complete faith that their restored government will redeem these receipts," he says. "Hundreds of these fighters have been shot because of their activities, but this never lessened their efforts."

"How did the natives treat the Jews?" I ask.

"In this little village, one Jewish lady was concealed in a basement for two years and another behind a false wall in the barn. A British airman was harbored for seven months until he could be secretly evacuated."

"They have taken extreme chances, haven't they?"

"Punishment for such crimes has been death. Every time someone was caught at it, a bold obituary of the offender was printed in a box on the front page of the daily paper," he says.

"Did you know about Reichminister Alfred Rosenberg? He was Hitler's philosopher; he declared that Holland could be assimilated because the people are Aryan—like those in the Scandinavian countries." (My interest derives from an article in *Stars and Stripes*.)

"No, but the German soldiers have been disgustingly smooth and polite to the Dutch girls they liked. The soldiers gave them money and bought them silk dresses and leather shoes, otherwise unobtainable. Some of the stupid girls went for the slick uniforms, polite treat-

Alfred Rosenberg

ment, and pretty presents and soon found themselves unhappy mothers. The German army has given an allotment of ten gulden [three dollars] a week to each mother for her baby's support."

"What happened when the German soldiers left?" I ask.

"When the American troops arrived, the Germans took every car, horse and wagon, and bicycle they could get their hands on. They used the small country roads, speeding with cars and trucks in the daytime, using the horses only at night."

"What kind of soldiers were they?"

"Many of the German soldiers were boys, 14 to 16 years old. Once in a while, the Dutch boys mocked them with the Hitler salute, lowering their raised arms quickly and saying, 'Down with Hitler.'"

"Did the soldiers leave anything behind?"

"Everyone will read their propaganda sheet. It says that while the Allies have more weapons and a large army, the reason for withdrawal is that the Germans are fighting for time to get out a secret weapon, the atom bomb that will end the war. It says their master strategy is to let Americans into Germany, then slaughter you all at once."

———————————

We wait to cross the last border from Holland into Germany—near Maastricht. Sometimes as I lie in our wet dugout at night, I think about a recent court-martial case I have defended: 1st Lt. James Lewis ran to the rear when the firepower of the massive artillery, both friendly and that of the enemy, became too much for him. General Gerhardt wanted the case to be an example for others who might have the same idea, primarily because the offender was an officer, supposedly leading his men into battle. Deserting a battle station is a capital offense calling for death or life imprisonment in the United States. Gerhardt appointed a court of senior commanders and, in the same order, named me the chief trial judge advocate for the defense.

I thought long and hard and concluded Lewis should not be subject to the M'Naghten rule (if the defendant knows the difference between right and wrong when he commits the offense, he is sane; otherwise, he is insane) used by most courts in the United States.

"What made you run to the rear?" I asked Lewis.

"I don't know. I can't remember."

"Why can't you remember?"

"My mind went blank. I didn't know I was running to the rear until a major stopped me and asked why. Then I came to my senses and said, 'I don't know.' I guess the heavy explosions made me lose my mind. He arrested me on the spot. So here I am in the stockade."

"Are you sure that is it, that you lost your mind?"

"Yes, it was blank until the major stopped me, and then it took a while to gain my senses."

After the questioning I was sure the M'Naghten rule should not apply. For expert testimony, I went to see our division's so-called psychiatrist, David Weintraub, a pediatrician from Brooklyn. He referred me to Col. Henry Schultz, a psychiatrist at our corps headquarters to the rear, about five miles away.

Formerly a full-time prison psychiatrist, Schultz was tall, about 50 years old, rather thin, and patient. When I told him about Lewis, he listened carefully, then said, "I agree with you. This is a case of irresistible impulse, and the M'Naghten rule is not applicable. How could he tell the difference between right and wrong when he couldn't think?"

Then the important question: "Will you testify?"

"I'll be happy to. I've already testified in a similar case where the evidence of desertion was almost identical. The explosions are so great that a man's resistance is easily overcome. Some soldiers have a greater threshold of resistance than others. Lewis obviously had a short threshold. He had an irresistible impulse to desert."

Schultz testified along this line at the trial, with the military bearing of a full colonel and an assuring tone of voice. He stood up well through cross-examination and questions by the members of the court. On final argument, I made the point that everyone in the room was a member of a citizens' army and that the war would soon be over. When all returned to their homes, the members of the court would not want it on their consciences that they had given the penalty of death or life imprisonment to an officer who lost his mind.

The court took two days to decide the case, finally coming in with the peculiar verdict that the defendant serve three years imprisonment in the United States. General Gerhardt was disappointed in his hope for an example. I was disappointed that Lewis was not acquitted.

(There are automatic appeals in such cases, one to the division and one to Eisenhower's staff judge advocate. Later I found out that the defendant received a dishonorable discharge with three years of probation in lieu of the three-years imprisonment.)

The author with a line of dragon's or tiger's teeth (top) made by the Germans to stop tanks, in the snow in front of an abandoned pillbox (right), and with fellow officers (above), all near the Siegfried Line.

Chapter 4

November 1944–April 1945

Our outfit is finally inside the Siegfried Line, the last great stronghold of the German defense. The replacement company is at Eschweiler.

I see many civilians. At first I wonder about their attitude and look for signs of it, but that is like looking at the *Mona Lisa.* I've never been able to decide whether she is smiling or smirking. These are the stubborn ones who have refused the orders of both their own and Allied armies to move eastward. They are mostly farmers, coal miners, and small-factory workers. For security reasons, we are ordered not to "fraternize" or talk with them. But I've spoken with our civil affairs and medical officers, who say, "In this section of northern Germany, the people are quite religious. They have cooperated with the Nazis because of their orders, but they resent their dogma. All they did was oppose their antisocial decrees, especially against Jews."

At any rate, they are here and very much in our hair. Some of the German civilians spot for their artillery, snipe at us, and transmit information with concealed radios. So we enforce strictly the rules for civilian conduct posted on the doors of German dwellings. Civilians must stay indoors from dusk to dawn and observe absolute blackout. They must also stay indoors during daylight, except that they may work the land adjoining their homes and tend cattle. One person from each dwelling may obtain a pass for one hour a day to shop for food. Those outside their homes are carefully watched by the newly recruited Dutch army and the MPs, as well as by the Intelligence Corps, Civil Affairs units, and others.

Our firmness is free of oppression. They have stated surprise that we have not taken their homes, furnishings, or cattle. They are not forced to work for us, but they may work for pay—one-and-a-half marks per hour for common labor and more for skilled work. This treatment must seem strange to them, knowing as they do that some of their possessions have been taken from German-occupied countries—France and Belgium—and that millions of laborers from other countries are working in German concentration camps against their will.

The bombed houses smell of something in decay. Lacking water, the people do not bathe, so they smell of sweat. Everything is old and musty. Our troops guard mines, factories, and warehouses against pillaging by German and Dutch civilians. Under the Rules of Land Warfare, captured military stocks are ours, but civilian goods are not. We can obtain coal stoves, coal, and beds for an American hospital only by requisition. A record of the amount and value is kept for final accounting.

Going through the northern areas in Germany, we see the civilians are farmers tending crops and cattle, work gangs along the roads, and

people looking out from windows and doorways. The lookers are the *Mona Lisas.* An elderly man leans against a doorway, a woman rests on her elbows in an open window, or a girl carries milk pails suspended from a neck yoke. Some look toward us but avoid our eyes. Others look at us with a sort of intent stare and half-smile, as if attempting to be pleasant. Most are women. Some are small children or elderly men.

The women sit by their windows for hours. The sidewalks are flush with the house fronts, and window sills about waist high. The windows are hinged on their sides and open in—when you look in, you feel as if you are already halfway inside. Women sit by the sills or on chairs close inside, watching us.

Increasingly disgusted with the luxuries enjoyed by some Germans at the expense of occupied countries, I have filed an amended application for transfer to JAGD and assignment to war-crimes investigation. Now in the 29th Division at Aldenhoven, Germany, I get word I'll transfer on January 4 to the Ninth Army headquarters in Maastricht.

Lt. Col. Henry Mize meets me there and takes me on a tour of the HQs, formerly an office building. Its size and my new assignment humble me. He shows me a desk in a large room housing a library on international law.

"This is where you will work. Feel free to read the books and articles as you choose. There is no decision yet on the form of the indictment against the leading Nazis. I would like to see a memo on your thoughts," he says.

"This must be a test," I think.

Colonel Mize is about my age, 35, a little taller, thin, and friendly. He goes on, "Now, I'll show you your quarters." He takes me to a fancy hotel less than a block away and talks with the manager, who ushers me into a splendid room on the third floor with bed, bath, a table and chairs, and two windows.

The next morning I start my research, making a study of the types of war crimes that might be prosecuted, the treaties and international law involved, and the kind of evidence needed for the trials to come. Among the papers I read is the October 7, 1942, speech of President Franklin Delano Roosevelt:

In August, I said that this government was constantly receiving information concerning the barbaric crimes being committed by the enemy against civilian populations in occupied countries, particularly on the continent of Europe. I said it was the purpose of this government, as I knew it to be the purpose of the other United Nations, to see that when victory is won the perpetrators of these crimes shall answer for them before courts of law.

I learn that the United Nations War Crimes Commission formed in the fall of 1942 and three months later started the Central War Crimes Evidence Library in London to compile lists of perpetrators. In Moscow on November 1, 1943, President Roosevelt, Prime Minister Winston Churchill, and Premier Joseph (Vissarionovich Djugashvili) Stalin issued their first public declaration on war crimes, in part:

We have received from many quarters . . . evidence of atrocities, massacres, and cold-blooded executions which are being perpetrated by Hitlerite forces in many of the countries they have overrun and from which they are now being steadily expelled . . . these German officers and men and members of the Nazi party who have been responsible for or have taken a consenting part in the above atrocities, massacres, and executions will be . . . judged and punished.

The end of the declaration suggests the Allies have not yet agreed upon the form of indictments against the offenders, the makeup of the trial tribunal, its procedures, or the types of punishments to be imposed. These matters will not be settled for several months. I write my thoughts in a 12-page memo to Colonel Mize. A few excerpts illustrate the problems:

We are not going to find precedent in the law or in the authorities as a basis for many of the types of violations we are going to see . . . The new totalitarian concepts arising since the last war have completely upset the lagging concepts of civilized laws of nations.

. . . [We] apparently are going to treat as war crimes any acts which are obnoxious to the fundamental principles of humanity and chivalry and which are not justified by military necessity.

Commission of a war crime under orders of a superior is not a defense, but it may be considered a mitigation of punishment.

———————

Completing my research in about a week, I give Colonel Mize my memo. The next day he introduces me to Lt. Gen. William H. Simpson, commander of the Ninth Army. He is a tall, lean man, unassuming and cordial. He wishes me well on my assignment and hands me a letter addressed to "Anyone Concerned" (meaning Allied commanders at all levels). The letter, signed by Simpson, calls for cooperation with me in my work.

I start to gather evidence in a broad area of northern Germany. The Ninth Army is the main force there, while the British and Canadians are along the coast of the English Channel. Some of the commanders I need help from say, "What the hell is this?" Others say, "What do you need?" In most cases, it is gasoline, food, a place to sleep, translators, and a large truck to carry personnel.

Once I have what I need, I visit a nearby subcamp (satellite of an administrating, or main, concentration camp) to interview witnesses,

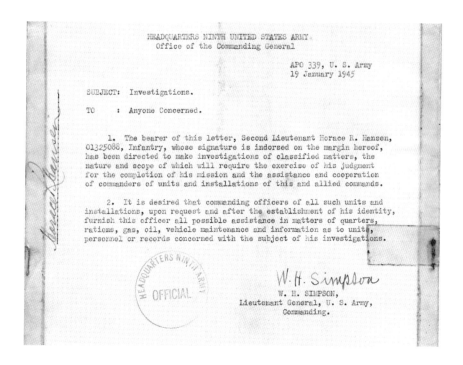

HEADQUARTERS NINTH UNITED STATES ARMY
Office of the Commanding General

APO 339, U. S. Army
19 January 1945

SUBJECT: Investigations.

TO   : Anyone Concerned.

1. The bearer of this letter, Second Lieutenant Horace R. Hansen, 01325088, Infantry, whose signature is indorsed on the margin hereof, has been directed to make investigations of classified matters, the nature and scope of which will require the exercise of his judgment for the completion of his mission and the assistance and cooperation of commanders of units and installations of this and allied commands.

2. It is desired that commanding officers of all such units and installations, upon request and after the establishment of his identity, furnish this officer all possible assistance in matters of quarters, rations, gas, oil, vehicle maintenance and information as to units, personnel or records concerned with the subject of his investigations.

OFFICIAL

W. H. Simpson
W. H. SIMPSON,
Lieutenant General, U. S. Army,
Commanding.

mostly former slave laborers. I get descriptions and names, when possible, of the SS men who have committed war crimes and try, with help from others, to apprehend them. In many cases, they are nearby, wearing civilian clothes. They are often identified by the tattoos of blood type near their left armpits. (Only members of the SS have such tattoos.) But most have fled. In such cases I make a special report, with a copy to the Central War Crimes Evidence Library in London.

Soon various intelligence sections and military governments report so many treaty violations and atrocities that I am able to handle only the worst ones. These include the starving, beating, and killing of slave laborers, mostly from France, Holland, Poland, and Russia, as well as the torture and killing of American prisoners and others in concentration subcamps. I'm almost too busy to notice how sick and angry I am at the cruel acts I hear about.

I inspect several subcamps recently liberated. One is like the next—in each, a group of six to ten one-story blocs (barracks) in the woods, painted light green and surrounded by a high barbed-wire electric fence, with a high guard tower at each corner. The blocks have housed the slave laborers from areas conquered by the Germans. The laborers have been marched daily to nearby privately owned factories or mines to work about 11 hours before returning to their blocs each night. They have been fed only a thin soup and a little black bread before and after work. They have slept on deep wooden shelves, stacked as in a warehouse, three men abreast on each shelf.

The prisoners were civilians, able-bodied men and some women, literally kidnapped from territory occupied by Hitler's SS men and herded into these camps. They were called "slave laborers" because their SS captors sold their labor to factory owners for two to five marks per head per day. This amounts to about 20 to 50 U.S. cents, the lower scale for common labor and the higher for skilled labor. The wages provided the only income for members of the SS.

I investigate war crimes at the scene and take a hand in arresting a few perpetrators. Some are indicted for trial. Most have fled deep into Germany. But their names, descriptions, and crimes—and conclusive evidence of guilt—are on the perpetrator list. A network of Allied organizations is alert to apprehend them. In addition, Col. Melvin Purvis, the former FBI agent who captured the notorious John Dillinger, leads a special organization in arresting the perpetrators.

The investigations are difficult, especially when dealing with the Russians. It takes three translators to learn their stories—one who knows Polish and Russian, another who knows German and Polish, and still another who can translate German to English. I become more confident with experience. In one case, a German lieutenant received a letter from his superior, taking him to task for mining too little coal. He became irate and took his 60 or more slave laborers outside, ordering them to remove their clothing. They stood naked in the cold weather while the lieutenant gave them a half-hour tongue-lashing, excoriating them to mine more coal and be fast about it. While he abraded them, some fell down from the bitter cold and starvation and died. Others died later. A total of about 20 died from the exposure.

The battlefield war crimes committed against Allied troops always come first and are investigated quickly. From prisoners we can often obtain information and net the perpetrators at once. Most crimes have been committed by SS troops and paratroopers, though on the whole the Wehrmacht has been treaty-abiding. At any rate, these investigations take me all over the Ninth Army front, and I seize every opportunity to check out crimes at the scene.

Many atrocities are reported in the liberated Dutch border towns, and I go back there to gather evidence. The quiet Dutch civilians have lived under a terrorism hard to describe. Since September 1944, men and women have been starved, beaten, robbed, and killed by Germans in desperation of advancing American planes and troops.

In Roermond, Holland, a city of 20,000, the SS units ordered all men and women aged 16 to 60 to dig tank traps and artillery emplacements. Few responded and almost all went into hiding, so the SS blocked off a section of the town at a time and searched each house. The units forced Dutch men under armed guard, by beating them with clubs, to do the digging. Because this went too slowly, they moved in 4,000 Russian and Polish slave laborers, mostly women. The searches continued, but the Dutch were clever in their escapes. In reprisal, the Germans looted homes and shops, taking away trainloads of living necessities and valuables to Germany. When these tactics didn't produce much, they called in paratrooper units. Immediately the paratroopers went house to house, smashing front-door locks with axes and hammers. They raided the homes at night, arresting all the able-bodied men and women they could find to dig the ditches.

Still more slave labor was needed for German factories, so the paratroopers used a scare tactic. They would pick a group of men, make them dig their own graves, then shoot them as a lesson to those who hid. The victims' only offense was hiding, and they had no trials. A warning was distributed to each house—any man 16 to 60 years found after 4:00 P.M. the next day would be shot on the spot. Before the deadline, more than 3,000 Dutch men reported to the market-place to be marched off in a long column to German concentration camps. On the second day, the Germans locked them in freight cars that took them on an all-night ride to the concentration camp Giebel near Wuppertal. There, for the first time in three days, they received some food—the soup and black bread. Then they were split into groups and sent to various factories.

During some of the marches, older men and women died on the roadside. Some women bore children in the cold. Both mother and child died. Those who made it were immediately put to work.

I spend eight days, with the help of the Dutch Underground, interviewing witnesses and escapees, taking photos, and collecting documents. The Germans' methodical record-keeping proves many gross crimes. The cases I handle make it clear that the Germans have violated every provision of the Rules of Land Warfare based on the Hague and Geneva treaties, and more. Their brutality has gone beyond anything the experts in international law could anticipate while drafting the rules.

My war-crimes investigations are interrupted by the long static defense at the Roer (or Rur) River. During a lull in the activity, I see at some distance a flock of ducks flying toward the enemy. I watch closely and think of the good old hunting days. Some more planes

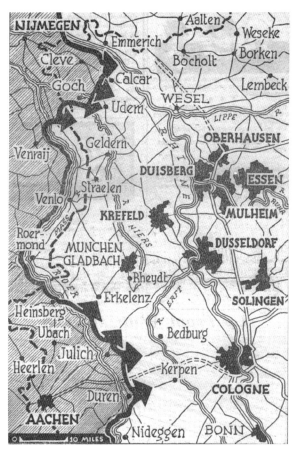

"Behind, the Roer—Ahead the Rhine," reads the headline for a Stars & Stripes map after the crossing.

come in, and flak suddenly bursts just ahead of the ducks. Black puffs fill the sky. The ducks turn suddenly right. The bursts progress, and the ducks must make another right turn, which puts them on a reverse course. I expect they will be hit or scattered, but they keep a perfect V-formation, and their wings don't miss a beat.

After crossing the Roer, I notice that many of the German towns remain untouched by the war. The citizens have good shoes and clothing, and the women wear silk stockings. They also have plenty of bicycles, and there are many cows and horses in the fields.

In France, Belgium, and Holland, the women were bare-legged and wore wooden or cloth shoes and cheap, worn clothing. There were not enough horses to plow the fields. In one Dutch community there were only four horses left to plow hundreds of acres for three years, so the fields were not plowed, and the people starved. And I can't forget Roermond, Holland, where many had facial sores for lack of proper nutrition and where every shop was cleaned out.

In April Maj. Gen. John B. Anderson, CO of the XVI Corps, orders me to prosecute some GIs for multiple rape. I am called back to the town of Altfeld (3,000 population) on the west side of the river, where the crimes occurred. The GIs are in an artillery battalion of 300 men. Some of the younger men were bored, restless, and looking for action as they awaited the buildup of troops.

Many of the GIs, in a short division of about a hundred, decided one evening to go in pairs into the homes of women and rape them. Taking turns, one held his rifle or pistol on the victim and others in the house, while the other GI assaulted her. In most cases there were two women and occasionally an elderly man. The younger men were away at war. The victims were of all ages; one was 80 years old. Afterwards the GIs looted the homes.

I interview some of the women in my makeshift office in a schoolhouse. All tell the same story—they can't identify the men. I must figure out a strategy, some way to identify the perpetrators. The women are so shocked that they are of little help. But they have come willingly to my office. All they know is that the men all wore the same uniform and that some were taller than others. Most of the women have somber faces. One woman tells me, "They were like animals, and they were rough and tore my dress."

"We will arrest and punish them," I say.

I have to find some other means of connecting the 40 involved GIs to the victims. My thoughts turn to the looting. Perhaps we can identify the men by the jewelry and other items they stole. But many may have mailed the items home. Only the inspector general has the right to open packages at random. His search yields a few items, subsequently put into envelopes marked with the sender's name. This is not enough. I must find a better way.

The inspector general cooperates, and we conceive an unusual approach. Borrowing a group of men from another outfit and instructing them carefully, we gather at the edge of the division area at 4:00 A.M., then walk in and wake the GIs. One inspector stands in front of each two-man tent and makes them strip and stand at parade rest. The inspectors then go through their pockets and duffel bags. We find hundreds of pieces of jewelry, coins, and other valuables. These items are placed in envelopes, marked in each case with the soldier's name and serial number, verified by the dog tag worn at all times on a chain around his neck. The evidence is sealed.

This procedure complete, we set up a line of tables at a school-house, laying out each group of valuables next to a numbered card matching the number on the soldier's envelope. We circulate a written notice in the town, saying we have the valuables and inviting everyone to the schoolhouse at an appointed time. Almost everyone comes.

We instruct the townspeople not to go near the tables until directed and not to touch or take anything. We queue them up, one line for each side of the tables, and they examine each pile. We hear exclamations and shouts of joy as they identify their valuables. A soldier writes down each identifier's name and address, saying she will hear from us soon. Then we run a lineup of the GIs whose numbers have been identified. The ravaged women silently indicate whether they recognize the rapists. Answering our questions afterward, some make positive identifications, from a look in the eye, from hair, profile, or weight and height. This identification is matched to the holders of the valuables, without the knowledge of the victims. I choose two of the men identified to be defendants at the trial.

Five senior officers, seated behind a table in the schoolhouse, conduct the trial. There is a table for defense counsel, another for me and my assistant. Almost all of the victims are in the audience. A captain second-chairs me. (I am now a first lieutenant.) He doesn't offer any suggestions throughout the trial, which takes two weeks.

The convictions are unanimous, and the men are sentenced to death by hanging. This is the first time someone I've prosecuted has received the death penalty. Even for so heinous a crime, the penalty seems unjust. Ten years seems plenty, but the military has its rules.

Afterwards, to my surprise, I receive the Bronze Star for "out-standing service" in the case, the solution of which appeared impos-

HEADQUARTERS XVI CORPS UNITED STATES ARMY

Award of the Bronze Star Medal
Citation

First Lieutenant Horace R. Hansen, 01 325 088, Headquarters Ninth United States Army (then Headquarters XVI Corps), for meritorious service in connection with military operations against the enemy from 3 March to 6 April 1945, in Holland and Germany. The unusual diligence, determination, intelligence, foresight and meticulous attention to details which this outstanding officer applied to his duties expedited the process of military justice in an extremely meritorious and efficient manner. First Lieutenant Hansen brilliantly performed an outstanding service for the XVI Corps and the United States Government when he expeditiously prosecuted and convicted two soldiers guilty of numerous heinous crimes, the solution of which had appeared impossible. The stellar performance at all times of First Lieutenant Hansen reflects great credit upon himself, the armed forces and the United States Government. Entered military service from Minnesota.

JOHN B. ANDERSON,
Major General, U. S. Army,
Commanding.

sible. The pattern of proof laid a foundation for other prosecutions. But I feel guilty about the sentencing. The perpetrators had to be convicted, and that's what I did. For now, the convicted men are kept in stockades, awaiting case review. I hope their sentence is commuted.

In the barn above, near Gardelegen, Germany, the Nazis burned 300 prisoners alive. Below, what was inside.

Chapter 5

With transfer to the 102nd Division on April 9, I am entered in a table of organization and told I will soon be a captain. The destination of the Ninth Army is the Elbe River, and the 102nd Division reaches Stendal, Germany, about a quarter-mile from the Elbe, on April 15. Between the river and Stendal is the site of a well-concealed, abandoned Luftwaffe airdrome. From the air it looks like a poultry farm. Fowl of all kinds are kept there as camouflage.

As soon as we arrive, a nearby atrocity is reported. I go immediately to the scene—a large barn near the town of Gardelegen. The 50-by-100-foot brick barn smolders. I park the Jeep and walk toward it. I see bodies and smell the strong stench of burned flesh. I feel sick and angry.

More than 300 slave laborers have burned to death in the brick barn. Bodies cover the entire floor, piled thickest at the four sliding doors. Nearby are mass graves dug—by slave laborers—five feet wide, six feet deep, and 15 to 60 feet long. More bodies lie in the ditches, some only partly covered. We find one person, a Hungarian lieutenant named Bondo Gaza, who has miraculously escaped this horrid death through a sliding door.

"At first there were 2,000 of us, transferred from a concentration camp and factory in East Germany where they were making airplane parts," Gaza says. "The Russians were about to capture the SS guards, who quickly put us on a train going west. American planes strafed the locomotive, and it stopped about 12 miles east of Gardelegen.

"We were marched farther westward, but only 1,200 reached Gardelegen," Gaza recalls. "The lame who fell were shot at the side of the road and left without burial. At Gardelegen, most of the 1,200 were shot, and their bodies were dumped into the recently dug mass graves. The 300 remaining were herded into the barn, where there was gasoline-soaked straw scattered almost knee-deep on the floor.

"SS guards herded us with machine guns into the barn. One guard opened the door slightly and threw in a lighted match. The prisoners tried to escape through the doors on the opposite side, only to be mowed down by gunfire. Some tried to put out the fire, and the SS guards threw signal flares into the spreading flames," Gaza concludes.

The 102nd Division chief of staff is furious. He orders all able-bodied men from the town to come to the barn immediately. When they arrive, he climbs onto the hood of a Jeep and in stinging language tells them the story in detail. Then he points to the barn and orders the German civilians: "Now, get in there and see what your fellow men have done. Stay in there 20 minutes. Then come back here."

The author points to the bodies of slave laborers who tried to escape the fire at one door. SS troops shot those who tried to escape through another door, below.

American soldiers show Gardelegen citizens a mass grave near the barn where the prisoners burned.

The people hesitate at the pile of bodies at the door, and one man faints. When they come back from the barn, Colonel Lynch orders them to dig more graves and bury the bodies. The next day, I drive the 12 miles of road over which the prisoners marched to their deaths. We see clusters of bodies along the roadside. We determine that the 2,000 were mostly Russians and Poles, with some French, Hungarians, Greeks, and Italians. They were marching to another concentration camp—farther behind German front lines.

The following day a message comes from General Eisenhower. It requires proper burial, in separate graves with markers, in an existing or new cemetery. One German civilian must dig each grave. Another, with perpetually designated successors, must care for it.

Fifty years later, a neat cemetery with a cross at each grave, except for about 40 graves marked with the Star of David, will prove Hitler's order, prove that his SS guards marched foreign workers out of many of the concentration camps, threatened them with capture, and when "necessary" killed them on the spot. He did not want any witnesses to his barbarism left in the camps.

Cemetery at Gardelegen

I report our findings to the Ninth Army HQs, which will forward them to the Central War Crimes Evidence Library in London for safe-keeping until the perpetrators are caught.

The new headquarters at the Luftwaffe (airdrome) provides us with first-class accommodations. The JAGD unit is in an office building, and I have a private bedroom on the second floor of an adjoining German officers' quarters. It is luxurious, the best so far. There is no electricity or running water, but we find a storehouse of canned goods, Polish hams, wine, and champagne.

A patch of woods conceals the whole complex. The Germans have left V-1 and V-2 bombs, loaded on railway cars (see below). An airplane hangar with a German jet fighter, the first I've seen intact on the ground, catches my eye. The Germans have left in a hurry. For us the hot war is almost over.

Author with V-1s

While waiting for the Russians to reach the Elbe, the Allied artillery spotter planes take turns watching eastward for prearranged flare signals (red if the Russians are stalled and green if they're moving toward us). It is a boring job. At the evening mess, I learn that the pilots have been in a playful mood. Seeing a large white goose flying about four feet above the road, they decided to give it a thrill, then added a rooster and a turkey to the experiment. Lt. Fred Campbell tells us:

"We tied a piece of cloth to the leg of each bird so we could identify it and took them all three to a height of 1,000 feet. First, we threw

The author, above with an intact German fighter jet at the Luftwaffe, below with a shot-down German fighter, also near Stendal.

the goose out. He made a straight nosedive, then suddenly came out of it and landed safely. Next, the turkey. He plummeted like a lump of lead, and we couldn't see what happened to him. Then the white rooster. He went head-over-tail but came out of it, feathers flying, close to the ground.

"When we landed and looked for the birds, we found two of them in the farmyard we got them from, with the cloth still tied to their legs. The goose was groggy, continually shaking his head and teetering. The rooster was back with the flock of hens, strutting around as if nothing had happened. I'll bet those hens don't believe a word of it," he says with a big smile.

———————

The Russians are entering Berlin, only 50 miles due east, and we have reached the Elbe River, the agreed-upon line dividing the Allies from the Russians. Organized resistance from the Germans has collapsed. Only some detached Germans on the Elbe to our front and an armored task force to the rear give real trouble. The day after the Berlin entry, American fighter planes bomb the Germans and clear us. On April 15, the fighting is over for us!

Over the next several weeks, until Victory in Europe (V-E Day, May 7, 1945), we accept the surrender of some 60,000 fear-crazed German soldiers trying to escape capture by the Russians. When we hear the great V-E news is announced, there is mild excitement lasting about five minutes. Then everyone goes back to work.

———————

A short way from the Luftwaffe airdrome is a demolished steel bridge crossing the Elbe, about 200 yards wide. When the Russians take Berlin in a mighty battle, fleeing German soldiers jam the bridge on the east bank. Unable to climb across the twisted steel, some Germans use boats and rafts; others swim. Our guards stop them because of the agreement that the east bank be the Russian zone of occupation.

I go down to the west bank for awhile each day, to watch the end of the war. Thousands of Germans, still armed, are trying to cross the river. Yet for them to fire a shot at us is unthinkable. Their one consuming thought is to escape the Russians. We alone can give them sanctuary. Like children in the shadow of the monster, they cry for protection. We give no quarter but don't fire at them. The guards discourage their crossing by firing into the water when any of them try. I've never seen anything like this before. I can't say I enjoy it.

One day some Russian Yak fighters fly over and strafe the

German soldiers crossing the Elbe River over the bombed-out bridge at Stendal.

Germans. Even that doesn't scatter them. The Germans move up about 40 white ambulances, and the mob gets bigger. Finally, the Allies make an agreement with the Russians, and we let the Germans come over to surrender. We give them no help in crossing but leave them to their own devices. They string planks through the wreckage of the bridge, but it would take a gymnast to get across that way.

One German, carrying a huge knapsack, falls off the bridge and drowns. Others use rubber pontoons, assault boats, or logs—anything that will float. The few boats take what seems forever to make a round trip, and some Germans wait for rides in cold water up to their necks. An American GI borrows my binoculars, then says, "It looks like a shipwreck." And these are only the deserters.

After about a week, German officers—a brigadier general and a lieutenant general—come with a white-flag party to a regimental command post of the 102nd in Stendal. They formally surrender what is left of two of the German armies. At first, they insist we occupy the areas across the river so they can save face, but finally they agree to *our* conditions. After surrender, the German soldiers cross over in droves. They funnel into the approach on our side, where they must walk down the street to a shakedown point. None tries to escape, though

we have only a handful of guards for every thousand of them. At the shakedown point, GIs search them, throwing the weapons into a big pile. Not one complains about anything. Not one German soldier cries "Geneva Treaty," as others have done. They are simply tired of running from the "Bolsheviks" and glad to be alive.

Afraid of capture by the Russians, as many as 18,000 German soldiers a day surrender peacefully to the Americans. Above, the officers; below, the troops.

The GIs like to frisk the German officers most. They know it nettles their dignity, and so they do a slow, painstaking job. To add to the humiliation, they make the officers take off their shoes.

One GI takes a box of cigars from a general (we take in 18 generals today) and hands them out to German privates coming through the line. Each takes a cigar with a startled, quizzical look. About 75 feet down the line, another GI takes back each cigar as the soldiers pass. They look back, trying to figure out the game.

As the line progresses, German civilians, mostly women, line up about six deep on either side of the street. There isn't a wave or a smile. They just stand sadly, perhaps looking for loved ones. Not a word passes between soldier and civilian.

We keep most of the prisoners at the airport, where a single strand of barbed wire encloses them. There are only a few roving guards in Jeeps, but again no one tries to escape. With typical efficiency, their ranking officers start a chain of command and organize the mob into squared-off platoons. Then they ride the privates as if they were in training camp.

A German soldier clicks his heels and stands like a board while the officer shouts at him from two feet away: "Dummkopf!" I ask my interpreter why they don't just take it easy. He lived in Germany until 1938, and his answer is simple: "They're Germans. They never relax."

———

The 29th Division, my earlier outfit, is demobilized at München-Gladbach (later Mönchengladbach), and I take a day off for some visiting. I see my friends—including a good buddy, Chaplain Joseph Shubow of Boston—at division headquarters. He tells me he held a traditional Jewish Passover seder in March in the dining room of the mansion of propaganda minister Joseph Goebbels. "It's retribution come home, for Goebbels' decree in November 1938 was to burn all the synagogues in Germany," he says. Just thinking about this delights me for days.

Back at Stendal, we talk with some of the German prisoners, who say that the Allied bombings have been pure terror attacks against helpless cities. That the Allied attacks might have been strategic targets and reprisals for bombing England doesn't occur to them—they haven't been "told" that. They have no conception of how their war has affected the "inferior" people from the east, or of the suffering of the slave laborers. They know nothing of mass atrocities, never heard of them,

The author at Stendal town square.

and do not believe they have occurred. Not one admits to being a Nazi, not even the cold, cocky Hitlerjugend. All have been "forced" into the Wehrmacht.

The Germans are all positive that the Allies will fight the Russians when they meet. The Americans have no business in the war, they say. Churchill has tricked them into it. They keep asking whether they can go home, as the war is practically over. One asks to go to nearby relatives tonight: "I'll be right back early in the morning. It's such a short distance." From the Bronx, he says he was visiting here and couldn't get back. He insists, but I tell him to go back to his unit.

———————

Gen. Kurt Dittmar, the Wehrmacht publicity chief, has surrendered at the River Elbe today. The interrogation team says it took no pumping whatever to get him to talk. Rather, it was hard to stop him. "The High Command was convinced of defeat after Stalingrad," he said. "No doubt was left when the German counteroffensive failed to split us in Normandy. Your air forces made the invasion possible. We couldn't get our reserves to the front. The Ardennes counteroffensive was a poor man's choice, the only object being to gain four months to build the Rhine defenses. That attack cost too much, and it would have been smarter to spend everything at the Rhine."

"Hitler is still in Berlin, running everything down to the details. The National Redoubt in the Alps is only a paper idea. He knew they would lose but never dreamed the destruction would be so terrible."

Col. Edward Beale, my immediate supervisor, and I will have a private session with Maj. Gen. Hermann Eicher for four hours tonight. Eicher is "judge general" on the staff at Berlin, a rank corresponding to our assistant judge advocate general in Washington. We are interested in the German system of military justice.

Eicher is a typical, poker-back Junker. He shows the marks of an elite military class in bearing, demeanor, and Heidelberg scars—two deep ones on his left cheek. He is 65, tall, with a long, severe face. His uniform is elegant, with several flashy medals. He tells us: "The Wehrmacht has only two courts—the central court that tries both soldiers and civilians for high crimes such as treason, espionage, and sabotage, and the single-division field courts with general jurisdiction that try soldiers only for military and social crimes." The sentences of the field courts are final (no appeal) and are executed automatically.

In contrast, the American military has three courts in each division command, having fixed jurisdiction and limited power of punishment for offenses of varying severity. Each offense is tried in the lowest court having jurisdiction. We have an automatic appeal, and there is a searching review of serious cases before a sentence can be executed. The

Maj. Gen. Eicher with the author.

penalties differ, too. A German soldier convicted of rape ordinarily gets one to three years while the American soldier gets mandatory life imprisonment or death.

We acquire some documents, elaborate plans for activities of the Werewolves, mainly Hitlerjugend. There are specific instructions on how to snipe and run, cut communication wires, blow up bridges and important American installations, contaminate the water supply, and disable enemy vehicles. The Werewolves are supposed to continue their operations against the Allies no matter what happens in the war. We do have some trouble with these brats, especially with their sniping and cutting wires, but not enough for real concern. From nearby woods they shot some men on the roads recently, and the other day we caught four of them red-handed, cutting our communication wire. The four boys are only eight, nine, 11, and 15 years old. MG (military government) sentences them to confinement. We catch another, older boy, who has planted dynamite on a pontoon bridge, and find several of their headquarters, including caches of explosives and weapons. Afraid the activities of the Hitlerjugend could bring reprisal, some German women tipped us off.

In Stendal, the division band assembles on the lawn in front of the regimental command post. A lot of German civilians gather, but no one knows the purpose of the show. After a while, a string of sedans pulls up, and the band blares out the "Internationale." Out of the cars step ten Russian officers, who face the band and salute. When the music stops, there is a spree of handshaking and backslapping all around. Then the officers obligingly pose for a mob of GIs snapping pictures with their "newly found" German cameras. The Russians look sharp in their smart uniforms. When they go into the command post, I notice that the civilians across the street stand as if fixed, their expressions a mix of disbelief and apprehension.

I find out later that the Russian officers' group includes Marshal Konstantin Rakossovsky and his aides coming from the Berlin area. We haven't yet met the bulk of the Red army, on the other side of the river. The Russian soldiers are waiting to cross until we take custody of all the German prisoners.

By the time we meet them here a few days later, several other contacts, including a meeting with Rakossovsky, have occurred. Because the river is difficult to cross, each side exchanges only small groups representing similar units in each army. The bang-up affair we had planned doesn't materialize, but it is a friendly, enthusiastic meeting.

I meet one of the first groups of Russian officers coming over to our side. At first, everything is formal—they exchange salutes and all that. But when we start chatting and they see what ordinary guys we are, they wring our hands, slap our backs, and hug us. We can't help but like their robust, straightforward manner. They grin all the time and throw a lot of action into the conversation. They are physically rugged and plenty lively—not the stolid, grim types we expected.

Linkup with the Russians opens a pathway for the return of GI prisoners of war. The Russians bring them to us first-class. They have motor-powered rubber boats and planes to get to our side of the Elbe. I spend a whole evening talking with a group of returning American POWs. They are housed temporarily in a school building without running water, electricity, and toilets, but they have no complaints. They are so happy they don't know what to do with themselves. But some are starving, skin-covered skeletons.

As tired as they may be, not one man lies down. They pace and talk excitely about how wonderful it is going to be to take a bath, to eat good chow, and to wear clean clothes. They

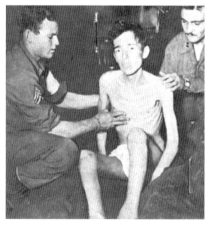

Yank taken at Battle of the Bulge.

are told that their shipment home will be as speedy as possible. I am interested in their treatment at the hands of the Germans because I wish to obtain evidence of treaty violations. But I soon find myself absorbed in their personal experiences.

Most of the men were taken in the Battle of the Bulge. One GI says, "Life in the German prison camps was rough. The guards didn't beat us, but the routine ground us down. We were up at five o'clock every morning and given a cup of bitter, ersatz coffee but nothing to eat. Then we were formed into work gangs. We protested at first because that treatment was an outright violation of the Geneva Treaty, but it didn't matter. The rule was 'No work, no eat.' We were made to work at repairing bomb damage, mostly the railroads, and building road blocks.

"At noon we took a half-hour rest but no food, then worked until 6:00 P.M. After marching back to camp, we got our one and only meal of the day—a cup of thin turnip or potato soup and some black bread, six men to a small loaf. Weeks of hard labor and a starvation diet of bad food made us stuporous and docile. We lost our will to attempt escape and could think of nothing all day but to get back to our straw ticks and lie down."

Another skinny GI tells me, "The only thing that kept our hopes and interest alive was war news, and we did everything we could to get it. Whenever a prisoner overheard guards talking about the news, he told the others through the grapevine. In one camp, a GI radio operator rigged up a crystal set from parts he pieced together. He kept the whole place informed of BBC broadcasts. Another guy wrote the headline news on a small piece of paper, which he folded in a wad and put under the fence almost every night."

Some others were prisoners much longer. One American taken at Tobruk 26 months ago dropped from 140 to 87 pounds and looks ten years older than his 24 years. A British soldier, starved to a rail, carries a shriveled right arm in a sling. He was taken at Dunkirk five years ago: "About two years ago, while working on a railroad gang, I picked up a handful of dried peas that spilled out of a freight car. The Nazi guard broke my arm with a rifle butt before I put the peas in my pocket. I received no medical care; my arm is now useless."

They all brighten when I ask about their liberation: "The Russians gave us everything we wanted, but liquor first. If you didn't drink with Ivan," one says, "he gave you everything he had."

What a few vodkas can do!
Author with Russian lieutenant.

Russian soldiers, American military personnel, and liberated prisoners alike—all are waiting for a big change around here soon. Everybody is busy overhauling weapons and equipment. We have all had physical examinations, and the re-organization program is going at top speed. Everyone is counting service points, with most finding themselves a little short of the 92 needed for discharge.

Chapter 6

I'm waiting to get to Bavaria, the center for war-crimes prosecution. Meantime, I'm involved in court-martial cases in the XVI Corps and the 102nd Division, both units of the Ninth Army.

We move south from Stendal into Bavaria in easy stages, as the Russians are not yet ready to occupy their zones. The frequent moving is a nuisance, but it gives us the chance to see central Germany. It is good to get away from Stendal. Our outfit has handled and screened more than 80,000 prisoners and countless thousands of displaced persons. Everyone has been on edge and dog-tired besides. We deserve a rest, and now we finally get it. In early June we move south to the city of Gotha in Thuringia, Germany.

I make my first trip on the continent in something other than a Jeep or a truck. We have a liberated bus with soft leather seats and a quiet motor, almost as good as a Greyhound. Our route takes us through the rolling country of Saxony and finally through the Harz Mountains into the state of Thuringia. The Harz chain is a dead ringer for the Tennessee Smokies—not as large but just as grand. Pine trees cover the mountains, and there is the same misty haze around the peaks. Even the blacktop roads look the same. The only difference is that in every valley a huge church with a high spire dominates a cluster of red-roofed houses. Ox teams pull the farm wagons. There are few roadside inns or billboards.

After a while, though, we see several of the legendary museum castles. The Schaufenberg at Friedrichrode contains armor and mail suits, lances, swords, shields, and other relics of the Crusades, the Thirty Years' War, and the campaigns of Napoleon. The Wartburg at Eisenach, the best preserved, is a storybook castle with battle wall, moat, and drawbridge. We see furniture and other relics of Martin Luther, who translated the New Testament into German from Greek

Wartburg castle, near Eisenach, Germany.

The Wartburg drawbridge, sole entrance to the castle (left),
and the author examining a water well inside.

while he was hidden here, and of Wolfgang Goethe, who wrote poetry
here. We also see the mementos of Franz Liszt, who played concerts in
the festival hall.

Everywhere in Europe is the sharp contrast between the common
folk and the members of the upper class, who have mansions and
castles on the high ground or at the edges of towns. There seems to be
no middle class.

By this time most of the slave laborers in the large cities have been re-
patriated or housed separately from the Germans, in DP (displaced
person) centers. Even after two months of eating double rations, they
are so thin as to be readily distinguishable from German civilians.
Some were hardly more than skin-covered skeletons before liberation.

Caring for these people is our first concern and a major headache. With few unbombed homes available, housing is the greatest problem. Often we must put them in Wehrmacht barracks, factory buildings, or even in the sanitized concentration camps whence they came. For a long time, 10,000 people have been housed in Buchenwald. Many have contagious diseases and require medical care. Food and other supplies can't be procured efficiently. A few of the slave laborers are understandably bent on plunder and violence, and some security is necessary. Many whose homelands are in the Russian zone of occupation do not want to go back.

I have been in many of these DP centers, and there is little difference among them. Despite the efforts of the American army to keep them clean, one is as filthy as the next. The army has been criticized for conditions in some places. In others the facilities are adequate, but the people have no will to improve their lot. Many never wash clothes

Erwin (above, far left, and at right) looks healthy compared to thousands of other skin-covered skeletons I see at Buchenwald. The Nazis forced 50,000 (on average here) prisoners to make weapons such as panzer fausts and cannon parts.

or take a bath. Some relieve themselves in any handy spot. They are fed and have beds; beyond that they don't care.

I've talked with some of the freed laborers about going home, and the response has never been enthusiastic. Many expect to find families gone, homes ruined, and the living hard. Some, especially those from the east, have left behind so little that they have no desire to go back.

Repatriation committees for each nationality (made up of its own people) practically have to push them around to overcome their inertia.

Despite the army's order to treat those who refuse repatriation as German civilians, hundreds of thousands of DPs remain. We can't force them to go, but we really don't want to treat them like Germans. I suspect a good many simply want to stay where they can see Americans. Others are still afraid of starvation. There is little we can do to make their lives better.

Yesterday we got an order, classified secret, that the Russians will take over Thuringia, their agreed-upon area, in one week. But today, the American-controlled German radio announced the news, and panic began.

Every day in the week that follows we see all roads jammed with German civilians fleeing south to Bavaria. From children to old women, they walk with packs on their backs, push overloaded baby buggies or pull carts, ride on everything from a wagon with ox team to a train of hayracks pulled by a tractor. This mass exodus has surprised us. We knew the Germans hated the Russians, but nothing like this. We know now, more certainly, that when a German abandons his property, he is moved by more than hate. It is more like pure terror. The GIs who comment on all this usually say, "I'd be scared too, knowing what I'd done to the Russians."

In two days the Russian advance party arrives to plan offices, quarters, and occupation details. The men come in the queerest-looking military convoy I've ever seen, with everything from three-wheeled pickups and jalopies to ambulances and long, black Mercedes limousines—all German civilian vehicles. About 50 men are in the party, and with great seriousness they immediately set about their work. The moment they appear, the window shades of the town are drawn.

The Russians come without complete messing equipment, so the officers eat with us, and the Ivans eat their emergency rations. I visit the soldiers in their separate billets at noon one day, but I immediately become more interested in their mess. They have black bread, margarine, and some kind of sour-smelling canned meat. First they cut the small loaf of bread in half and scoop out the center. Then they mix the crumbs with margarine and canned meat, kneading it with their hands on a dirty table, and stuff the mixture into the hollowed loaf. They eat it like an ice-cream cone and wipe their greasy hands on their jackets afterwards.

"A *real* mess," I think.

After dinner one night, I invite one of the Russian officers to my quarters, a single-family house that I share with another officer. The

A Russian major and his assistant (left) and a Russian soldier consorting with fräuleins on the American side of the Elbe.

Russian is intelligent, speaks fair English, and says his home is in Vladivostok. He plays the piano well, if loudly, and like most Russian soldiers drinks cognac like water. His tunic is loaded with medals, and after some urging, he explains that several are for major battles including Stalingrad, and five are for wounds. Despite all this combat he still wants to get in the fight with the Japanese. He chews gum vigorously all the while, and leaving, he asks, "Do you have some new gum? I chew this one for two days."

Finally, we are told that everything is organized in Bavaria and to come at our convenience. When our troops leave Thuringia, the civilians are apprehensive. They gather to watch us load the trucks, and they ask a lot of questions: "Do the Rooskies stay long? Come you back? Don't some of your soldats stay here?" They are clearly apprehensive. I don't feel sorry for them.

The trip takes two days, south through most of Bavaria to an old town on the Danube River called Vilshofen, near the Czech-Austrian corner. The country is beautiful the entire way—hills, valleys, neatly kept forests, lots of villages along highways and rivers, picturesque inns and houses, and no signboards.

The most noticeable wartime mars on the landscape are the dozens of work subcamps, each usually adjoining a small factory set against a hill or in a wooded valley. Each subcamp is fairly well concealed and a little apart from a village. The obvious intent was to decentralize industry and avoid air-bombings. These are subcamps of mother camps like Buchenwald, Nordhausen, and Dachau, where the parts of all kinds of military equipment—telephones, tanks, artillery, mortars, machine guns, uniforms—from the subcamps are assembled. Some of the sanitized subcamps still house some DPs. Most are decorated with antifascist signs and the DPs' national flags.

Out of the blue sky, on August 5, the radio announces the dropping of an atomic bomb on Hiroshima. There is almost complete disbelief until *Star and Stripes* carries the story the next day. Just about everyone stops work to talk about the greatest excitement since the crossing of the Rhine. This excitement is sweet because it counts us out of the war with Japan. Going home soon becomes a real possibility.

I ask Col. Edward Beale, who in civilian life was a patent lawyer specializing in chemistry, "Is the atom bomb related to chemical or physical science?" He says some of both.

I soon leave southern Bavaria for Bayreuth in central Germany, to obtain war-crimes evidence. Here I live in and take my meals at a modern building, used earlier for Hitler's visits. It was built within the walls of the Villa Wannfreid, the home of composer Richard Wagner.

One day I visit Wagner's mansion and meet Winifred Wagner, about 50, who shows me around the huge place. She is the widow of Siegfried Wagner, son of the composer by his second wife. She is English-born-and-raised and a graduate of Cambridge University.

She takes me to the music room, and there I see the instruments on which the composer wrote his music. One is a large concert piano and the other a pianoforte. There has been no damage to the mansion or the high stone walls surrounding the large area of the villa, except for one artillery shell that struck the corner of the kitchen.

Winifred Wagner, above with Hitler, ca. 1938, at the entry to Fespielhausen (Festival House), built for her father-in-law, composer Richard Wagner. (Paul) Josef Goebbels is partly visible, right. With back to camera is Hermann Goering.

Richard Wagner's home, Wahnfried. Facility at left was built for Hitler's visits.

Mrs. Wagner is most gracious and reminds me to go the operetta at the concert hall called Festspielhausen, built for the composer. *Rosalinda* is beautifully performed, and the acoustics in the amphitheater are nearly perfect. Later I think about Mrs. Wagner and her musical heritage. I again wonder how a man like Hitler could lead a country rich in the arts into the depths of barbarism.

After 16 months in Europe, I finally get a leave for nine luxurious days on the Riviera. We come back to find the de-Nazification program in full swing. Flour mills and clothing and shoe factories have shut down—their owners departed Nazis. No provision has been made to reopen them.

We've known for months that there will be inadequate fuel for the winter, but the woodcutting program won't start until fall—too late. Military government detachments are filled with inept personnel who duck responsibility and pass the buck. One MG detachment replaces another, five times in less than three months, with utter confusion. We are probably the world's worst occupation force. The long, tough occupation job should be turned over to interested career people as soon as possible. The troops here now have no stomach for the job. They are sick and tired of Europe and want to go home.

I don't have enough points to leave, but still there is a welcome surprise—transfer to the concentration camp at Dachau, Germany, to take part in the camp's war-crimes cases. This is what I've been waiting for.

The author and Capt. James Feeks with army nurses at the Carlton Hotel on the French Riviera, not long before Horace's transfer to Dachau.

Maj. Gen. Lucian Truscott (overcoat) bids farewll in October 1945 to Col. Edward Cheever (Third Army JAG, stationed at Munich) after touring the Dachau camp and trial facility. The author (far left) led the tour. Truscott succeeded Gen. George Patton as commanding officer of the Third Army after Patton died in a car accident.

Chapter 7

Early October 1945

After my assignment to Dachau, Gen. Frank Keating, CO of the 102nd Division, advises Gen. Lucian Truscott, CO of the Third Army—through a hand-carried message—that I will be delayed in arrival due to my trying a murder case. The order states that I will report to Dachau on October 1, 1945.

I see the judge advocate general (JAG) of the Third Army headquarters in Munich and am told I will replace a lieutenant colonel who has left for home. The JAG is Col. Edward Cheever, about 50, my size, a quiet speaker who gets quickly to the point.

I am only a captain in the JAGD, and I ask how I can replace a higher-ranking officer. He says this will be no problem because the ten officer-lawyers on the staff at Dachau are lieutenants. He notes the obvious: rank and qualifications do not always coincide in a war-time army.

He looks at my personnel file, then says my experience with courts-martial law in Europe—war-crimes investigation for the Ninth Army, my assisgnment as trial judge advocate for the XVI Corps head-quarters and the resulting Bronze Star Medal, as well as my six years as a felony prosecutor before enlistment—qualifies me for this post. He says he will communicate my background to the staff at Dachau and that my title will be chief prosecutor, as used by my predecessor. He personally takes me to Dachau, introduces me to the staff, and sees to my living quarters, a mansion formerly occupied by the German camp kommandant.

I function as chief of staff, although I will also try two cases. The mission of the staff is to sort out, from more than 32,000 automatic arrestees, those to be prosecuted and those to be released. The sanitized compound holds as many arrestees as it formerly held slave laborers. The Dachau camp is the central compound for all automatic arrestees in the American zone in Bavaria. They are Nazis of various ranks, picked up in the American zone and western Austria. The French zone to the west and the British zone to the north each have similar facilities.

Enclosing the Dachau compound are an electrified fence, high guard towers, and a deep moat formerly connected to a nearby river, all fringed by tall pines. The countryside is slightly rolling farmland. The pines help conceal the camp from travelers along public roads.

The automatic arrestees in the compound are mainly ranking members of Hitler's many organizations—the Nazi party officers, his private army of SS, Gestapo, SD (security police), and others. Among the arrestees are the special SS Death's-head units, who have run the four mother camps in this area—Dachau, Flossenburg, Mauthausen,

The Nazis forced prisoners at Dachau (lined up along the electric fence, moat, and guard tower) to listen to Hitler's radio speeches.

and Buchenwald. (See appendix.) The latter two camps fall within what will become the Russian zone of occupation, with prosecution tendered to the Russians. (Later we learn that they have declined the responsibility.)

Linking the beatings and murders committed against the slave laborers (taken from conquered countries by Hitler's SS forces) to the specific officials and guards of the SS operating these camps is a laborious job, one yielding hard evidence too slowly. (The SS—or Schutzstaffel—is Hitler's private army for dirty work like running concentration camps and persecuting the Jews.) I hold a meeting of the officers on the staff to determine a quicker method.

A lieutenant who spent his early years in Austria before the war understands the mentality of the Nazis. "A profile questionnaire would be the best to get primary evidence," he says. "We could take

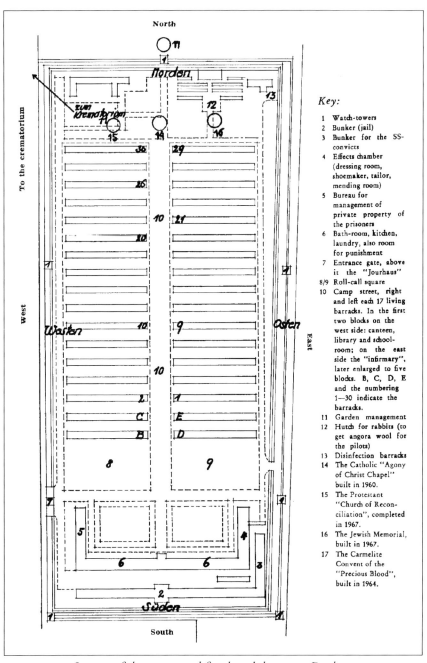

Layout of the compound for slave laborers at Dachau.

one barracks at a time, starting with the 1,500 who have been specifically denounced by their victims."

He prepares questions and presents them the next day. They ask for the background of the arrestee, where he was born and raised, location of occupations, and particularly, a list of duties at concentration camps or subcamps, specifying times and places. We decide the forms will shorten our chore, and they do.

The Germans are accustomed to filling out forms and do so rather truthfully, as they are afraid to lie. The arrestees apparently think we have evidence against them. Nevertheless, I am sure that some admit to lesser or fewer atrocities in the hope of gaining leniency or of dodging connections with greater crimes.

After the questionnaires are returned, some of the perpetrators in the camp ask to talk with us. In some cases, the wrongdoers make voluntary admissions and denounce others. This widens our net. Many arrestees are later found to have been functionaries only—messengers, truckers, janitors, kitchen help, and the like. Some of these are released.

Besides the three courtrooms and administrative offices, we have an office building made into a hotel to accommodate witnesses. The former chef of the steamship *Bremen*, a luxury liner, runs the hotel's large dining room. The food is excellent.

In a house at the end of a long row of stone structures formerly housing the rest of the SS staff, outside the prison compound, I have a large bedroom at the top of the stairway to the second floor. Next to the mansion are formal gardens, statues, and a pool. We use the mansion for receptions and lodging for visiting dignitaries.

The Dachau compound, the camp at upper right.
Buildings to the left housed staff. Buildings along the street housed officers.

Members of the U.S. Congress and other representatives of Allied governments come to tour the camp. These occasions are welcome breaks from my staff duties. The mansion is a fine place for after-hours visits with staff friends and English-speaking former prisoners.

Paul Husarek, an anti-Nazi radio commentator from Prague, Czechoslovakia (later the Czech Republic), is highly intelligent. He tells me he stayed alive for three years by hiding from the guards in any way he could and by filching food intended for the guard dogs. After the end of the war, he was elected chief of press of the newly formed International Prisoners Committee. He issued a reproduced letter to slave laborers, telling them the latest news, asking them to remain calm, and saying that justice would eventually prevail. He speaks good English, answering my many questions without hesitation.

Friedrich Leopold, Prince of Prussia, has a *schloss* (castle) at Salzburg, Austria. He also speaks good English and has many connections. One is the president of a sound film company at Munich, and the prince invites me to a party at the filmmaker's home the following week. (His company will take films on certain days of the Dachau trial.) I decline and suggest he ask a first lieutenant on my staff.

Later I learn that the party was specifically targeted to me—its real purpose to obtain a submarine to take the filmmaker and his wife to Argentina. As an opener, he has offered to pay $100,000 plus expenses, in American money. I suspect he was an active Nazi—now afraid of arrest.

Before the proposition was stated, says my proxy, many drinks and a superb dinner were served—along with a voluptuous blonde in a black satin dress. She took him to another room and tried to seduce him by fondling his genitals and lifting her dress to show she wore no underwear. He was hard-put to restrain himself but managed to do so.

Another time, when I am having breakfast with a German lawyer in the witness dining room, I see the prince with his male "secretary" having a breakfast that includes a large glass of orange juice. I call the chef over and tell him never to give the prince a large glass of orange juice again, as everyone else dining there will want the same. The chef agrees. Apparently he has been struck by the presence of royalty.

Later, when the prince hears I have five of Hitler's former recorders on my staff, he comes to see me in my office. Greatly excited, he wants to see them right away to determine why he is at Dachau. I tell him I will convey his inquiry to the recorders and let him know. He is disappointed that he cannot see the recorders personally and tells me so. Obviously he is used to getting his way, without question. I tell him he is in Dachau for listening to a BBC broadcast on his radio, contrary to Nazi rules. He huffs and leaves my office without another word.

Another former prisoner, Franz Blaha, a pathologist and surgeon from Prague, operated a 900-bed hospital there. His memory is keen, and he recalls all the forms of torture and killings at Dachau. He states that though it has been difficult for him to leave his work in Prague, he feels it is his duty to testify at the Dachau trials.

Speaking fair English, Blaha recounts his personal experiences in Dachau. Before he became a camp doctor, he says, he was hung by his wrists, which were tied behind his back, for one hour. This caused his arms to dislocate at the shoulders. It took three days to get the joints back to normal and another two weeks to regain feeling in his arms.

Wrist hanging, a Nazi form of torture for slave laborers.

He was beaten on the back by a stick a yard long until he bled—all for doing heavy physical labor too slowly.

After his appointment as camp physician, he observed beatings, torture, and killings of prisoners, as well as typhus, typhoid, and dysentery epidemics, medical experiments on healthy prisoners, and prisoners dying from malnutrition.

Blaha has done hundreds of autopsies at Dachau, keeping written reports on the causes of death. Before coming to Dachau, where he was imprisoned for year and a half, he was detained at Prague by the Gestapo for two years. He becomes the chief witness at the Dachau trial.

Heinz Buchholz (right) and Hans Jonuschat (below), two of the five non-Nazis required to take verbatim notes of Hitler's twice-daily military conferences. At war's end the recorders offered their translation skills to the Americans.

Chapter 8

My master sergeant comes into my office on the second day of my assignment at the Dachau concentration camp. He is tall, with a fine appearance, and is competent in seeing to the performance of my staff. He introduces himself, then says, "Did you know we have new additions to our staff of translators? They were recorders for Hitler."

"No, I didn't. How did they get here?"

"They came from Berchtesgaden, where Hitler sent them. They speak good English," the sergeant says, standing at my desk.

"Why are they here?"

"They came here a couple of days ago with a letter from the U.S. Counterintelligence Corps at Berchtesgaden. Here it is." He takes a letter from his shirt pocket and gives it to me.

"Thanks."

The letter states briefly that the recorders voluntarily surrendered to the American army on May 5, 1945. They were cleared as non-Nazis but chose to stay at Berchtesgaden and translate documents. Finishing with that work, they were told not to try to go to their families in Berlin (because of the Russian occupation) but to go to Dachau, where their talents could be put to good use.

"This is very interesting," I say. "They could be useful on the staff. They are here in this building?"

"Yes."

"I would like to talk with them. Could you bring in a few chairs and ask them to come here?"

"Certainly." He brings the extra chairs, then leaves.

In a few minutes, the recorders arrive.

"How do you do, gentlemen? I am the chief prosecutor here. Please have a seat. How is everything?"

"We are fine," they say, almost in unison. They sit down, not knowing what to expect.

"I understand you were recorders at Hitler's military-situation conferences."

"Yes, we were."

The recorders introduce themselves as Ludwig Krieger, age 58; Ewald Reynitz, 44; Karl Thoet, 39; Hans Jonuschat, 44; and Heinz Buchholz, 39.

"You may be of special help, as the interviewing lieutenants on the staff will see top German officers. Do you have any trouble with that?" I ask.

"No. We would be glad to help. We have just discovered the horrible treatment of prisoners here. This is a situation we knew nothing

Hitler in conference with Field Marshal (Fritz) Erich von Manstein at his right and Gen. Kurt Zeitzler at his left. Seated is recorder Hans Jonuschat. The back of the photo reads in German and appears to be in Jonuschat's tidy hand.

about before we came here," says Krieger. He chose the staff for Hitler from the Stenographic Office of the Reichstag (German parliament).

I am interested in Hitler's reactions to the first things the Allies encountered in Normandy, France, and so we begin our interviews:

"How did Hitler react to the Allied invasion by the Americans, British, and Canadians on June 6, 1944?" I ask.

"[Erwin] Rommel had complained to Der Fuehrer that building steel and concrete fortifications along the French coast would be inadequate. Besides there would be a shortage of men and firepower. The Allies had command of the air and 75 percent of the German forces, including tanks and planes, on the Russian front." Jonuschat leans forward in his chair.

"Der Fuehrer made only one comment when the Allied invasion was successful," he recalls. "'Rommel is always complaining of shortages, just as he did in Africa.' He said no more."

"Why do you always refer to him as *Der Fuehrer?*"

"We were all required to use that term, and I guess it is just a matter of habit."

"What were Hitler's reactions to the July 20 bombing attempt on his life and the breakthrough at Saint Lô?"

Heinz Buchholz says he made a memo for the U.S. Counterintelligence Corps at Berchtesgaden, on July 14, 1945 (almost a year later) regarding the attempt on Hitler's life. Of average height and rather thin, Buchholz has a long face and a short haircut. But his appearance belies his accomplishments. He has been a lawyer since 1929. Finding that the law paid poorly, he became a verbatim recorder for the Prussian Diet, for Field Marshal Erhard Milch's headquarters, for the German Reichstag, and finally for Hitler's headquarters in 1942. He has lived an arduous life and is a competent recorder. He smiles frequently, showing all his teeth as he tells me of the bombing. I notice his upper left incisor is missing.

"When the bombing took place on July 20, 1944, Hitler immediately called for a news blackout. The bomb had been planted at the conference by Lt. Col. Count [Claus Schenk Graf] von Stauffenberg, who was introduced by Field Marshal Wilhelm Keitel, one of Hitler's inner circle, as the man working on new activations for the replacement army in Berlin. If you don't mind, I'll go through the whole story."

"Certainly."

"The bombing was at Hitler's headquarters, called *Wolfsschanze* [Wolf's Lair], a compound of bunkers and barracks in a forest about three-and-a-half miles east of Rastenburg in East Prussia. The conference was not in the bunker but in a room above ground with windows. Near the middle was a large map table supported by two thick, massive table plates instead of legs.

"Stauffenberg's left lower arm had been amputated from a wound in the African campaign. He wore a patch over his right eye. He was carrying a brief case, which was not unusual, as those who attended these conferences usually had maps and papers.

First, his background:

Note for Capt. HANSEN

H E I N Z   B U C H H O L Z

My home-address is: BERLIN-FRIEDENAU, Bachestr. 8 III

I am 39 years old (born on 14 March 1906 in Berlin).

I attended the Elementary school from 1912 till 1915, the Public school from 1915 till 1924. From 1924 to 1929, I studied for the laws at Berlin University. Besides that, I was employed as verbatim reporter at the Prussian Diet, starting 1 September 1925.

After Hitler took over, I was transferred to the stenographers office of the German REICHSTAG. There I was employed till 1945 as Reichstagsstenograph, i.e. an official of senior civil service, with the title "Regierungsrat".

Since October 1939, I was a member of the Wehrmacht (air force, air base troops), at last as Sgt. on the Eastern front. In August 1942, I was ordered to Field Marshal MILCH's headquarters in Berlin as verbatim reporter.

In December 1942, I was detached to the stenographic service in the FÜHRER's headquarters, although I was not a member of the Party or SS; but there were no other stenographers who could do this difficult work of noting down the military discussions verbatim and accurately.

I was present at the briefing on 20 July 1944 when an attempt on HITLER's life was made. I refer to the special report I gave about this attempt.

Dachau, 13 Dec 1945

"He set the briefcase on the floor, leaning it against the solid wooden plate where Hitler stood, near the middle of the map table. Stauffenberg was called by telephone, and he left the room with the remark that he had to go to the office to take the call. We learned later that the call was prearranged.

"One of the generals near the briefcase stumbled into it and moved it to the other side of the plate. Soon the briefcase exploded. At that moment, Hitler was looking at a map on the table, and he leaned over it, supported by his right arm. I remember the blast as a thundering roar, with a bright yellow flame and thick smoke. Glass and wood splinters flew through the air. The large table collapsed. I heard a voice calling, 'Wo [where] ist Der Fuehrer?'

"I saw Hitler, supported by a general and a valet, walking from the barrack to his bunker quarters, approximately 70 meters away.

"There were 23 persons in the room with Hitler. Four died: a colonel, two generals, and my colleague, Heinrich Berger. Twelve were seriously injured and seven slightly injured, including me.

"Hitler suffered a strong shock of the right lower arm, some lighter burns and injuries on the right leg, and slight scratches of the skin from the splinters. Besides that, both eardrums were injured. One became perforated, so his hearing ability was reduced for a long period after the attempt. This became especially obvious during telephone conversations.

"I have a sketch of the room that I'll give you later. It shows locations of the windows, door, and the wooden plates of the table. Position (b) shows that all who died from the explosion were on the open end of the wooden plate, while Hitler stood in the middle, between plates, almost two yards away. I can't remember where everyone

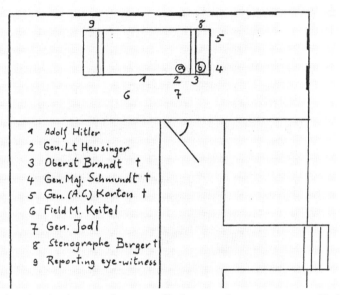

Buchholz's sketch of room where Stauffenberg made an attempt on Hitler's life.

stood, only the nine shown on my sketch. Crosses mark the positions of the four who died." Buchholz ends his narration.

Reynitz continues: "Hitler assigned his favorite general, Kurt Zeitzler, now suspect, away from headquarters to an obscure post. He was sure of Field Marshal Rommel's part in the bombing and ordered two generals to see that Rommel died. Rommel was at the time at a nursing home, recovering from wounds he received in a strafing of his vehicle. The generals were told to give him a cyanide capsule or shoot him on the spot if he didn't take it. He took the capsule."

"That is a good bit of history. You certainly have a wonderful memory. Did Hitler make changes in chief commanders?" I ask.

"Hitler named Goering the director of mobilization and Himmler the director of the home front. They were to increase the number of replacements for units at the front lines. The inner-circle people were to stay at headquarters. They were Field Marshal Wilhelm Keitel, chief of the high command; Gen. Alfred Jodl, chief of operations staff; and Adm. Karl Doenitz, commander of the navy. Herman Goering remained as chief of the air force."

"What happened next?" I address Reynitz again. He seems to have a good command of the facts.

"On the afternoon of the bombing Hitler had an appointment with Benito Mussolini, dictator of Italy, at Hitler's headquarters, which he kept. Mussolini expressed surprise at the lack of security. Hitler said, 'I think the bombing is a good omen. I am still living, and my right hand has quit shaking.'" Reynitz's answer surprises me.

"What did Hitler say about the breakthrough at Saint Lô?" I ask Buchholz.

"He said, 'It's all Rommel's fault.' That's all he said in spite of the fact that he himself had sole command of the war."

"Thank you, gentlemen," I say. "You have been quite helpful, and I now understand a little more of Hitler . . . I will see you soon."

"It was a pleasure. We will be happy to see you anytime," says Krieger.

"Auf Wiedersehen."

They leave with smiles on their faces.

———————

The recorders have little but the clothes they wear. They are housed in the barracks with other translators, and they eat in the staff's restaurant. I am able to improve their living conditions by putting them in private rooms, raising their translator's pay, and arranging for them to eat in the witness restaurant. Then I get them decent clothing—underwear, socks, and shirts—in Munich. New suits are made for them by Jacobs, formerly the private tailor for Reichminister Heinrich Himmler, a member of Hitler's inner circle. They can't seem to do enough for me in return, and I continue to invite the recorders to my living quarters or office on evenings and weekends. I want to learn all I can about Hitler.

Entrance to the main courtroom at Dachau concentration camp.

The court, showing reporters (left) and the defense table (right).

Chapter 9

I am engrossed in my position as chief prosecutor of the war-crimes division for the Third Army, whose present sector of occupation includes all of Bavaria and western Austria. Under my command are ten lawyers and about 55 translators and clerk-typists. We are preparing the trial cases for all four concentration camps in the area—Mauthausen and Buchenwald in the Russian zone, as well as Dachau and Flossenburg in the American zone. (Dachau has 85 subcamps, Buchenwald and Flossenburg about 60 each, and Mauthausen 19, as it was mostly a gas-and-burn murder mill, commonly called Auschwitz West.) The work here engages me about ten hours a day, 6½ days a week.

Dachau is the first case scheduled for trial. This seems natural as it was the first concentration camp (called a "mother" camp) in Germany, built when Hitler became chancellor in 1933. All camps since constructed have been patterned on Dachau. Reichminister Albert Speer had a hand in designing the subcamps.

I am trying two cases at Dachau, the central place for trial of all cases arising in the American sector. The first involves unarmed American fliers who were shot dead by German SS following Hitler's order to kill all captured American fliers. The second case, also involving the killing of American fliers, is unique for two reasons. It will, for the first time, follow a new procedure designed by General Eisenhower's JAG, and it will provide an orientation for the court named to try the Dachau case that immediatcly follows.

I study the new procedure. It combines parts of the pre-Hitler German court system with parts of the American system and is designed to give defendants maximum protection. Defendants know they will be afforded a fair trial. In fact, in my cases and in the Dachau case, no objections to the procedure are made by the defense. The court, its president, Gen. Reese M. Howell, and six full colonels are eager to comply with it.

The courtroom is formal. The court, which acts as judge and jury, is seated behind a high bench. At its left is defense counsel, and at its right I sit with my assistant. The table I use is from Hitler's "Eagle Nest" retreat. In the middle, in front of the court, is the reporter and a witness chair; the translators sit around the witness. Behind a railing is seated an audience of 300.

The defendant, Heinz Endress, is accused of killing four unarmed American fliers in March 1945, while standing at parade rest in the town square at Neckarsulm, near Mannheim. The fliers were being transported from Verona, Italy, and they parachuted from their disabled plane to the POW camp at Oberorsel, near Frankfurt. When

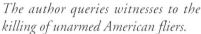

The author queries witnesses to the killing of unarmed American fliers.

the truck failed to function at Neckarsulm, the German sergeant and a corporal went to find a mechanic, leaving another corporal as guard.

Heinz Endress and Clemens Funder, local leading Nazis, saw the fliers, dashed out of their houses, each with a pistol, shouting, "They must die." Disregarding the corporal, who objected but later helped them, they shot four of the fliers. Two other fliers began to run. A German officer interceded, and the Nazis captured them unharmed.

Investigation for the case is incomplete, so I go to Neckarsulm to get all the facts. I find that Funder has died, but I interview several German civilians who saw the shootings and are willing to testify. They are as appalled at the murders as I am. I take measurements and order a large-scale drawing of the town square, the positions of the American fliers when they were shot, and the positions of the witnesses across the street from the town square.

The case is tried according to the new rules, but because of defense objections to the evidence, the court recesses a few times to be sure its rulings are in compliance. (See appendix.)

The author, left, addresses the court in final argument. Endress is at lower right.

Defendant Endress, SS, was a gardener before the war. He is an impressive, tall figure. His loyalty to Der Fuehrer is unbounded. Finally, the court finds the defendant guilty and sentences him to death by guillotine at the Landsberg prison, not far from Dachau.

After automatic review by the Third Army JAG, the trial record finally reaches Eisenhower's headquarters. I hear he blows up and orders death by hanging only, the most ignominious execution. The order is carried out by a special session of the court.

The Third Army chooses the trial judge advocates (attorneys for the prosecution) for the Dachau trial. Lt. Col. William D. Denson, ideally suited for the job, leads the team of several men. He is a 1934 graduate of West Point and a 1937 graduate of Harvard Law School. The JAGD chose the rest of the team of seven from the regiments, battalions, and divisions of the Third Army.

The trial team arrives at Dachau about the same time I do, on October 1, 1945. Denson tells me later that his team has worked long hours to select 40 defendants representative of the camp staff. They include the kommandant, the Gestapo, protective custody people, the labor allocation and medical department heads, and the crematory and administrative chiefs.

Forty defendants in the Dachau concentration-camp war-crimes courtroom.

L-r, Row 1 from bottom: Martin Gottfried Weiss, Friedrich Wilhelm Ruppert, Josef Jarolin, Franz Xaver Trenkle, Engelbert Valentin Niedermeyer, Josef Seuss, Leonhard Anselm Eichberger, Wilhelm Wagner, Johann Kick, and Dr. Fritz Hintermayer.

Row 2: Dr. Wilhelm Witteler, Johann Baptist Eichelsdorfer, Otto Foerschner, Dr. Hans Kurt Eisele, Dr. Klaus Karl Schilling, Christof Ludwig Knoll, Dr. Fridolin Karl Puhr, Franz Boettger, Peter Betz, and Anton Endres.

Row 3: Simon Kiern, Michael Redwitz, Wilhelm Welter, Rudolf Heinrich Suttrop, Wilhelm Tempel, Hugo Alfred Erwin Lausterer, Fritz M. K. Becher, Alfred Kramer, Sylvester Filleboeck, and Vinzenz Schoettl.

Row 4: Albin Gretsch, Johann Viktor Kirsch, Emil Erwin Mahl, Walter Adolf Langleist, Johann Schoeff, Arno Lippmann, Fritz Degelow, Otto Moll, Otto Schulz, and Friedrich Wetzel.

The court also named Hans Aumeier and Hans Bayer on its charge sheet.

Denson has drawn the indictment alleging violations of the Rules of Land Warfare—namely, the killings, beatings, torture, starvation, and other abuses from January 1, 1942, to April 29, 1945, when the Americans liberated Dachau. He says the worst offense was the starvation of prisoners through embezzlement. The administration of each camp received a check by mail from the Himmler headquarters in Berlin, the amount depending on the number of prisoners. But they bought as little food as possible for prisoners, pocketing the remainder of the funds. (See appendix.)

Many prisoners will testify in their native languages. We will require many interpreters, in some cases to arrive at English only after a series of translations.

From rear, the audience, court, prosecutors (upper left),
and defense plus tiers of defendants (upper right).

For each day of the trial, we issue 300 tickets to civilians in different towns near Dachau. American personnel trucks will pick them up. They will receive a

DACHAU WAR CRIME TRIAL
Admit Bearer to court room, Dachau, Germany,

on **Friday,**
16 November 1945

warm lunch and be returned to their homes about 5:30 P.M. Signs to this effect are posted in each town. The tickets go quickly. The German civilians who attend the trial see each prisoner point out his torturer, according to a defendant number (1 to 40) hung on his chest. This is the first time that most of the spectators hear the truth.

American soldiers who dress as locals and speak in the local dialect give us before-and-after reactions of the civilians. Before distributing tickets for each town, two soldiers listen to groups of civilians, who usually say, in effect: "Those Americans on the radio are lying about what went on in the Dachau camp." The two then return to the town to listen again, after the civilians have heard some of the testimony. This time they say, "It was terrible what went on in that camp."

From the accumulation of evidence, we know that German civilians living near main camps or subcamps occasionally saw the gaunt, ill-clad prisoners being marched along roads toward nearby factories. At times, a civilian close to a main camp caught the stench from a tall chimney and perhaps deduced cremation. The civilians certainly knew the prisoners were foreigners working against their will. But the only information the civilians received from the controlled media was that the workers were common criminals or enemies of the Reich.

We learn from *Stars and Stripes* that Hitler ordered Himmler to haul the prisoners by truck or railroad car from any concentration camp in danger of being overrun by American troops. If no transportation was available, they were to be marched toward Bavaria. Those who couldn't walk were to be killed and buried in mass graves. Hitler wanted no witnesses to fall into American hands. He told Himmler to give the order in secret. This accounts for the mass graves and burning alive of prisoners at Gardelegen in mid-April 1945 and the burning alive of Jewish prisoners at Landsberg near Dachau on April 28 (see (chapter 23). What amazes me is that the killings continued even after Hitler's death (April 30). The SS was indeed loyal to Hitler.

One day the master sergeant comes to my office and says, "There is a guy waiting to see you. I don't know if you want to see him. He is dressed so crazy. He is in formal dress with a silk hat. He says he was the official executioner in the pre-Hitler time at the Landsberg prison. Do you want to see him?"

I hesitate, then say, "Show him in."

A tall man, about 60, with severe demeanor and a long face, enters. I ask him to be seated. He is wearing a black swallow-tailed suit and a black silk hat. He tells me about his long experience as an executioner by hanging, guillotine, and three types by firing squad. He says his dress is the same he used at executions. He wants to be our executioner. He shows me a certificate stating he is the official executioner at the Landsberg prison.

"What are the three forms of execution by a firing squad?" I ask.

"The worst is when the victim has a hood over his head with his hands tied behind his back, and the captain orders the squad to fire. The next worst is when the victim has no hood on his head, but his hands are tied, and captain makes the order to fire. The last is when the victim has no hood, his hands are not tied, and *he* gives the order to fire. The type used depends on the severity of the crime."

"The victim's grandchildren can be told of the last type with pride, as if he were a hero," I say.

"Exactly," he concludes.

I stand up, indicating that the conference is at an end. "I will find out who has charge of executions."

He stands up, clicks his heels together, bows, and hands me his fancy card. With military precision he does an about-face and departs.

Denson and his team take six weeks to get the Dachau case ready for trial. Meanwhile, I have time to visit Mauthausen, near Linz, Austria, and subcamps in Austria and Czechoslovakia.

*U.S. Sen. Claude Pepper, Florida, congratulates the author
on his win in the Endress case.*

Chapter 10

After my first few days at Dachau, I visit the large facilities for the trials at Nuremberg, 70 miles north. The main trial there, originally scheduled to start four months before the trial at Dachau, has been delayed because of a weak courtroom floor needing considerable shoring. The Dachau trial thus starts five days earlier than the one at Nuremberg. The latter trial is nonetheless more heavily publicized because of its top Nazi defendants.

The indictment against the 24 defendants at Nuremberg contains four counts: Crimes against Peace, Waging Aggressive War, Crimes against Humanity, and Violations of the Rules of Land Warfare. Except for the latter violations, they are innovative charges *after the fact* and are based on treaties and assurances of nonaggression, some executed shortly before invasion of a country, to which Germany was a party. None spells out actions against individuals or their punishment.

U.S. Supreme Court Justice Robert H. Jackson has worked out the Nuremberg indictment. According to the June 18, 1945, issue of *Time International*, the victors have very little written law to work with and so plan to remedy that deficiency by making law to suit the case. In the United States, crimes and their punishment against individuals must be spelled out by statutes *before* the offense is committed. The merit of prosecution for acts against laws made after the fact likely will be argued for years.

By contrast, all of the cases prepared and tried in the Dachau courtrooms come under two treaties to which Germany is a signatory. The 1907 Hague Treaty, as amended, prohibits ill treatment of civilians in conquered countries, and the 1929 Geneva Treaty, as amended, prohibits ill treatment of disarmed enemy prisoners of war. These long-recognized treaties, the basis for the Rules of Land Warfare, permit the prosecution and punishment of individual perpetrators. In addition, the crimes prosecuted at Dachau come under the criminal laws of Germany and of the conquered countries in which they have been committed. That is, the laws specified such crimes as assault, kidnapping, mayhem, murder, and their punishments *before* the criminal acts were committed.

On another trip, I go through several towns in Czechoslovakia, finding many subcamps, carbon copies of those in Germany. I interview some of the subcamps' inmates to obtain evidence of war crimes.

In Czechoslovakia, buildings and towns look poorer, more ill-kept than in Germany, but the people cheer us wherever we go, a refreshing change. Czech and American flags hang side by side in many places. The Czechs are thoroughly pauperized, but they are busy kicking the

Sudeten (southern) Germans out of the country with considerable spirit.

Our trip into Austria is more scenic. The Alps and the pine-rimmed lakes are breathtaking. I find the mother camp Mauthausen near Linz and interview some slave laborers who were beaten and tortured. I have names and descriptions of the long-gone staff members who tortured them. I keep careful records of all the evidence I find.

In my investigation of the Mauthausen concentration camp, I discover a subcamp of the Berlin mother camp, Sachsenhausen, where the Nazis made counterfeit money for most of the countries of Europe plus Great Britain (according to the natives). I later obtain a memo by American Capt. R. Hrbeck stating that after the official end of the war on May 7, 1945, affidavits were taken from Oska Skala and Dr. Franklin Klein, both prisoners of the Nazis who escaped execution. The affidavits detail the forging of foreign currencies and identity cards on direct order from Heinrich Himmler. Attached to the memo is a list of 29 people, describing the involvement of each and naming Bernhard Krueger as head of the counterfeiting projects at Sachsenhausen and its subcamps. The plates, plans, and production records were put in boxes and thrown into Traun and Atter Lakes near Salzburg, Austria.

Here, too, the owners of any of the phony currency are required to bring all they have to a bank. The bank issues deposit credits against which depositors may draw up to a certain amount each month in the new currency. The policy outlaws all the old money and minimizes inflation and the black market. The wealthy German natives cry "bloody murder" and "communism," but there is no alternative.

Back at Dachau, we have many official visitors from the United States. The most serious is Sen. Claude D. Pepper, of Florida, who has two staff persons making notes during my tour of the camp. Some other members of Congress seem more interested in frivolity (liquor and women) than the history and horrors of the camp.

We lose a few prisoners every night. They escape by burrowing under the fence, which is no longer electrified. And there is no moat. The guard towers, searchlights, and guard dogs are all in use, but somehow a few prisoners manage to find a way out.

One day we discover a cache of gold teeth inside a mattress. The Nazis always knocked out the gold fillings and bridges from the mouths of killed slave laborers before taking their bodies to the crematory. We know that many slave laborers, especially Jews, converted their valuables into diamonds, then had dentists drill holes in their molars, place the diamonds in the holes, and cover the holes with silver fillings. The Nazi guards discovered this by accident while extracting gold from the prisoners, we hear. The American guards search everywhere for the diamonds, even in what appears to be freshly turned earth. Nothing is said of what they will do should they find any.

On one evening I take 40 Radio City Rockettes on a tour of the camp. Then they come to my living quarters for cocktails and dinner. Their chaperone, a woman of about 45, tells me many stories, in a coarse voice. I spend most of my time with her, laughing at her bawdy jokes—not so much for the content as for the way she tells them.

The Rockettes, all about the same size, have beautiful figures, but their faces don't match their bodies. After dinner they return to Munich to perform for the American soldiers.

———————

My perquisites include an elderly housekeeper who keeps my large bedroom immaculate and is proud to show me how she has pressed everything, including my socks, and neatly placed my clothes in the drawers of a large bureau. One day I come home at lunch time to get documents and find her cleaning the bathroom. I ask her why the bathroom doesn't contain the commode, which is located in another small room down the hall, as in many German homes. She replies in broken English, "Suppose you shaving and you Frau come to sit. Romance goes out the vindow."

Hitler's home—Der Berghof Obersalzberg (also known as the Eagle's Nest) at Berchtesgaden, Austria, with underground bunkers. Here he could be with Eva Braun and dog Blondi.

Chapter 11

I arrange for Hitler's former recorders to meet in my living room at 7:30 P.M. It is a large room, with upholstered furniture arranged in three conversational groups. I greet them and say I am glad they could come.

"Sit down, men, and have some wine." I pour, and after a few bits of opening conversation, say, "I'd like to know about some of Hitler's characteristics." With this broad question I hope to draw a variety of responses.

Reynitz sits forward in his chair and starts: "Hitler was smarting for a long time after the bombing attempt on his life on July 25, 1944. His actions were bizarre."

"Bizarre in what way?"

"He ordered that, instead of the usual army salute to a superior officer, henceforth the troops meeting an officer should use the Hitler salute—right arm straight and upraised, heels together, with the salutation, 'Heil, Hitler.'"

"That was a crazy order, don't you think?" I ask.

"It certainly was. It shows some of his character, demoniac to say the least." Reynitz is tall and thin, with a long face. "He also ordered the formation of the Volkssturm (People's Militia) by drafting all able-bodied people, ages 16 to 60, regardless of sex. It wasn't very effective."

"What did the SS do?" I glance at Buchholz, who sits with his legs crossed. He is of medium height, with a heavyset, roundish face, and precise in his answers.

"The SS, who followed the front lines of the German army, destroyed all statuary, burned books, libraries, museums, and land-office records. The purpose was to destroy any reminders of a conquered nation's heritage," says Buchholz, without wasting words.

"Even land records, imagine that. That would make it almost impossible to prove ownership. He certainly was thorough." As a lawyer, I thought this was a terrible thing to do and told them so.

"What was Hitler's outstanding characteristic?" I ask Reynitz.

"To Hitler everything was black or white, never anything in between. Compromise was a sign of weakness, he thought, because it might show uncertainty. When he adopted a position, he stuck by it even though in many cases it made no sense. This was his most revealing characteristic. I cannot emphasize this enough," Reynitz replies. He seems to have been an unusual observer, even of obscure events.

"Why did the generals carry out his orders if some of them made no sense?" I ask Reynitz.

"Because of two things—the oath and the chain of command,"

Reynitz answers, pulling out a copy of the oath from his pocket. "I brought it along as I knew it would come up.

"The oath was taken in groups standing in formation with right hands raised. The leader held the flag bearing the swastika in his left hand and held his right hand straight up as he told the group to repeat after him:

I swear to God this holy oath, that I will render to Adolf Hitler, Fuehrer of the German Reich and People, Supreme Commander of the Armed Forces, unconditional obedience, and that I am ready as a brave soldier, to risk my life at any time for this oath.

"The Bible was not used. The oath was meant to maintain discipline in the event of a coup or rebellion in Germany. The groups taking this oath included *everyone* in the armed services," Reynitz concludes.

"In this chain of command, each person had a superior and was afraid to oppose Hitler's orders. All had taken the same oath, and even speaking against an order could bring swift punishment too dreadful to contemplate. The oath instilled this natural fear," Reynitz concludes. He is sharp. I admire him.

"Did Hitler have an excuse for his invasions?" I ask Buchholz.

"Hitler's excuse for all his invasions of other countries was Lebensraum (living space for a greater Germany). He didn't trust his regular soldiers, who were drafted, leaving this chore for the SS, the loyal private army who did his dirty work. The SS followed the regular army like a giant vacuum cleaner and decimated each invaded country to make it more manageable for Lebensraum," says Buchholz, sipping his wine.

"That is a great statement, full of meaning and said in few words."

"Thanks," is all Buchholz says.

"How did Hitler manage to kidnap the men who were sent to concentration camps?" I ask Krieger. He rubs his chin thoughtfully before beginning.

"The SS would post signs in a city or town to the effect that, 'All men ages 16 to 60 will gather in the town square next Tuesday at 7:00 A.M. Anyone disobeying this order will be shot.' A good number of men came on time, but some went into hiding. The men who reported were put into railway boxcars and sent to German concentration camps at night, to avoid Allied bombers. If trains were not available, they were trucked or marched."

"What about those who failed to show?" I ask.

"Terrible things. Those who hid were hunted down by the SS and shot. They were left lying in the street as a lesson to others."

I think for a moment about Krieger's reply. "You certainly have the facts. Where did you get them?"

"Read it in two foreign newspapers I bought at a kiosk in Berlin. You see the papers were available because so few Germans could read them, and Hitler needed information on what other countries were saying about him."

"The SS were downright ruthless. I guess Hitler wanted them that way. Did he make any friends in his daily life?"

"Hitler was aloof and did not make friends. His thinking was that his orders would less likely be followed by friends. They might try to talk him out of it. He had an inner circle of those he trusted, but they were not friends. I mean he didn't warm up to anyone," says Krieger, standing up to stretch. He is of average height, getting bald, long-faced and rather good-looking. He is serious to the extreme. After all, he was in charge of the Steno-graphic Office of the Reichstag.

"Hitler permitted no one to know any more than what was absolutely necessary to do his job. This requirement helped him to maintain centralized control," Reynitz adds.

"Extreme secrecy. I would say. What about Lidice?" I suddenly think of what I have read in the *Stars and Stripes*.

Reinhard Heydrich

"The town of Lidice, Czechoslovakia, was decimated by the SS on June 9, 1942, owing to the murder there of Czech Commander Reinhard Heydrich. He was responsible for the evacuation of over 300,000 Jews from Germany and the submission in 1941 of a plan for a 'Final Solution' [extermination] to the 'problem' of the Jews. It was adopted at the Wannsee Conference near Berlin, in January 1942.

"Hitler gave the eulogy at Heydrich's funeral," Krieger continues.

"Did Hitler order the destruction of the town of Lidice?" I ask.

"Yes, and he personally went to Heydrich's funeral because of Heydrich's actions against the Jews."

"Did those at the military-situation conferences object to any of Hitler's plans?" I inquire of Jonuschat. He sits perfectly relaxed.

"Yes, at first. Only two had the nerve to do that—Alfred Jodl and Erwin Rommel. When this happened, Hitler would make a speech in a rage (he was strongest at this), sometimes for 20 minutes. This would quiet them. That is why the top brass attending military-situation conferences thereafter made only constructive suggestions."

"What about uprisings within Germany?" I ask Reynitz. He sits up straight. All eyes are on him.

"He had a plan to put down any demonstrations or riots in any place in Germany. If one began, the place would be crushed with air bombing, artillery, and tank fire. Heinrich Himmler was in charge of the plan and was ready at all times to implement it. Hitler made no announcement until the day of invasion of a country, so that no one would have time to demonstrate. The invasion would be a fait accompli." He says this casually, though it is tremendously important. Typical Reynitz.

"How did Hitler act at his military conferences?" I ask Buchholz.

"Hitler listened to the reports at his military conferences and asked many questions. There were a dozen-to-two-dozen officers— army, navy, and air force. When the reports were concluded, he gave his order of battle, many times opposed to the advice of his military brass."

"How could he do that?"

"Hitler relied on his intuition, stating, 'You know nothing of politics.' All the recorders think he was psychologically sick, especially when he acted against the advice of the generals to retreat and regroup."

"This is important. Did he say he was relying on his intuition?"

"Yes, he said it many times, as if the military chiefs knew little compared to himself."

"Did he have any spies?" I glance at Buchholz again.

"He had *two* spy systems to check on whether the field commanders were following his orders. A party member would secretly report to Martin Bormann by scrambled radio message, and an SS man would report to Heinrich Himmler or his stand-in, by the same method. The field commanders didn't know who was a loyal party member or who was an SS man. One field commander who didn't follow orders was never seen again. I don't know what happened to him."

"Did Hitler have any humor?" I look at Reynitz. He seems ready.

"His humor was rare. I recall one occasion. My colleague Ludwig Krieger and I entered the conference room where Hitler was alone. Krieger saluted, kicking his heels and raising his arm, almost falling down. Hitler said, 'For God's sake, don't fall down here. We have enough casualties.'

"Hitler laughed only twice that I ever saw. On one occasion the military situation was severe, and he was pondering how to get out of it. He asked those around the room, 'What do you think?' But he didn't wait for an answer. He said that we would always tell him, 'Fuehrer, give us the order and we will follow.' Then, as if he had made a big joke, he was laughing heartily," Reynitz continues.

"The other time he talked about many things, then switched to the subject of lawyers. All of a sudden he said, 'I want to know who, if any of you in this room, has studied law?' To his astonishment, it was a majority. Some were generals, adjutants, and one SS man. Then he laughed and said, 'What did I tell you?' Those in the room knew Hitler didn't like lawyers and didn't trust them. They also knew he didn't like intellectuals—professors, scientists, journalists, even college graduates."

"What peculiarities did he have?" I ask. Buchholz is eager to talk.

"Hitler was a vegetarian and usually ate by himself, unless there were foreign leaders visiting him. He was afraid of canned string beans because, he said, they were often poisonous. He never ate them."

"At most of his headquarters he had greenhouses where fresh vegetables could be grown. All his vegetable dishes were prepared by an elderly woman who had been with him for many years. She knew how he liked his vegetables prepared, and he trusted her completely," ends Buchholz.

Reynitz picks it up: "Next to poisoning from green beans, his main fear was toothaches, although he never mentioned having one. He always kept two dentists at headquarters to be ready in case he should get a toothache. His medical doctors gave him pills for his wild tremors and nervousness, and some of us thought he was taking too many pills. It was very noticeable in 1943 that his health was failing.

"He was even irritated by flies in the conference room. If an adjutant failed to keep them out, he disappeared the next day," Reynitz finishes his interesting little tale. There seems to be no end to his knowledge.

"What kind of life did Hitler have?"

As if tired of sitting, Jonuschat stands to answer: "Hitler lived a spartan life. He always had a small bedroom with scant furniture. Once I was called there to record what he said with an officer present. I had difficulty finding a place to write." After stretching, Jonuschat sits down.

"Were there any religious services?"

Reynitz, who seems the most religious of the group, plunges in: "No, there were no religious services or singing of hymns at any time at headquarters. Hitler hated the Roman Catholic Church, although he was raised as a Catholic."

"Did Hitler complain about anything?"

Reynitz sits upright and continues: "He complained that there was too much work and not enough relaxation during the war. He was always moving, except when looking at a map. Eventually this routine and the setbacks on the war fronts affected him, and he slowed down considerably. He gradually became worse in 1944 and 1945, more bent over and walking in a shuffle. His hands were trembling more. He became red in the face. We learned later that he had the onset of Parkinson's disease. He never said anything about his health." (Later I learn that Hitler actually showed signs of Parkinson's disease about the beginning of October 1944. A progressive disease, its origin and cure are unknown, and no medications were then known to control it.)

"What about foreign leaders?" I ask Krieger.

He stands up, stretches, and says calmly: "Benito Mussolini had meetings with Hitler many times, and Hitler often mentioned that Mussolini was a strong man and led a party like his own Nazis, called the Fascisti. When Mussolini was still in power, Hitler said at a conference, 'His Fascisti can hold their own.' General Jodl responded, 'I have been to Italy, and I saw no Fascisti.' Mussolini had been in power for over 20 years in Italy, and Hitler admired him. But Hitler lost faith in him even before his downfall."

Krieger carries on: "One time Mussolini came to headquarters with Gen. [marshal and president] Ion Antonescu of Romania, another ally of Hitler. Fake maps were placed on the table to show German forces in Russia at much better positions than actually existed.

"He didn't get much help from Francisco Franco of Spain, and he called him, 'That sausage.' He spoke one time about Marshal Josip Tito of Yugoslavia, saying: 'I wish he was on my side. He is a tough guy. I would give several divisions for a guy like him.'"

"What about you recorders? Did he say anything to you?" I ask Buchholz. He is relaxed but has a ready answer.

"For our part there was nothing to complain of. For example, one day before the conference started, he asked about our families in Berlin. He asked where we lived and inquired, 'What kind of food do you get on your ration card?' 'Very little,' I said. He made no further comment but looked at me thoughtfully for a moment before an adjutant called in the military men for the conference." Buchholz straightens.

"Hitler would not permit the conference room to be over 14 degrees Centigrade [about 58 degrees Fahrenheit]. He noticed that our hands and legs were cold, as we sometimes rubbed them.

"When we were alone he would ask my colleague and me if the cold room made it difficult to write our notes. We both said our hands and our legs were cold. He ordered electric heaters placed under both ends of the conference table. For our hands, he said to use wristlets, which could become fingerless woven gloves when we wrote." Buchholz relaxes in his chair.

"Why did he like it so cold?"

"Apparently he would sweat from being so vigorous at the conferences," Buchholz answers and goes on. "Hitler said he and others, during cold weather in World War I, used wristlets to keep their hands warm so that their fingers would be free for using weapons. Of course, we tried his suggestion, but we found it interfered too much with our rapid writing of shorthand." Buchholz is direct as usual. His face shows his disgust with Hitler wanting it so cold.

Karl Thoet hasn't said anything. He is a short man of medium build, with heavy brown hair and brown eyes set in a round face. Choosing to listen, he doesn't usually volunteer. Now he surprises me.

"I noticed Hitler sometimes used a typewriter, pecking with two fingers. The tremors in his hands made longhand impossible."

"Was Hitler afraid of anything?" I ask him.

"He was afraid of poison gas coming into the vent system in the bunkers in Berlin, so he had special filters installed. There were always emergency generators at the bunkers to run the fans, lights, water, and toilet facilities."

"Did you notice anything else?"

"He always demanded that the whole office staff go down into the bunker in Berlin when an air-raid warning sounded. He would go down last. At headquarters we usually worked above ground, and the fortified bunker was always underground," Thoet continues.

"I think Hitler was kind to his office staff because all of them were so subservient, and he felt it so easy to dominate them. We learned later that when he visited the staff lounge, unannounced, he sat down and did all the talking. It was a rambling monologue—then he abruptly left."

"What about friends, did he show any friendship to anyone?" I ask Reynitz, repeating my earlier question to Krieger.

"Hitler had no friends, even in his inner circle. I think he avoided friendships so his orders would be followed by everyone without hesitation. Eva Braun was the exception, though he rarely had time to see her," Reynitz remembers.

"This is a good place to stop," I say.

"Yes, indeed," says Kriegcr, and all of them leave.

In Frankfurt, Germany, at the structure where Hitler spoke to cheering crowds. The author at the podium, right, and with his Jeep driver near an abandoned American tank at the stadium, below.

Chapter 12

October 1945

The five recorders meet with me again in my living quarters at 7:30 P.M. They seem happy to answer my questions. I sometimes wonder about that. But, after all, they were not Nazi Party members, and they didn't like Hitler. They were recorders and have good memories.

I have two bottles of dessert wine that I know they like, and I fill their glasses. We engage in small talk for a while, as we settle into our chairs.

"We last discussed some of Hitler's characteristics. I thought this time we should talk about the early days. You were all members of the Stenographic Office of the Reichstag?"

"Yes," says Krieger. "All except Thoet and Buchholz, who weren't there when Hitler first came into prominence—when he was convicted and sent to prison in Munich. They came a little later."

"What did it require to get into the Stenographic Office?"

My question is to Krieger, the mentor of the group. Born February 16, 1887, he attended the University of Leipzig from 1906 to 1908, then studied political science at the University of Berlin until 1912. He began his stenographic career in 1907, while he was in school. In 1920 he joined the Stenographic Office of the Reichstag, and in 1941 he became its chief. The next year Hermann Goering called him to name the recorders for Hitler's headquarters. The most experienced, he is also the most respected of the five recorders.

Krieger's interest in precise facts is most helpful, and I take a sip of wine as I arrange my notebook to record his answer.

"First, there were competitive examinations for aspirants. They came from all over Germany and the competition was fierce. Then came the examination for associate members. Finally, the exam for membership, which was the hardest of all. Only a few made it," says Krieger, slowly and without humor.

"What happened in Munich?" I ask Reynitz.

He moves forward in his chair: "I was a student at Berlin University. I read of Hitler's arrest, conviction, and imprisonment because of the so-called 'Beer Hall Putsch' in 1923. He led his Nazis in a street revolt against the seat of the government of Bavaria in Munich. Before that, I paid little attention to the Nazi street fights with the Communists or to Hitler's rallies and speeches, mostly in Bavaria, as reported in the press and on radio."

"What did Hitler do after his imprisonment?" I ask Reynitz, as he seems knowledgeable.

"After 13 months in prison, Hitler began to make speeches to larger and larger crowds. I was assigned by the Stenographic Office of the Reichstag to record his speech at the Sportpalast in Berlin in 1928. Thousands packed the big hall. A loud band was playing. Colorful banners were hoisted in neat rows. The dazzling spectacle of thousands of swastikas on armbands was startling, especially during such a drab time in Germany."

"Did he have protection?" I look at Jonuschat.

Jonuschat sits forward in this chair and rubs his chin as he answers: "Hitler had protection at such rallies, which the Communists tried to break up. The SA [Sturmabteilung or stormtrooper units, also called Brownshirts] warded off the Reds at Nazi party gatherings. The SS [Schutzstaffel—protecting platoons or guard detachments, also called Blackshirts] protected Hitler's person. They all wore uniforms and used sticks because firearms were then forbidden by law. These were the beginnings of his private, personal forces."

I call on Reynitz and he begins: "All attention was on Hitler as he spoke. I could feel the excitement of the audience, and it was difficult to concentrate on my shorthand. The crowd was almost hysterical."

"What was his appearance as he spoke?" I rise from my chair. The room is stuffy, so I open a window.

Reynitz carries on: "His appearance was quite plain. About five feet, nine inches tall, with a narrow mustache and sometimes unruly hair, he had striking blue eyes."

"Did any of you see him up close?" I sit down again.

"The first time I saw him eye-to-eye was in 1930 or 1931," recalls Hans Jonuschat. "Hitler was a witness to the aims and ends of the SA at a trial, and I, together with another recorder, had to write down his testimony. When the session was finished, he approached us, giving his hand to each, looking us full in the face.

"I do not know whether there was something demonic in his eyes, but I should not have liked to work near him for fear of losing the power of my own will and in the end approving everything he did. But maybe he only intended or was accustomed to looking in such a way at strangers so as to change them into blind followers."

"Go on." I flip to a new page in my notebook.

"When, after 11 years, I had to work in his presence, my former impression had vanished, and I did not suffer myself to be constrained by his spell. It struck me, however, that he occasionally, when talking to a person, seemed to look not into his listener's eyes but through his eyes at a point far behind," concludes Jonuschat, sipping his wine and leaning back into the davenport.

"What was the effect of his speeches?" I look at Reynitz.

"At that rally in 1928," Reynitz says, "and at others that I recorded later, it was obviously his speeches—not what he said so much as how he said it. Hitler, all of a sudden, discovered that he could hypnotize the audience. He was forceful and he shouted at times, like a man in a rage."

"That's a good description," Jonuschat agrees.

"What did he say? How did he say it?" I ask Jonuschat.

"He used the common man's language and made promises he knew people wanted to hear. He was a politician, and he knew people wanted a leader to bring order to the country. Politics was the only job he had had since leaving World War I. Many people thought he could save Germany from Communism, which Germans feared. Also, many thought he could restore national pride."

"What was the effect on the crowd?" I look at Reynitz.

He moves forward in his chair and says, "As he shouted promises, he received salutes from the audience—right palms upraised and the cries 'Sieg Heil' [Hail Victory]. The excitement always increased and some people fainted. Scuffles on the edges of the crowd occurred as the SA fought the Communists, who were always trying to break up the rally."

"That's interesting. Could you tell me more?"

"You must remember that the tension and spell on the audience came from several factors—the large crowd, the colorful pageantry, and the loud band music played to stir up the crowd. Then came Hitler's forceful speech and the roar of 'Sieg Heil,' which helped the audience mesmerize itself. Hitler's rallies were a contrast to the dull political life in Germany before he came on the scene." Reynitz leans back in his chair.

"What promises did he make?" I am eager to know, as this had a bearing on his later successes. I glance at Jonuschat.

"He said he would put the unemployed to work. Most in the audiences were unemployed or had menial or part-time work. That promise was immensely popular. Germany's economy was in a shambles after World War I. There was runaway inflation until 1924, then a growing depression," says Jonuschat, warming to the subject. He moves forward in his seat and continues.

"He promised to get rid of the huge reparations imposed by treaties after World War I and said he would regain territories and colonies taken away by the treaties. Besides, he would gain Lebensraum so that Germans could live better.

"He appealed to nationalism and hammered on the theme that true Germans were the master race in Europe. He ranted against Gypsies and other 'undesirables.' He said if there was a war in Europe, it would not be the Germans, but the Jews, who would be destroyed," Jonuschat concludes and leans back.

"What did you think of his promises?" I ask Reynitz as I get up from my chair and pace, amazed at what I am hearing.

"When I read the transcripts of my notes of his speeches, I saw that he never said how he would fulfill his promises. His other themes, like Lebensraum, master race, and the destruction of the Jews, didn't make sense to me. From conversations with others, I gathered that most people were not moved much by those themes if they understood them.

"His themes about putting people to work and regaining lost territories had the greatest appeal—even to those who had jobs. Those two themes worked together and drew the noisiest responses from the crowds at his speeches," says Reynitz as he stands. Two of the others follow, as if for a seventh-inning stretch.

Catching the spirit, I take the time to fill their glasses with wine.

"This is delicious," says Krieger. The others lift their glasses toward me, indicating their approval.

"Glad you like it." When all sit down, I change the subject.

"About the Communists—did they give up?"

"Not in the least. Many riots in the streets occurred between the Communists and the Nazis. They beat on each other with sticks and the buckle ends of belts. The uniformed SA and SS were growing rapidly, holding their own, and winning in the street riots. Hitler stirred up people by leading marches, ending with a rally where he made a fiery speech. I was assigned to record some of his speeches. Germany was near anarchy, and martial law was declared in some areas by President Paul von Hindenburg," concludes Reynitz.

"What did he say about World War I?" I turn to Jonuschat. He sits up straight, the eyes of the others upon him.

"Hitler had special appeal to World War I military and other leaders with his tirades against the 'November Criminals.' He was referring to the politicians, not the military chiefs, who arranged and signed the Armistice of November 11, 1918. He cried that these criminals agreed to the unbearable burden of reparations to the Allies," Jonuschat explains.

"I suppose that appeal was popular?" I interject.

"That appeal had two impacts. The people agreed that reparations couldn't be paid at a time of deepening depression. The World War I military chiefs kept claiming that they hadn't lost that war. They said politicians had stolen victory from them," he continues.

"Hitler vowed he would regain territories lost by treaties after World War I. This would provide more employment. National pride was aroused in many people when he said this. And this promise won even more support from World War I military chiefs who became important to him later on."

"Was he an effective politician?" I direct my question to Reynitz. He leans forward and rubs his nose.

"From what I know about how he gained power as Der Fuehrer, he was an extremely clever politician. His actions and speeches, and his writings in *Mein Kampf [My Struggle]* show that he appealed to the masses through their emotions—to their hearts, not to their minds. He was attuned to the people." Reynitz comes through again. From their facial expressions, I can see the others agree.

"Did he dislike anyone?" I ask Reynitz, not knowing what the question might bring.

"He disliked professionals, like teachers, journalists, engineers, and lawyers, because they were trained to look at both sides of an issue and might come out in a gray area and take no stand," ends Reynitz.

"That's very interesting. Shows his character. How did he use propaganda?" I ask Krieger.

He always takes time to answer, and he speaks calmly now: "Hitler and his close associates used propaganda to take a position on an issue. By constantly repeating a position, even if false, the propaganda took on credibility. The Americans and British were saying in their newspapers that this was use of the Big Lie. He was good at it." Again, I see the others agree.

"The Weimar Republic was still in power, wasn't it?"

Krieger answers in his usual manner, not bothering to move from his relaxed position: "The government was ineffective. President Paul von Hindenburg was old and really a figurehead. Chancellor Heinrich Bruening was losing general support—he was ousted in May 1932. There was extreme confusion in German politics." The others take great interest in this subject. They watch Krieger as he continues.

"Keep in mind the craving of Germans for social order, which requires strong leadership and a chain of authority. It is inbred from a long history of rulers: monarchs and emperors. The last of them fled at the end of World War I. Germany had great difficulty adjusting to the democratic system of the Weimar Republic. The system was constantly vilified by the monarchists, Communists, and the Nazis. No one seemed to be in charge. There were also too many political parties.

"The inbred idea of social order in Germany starts in the family. The father rules; the oldest boy rules his younger siblings. In local government, the burgomaster rules, and so on up the line.

"Germany was ripe for a strong leader, and Hitler was eager to be the leader. More than that, he was driving to be the dictator of Germany, just as he had achieved dictatorship of the Nazi party," concludes Krieger. He stands and walks around a bit after his long dissertation. The others watch as he paces the floor, agreeing with him almost to the point of applause.

"Did Hitler ever run for office?" I look at Jonuschat.

"Yes. The weak government and economy were natural material for his speeches. He repeatedly assured the people that everyone would have a job.

"He said he would get rid of the Communists, the crippling strikes, and the labor unions. Industrialists openly supported his ideas and helped finance the Nazi party when it was increasing its seats in the Reichstag, especially in 1930. He had support from both ends of the economic scale, although he was an extreme rightist," Jonuschat says as the others nod.

"You're so right." Krieger chimes in.

I look at Krieger, and he adds, "The Nazi party continued to win state elections and more seats in the Reichstag, while the Communists were falling far behind. By 1932, the party doubled its seats and Goering was elected president of the Reichstag. But the party itself never controlled a majority of seats.

"In the national election in 1932 Hitler ran against President Hindenburg. He received less than half of the votes and lost, but it demonstrated he was gaining." Krieger is pleased with his answer.

"How did Hitler become chancellor?" I look at Krieger again.

"Hitler finally gained power by a combination of persuasion and relentless pressure. The uniformed SA and SS troopers more and more filled the main streets in the cities, and there was fear of civil war. There was pressure in the Reichstag and maneuvers by its president, Hermann Goering, Hitler's strong man.

"Pressure was put on the cabinet and on President Hindenburg, who, though he disliked Hitler, finally gave in and appointed Hitler chancellor on January 30, 1933. Up to that point Hitler had taken steps that had the appearance of legal means, apparently to achieve acceptance by the people," Krieger finishes. The others are strongly with him on this.

"It's getting very late," I say, looking at my watch. "I'm sorry to keep you so long, but all of the discussion is so interesting. The indictment has been served on the 40 defendants in the Dachau case, so the trial should begin soon. Then you will have a little more time to tell me about Hitler. I'll call you."

Several of the recorders stretch and look at their watches. Then they shake their heads and stand up.

"I want to thank you for your insights into Hitler's mind and actions," I say as they leave.

Chapter 13

The Dachau Trial, November 1945

The indictment in the Dachau concentration-camp case is served on most of the 40 defendants on November 2 and on the remaining seven defendants on November 4. The case is set for trial on November 15. While Dachau was the first concentration camp established in Germany and in existence from March 1933 to April 1945, the indictment covers only the period from January 11, 1942, to its liberation on April 19, 1945.

The beginning of the trial is devoted to a summary by the prosecution and to acting upon motions of the defense in attacking the charges in the indictment. I sit at the wall behind the prosecution table to watch. The arrangement of the court is identical to that for the Endress case that I participated in earlier.

Lt. Col. William D. Denson of the prosecution summarizes the main facts. He says that the Germans in Dachau were civilians, the remainder prisoners of war. None of them was tried by a court before incarceration. In April 1945, about half were Slavs (mainly Russian, Poles, and Czechs). The other half of the total of 41 nationalities in Dachau included citizens mainly of Italy, Hungary, and Germany.

The camp was equipped for 8,000, but in April 1945 it contained 33,000 prisoners. With its subcamps, it could accommodate 65,000 more in April 1945. A typhus epidemic raged in the camp from December 1944, killing approximately 15,000 prisoners, due to a lack of quarantine, latrines being constantly blocked, and hospitals being overcrowded. Nothing was done to combat the epidemic.

Food was grossly inadequate for workers laboring more than 11 hours a day. The additional cleaning of barracks, roll calls, and marches to work made for 17-to-18-hour workdays. When American troops came into the camp, a great majority of the prisoners were starving.

Clothing was insufficient to protect the prisoners from the cold; clothing was not washed for periods up to three months. But a large warehouse full of clothing was found on April 29, when the camp was liberated.

Medical experiments consisting of immersing prisoners in cold water for up to 36 hours, puncturing the lungs of healthy prisoners, and injecting them with malaria bacteria and phlegmon (diseased blood) so as to observe their reactions, were carried on constantly. Numerous prisoners died as a result of these experiments.

Invalids and emaciated prisoners were periodically gathered in large convoys to be gassed at the Hartheim Castle and cremated at the Mauthausen concentration camp, both near Linz, Austria. Prisoners were subjected to strict discipline, enforced by severe

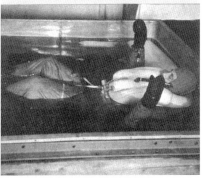

A freezing-water experiment at Dachau, conducted at the request of the Luftwaffe, determined how long a pilot could live wearing a certain type of clothing should he have to bail from a disabled plane over the English Channel, for example.

punishments such as working longer hours, hanging by their wrists tied behind their backs, lashings, solitary confinement, and death.

In 1942, 8,000 Russian prisoners were killed. In 1944, 90 Russian officers were hanged. The total death toll is unknown.

All concentration camps were administered by Himmler's Central Security Office in Berlin. The Dachau group of camps contained 85 subcamps, all under the camp kommandant. The accused, under him, all participated in a common design to run the camps in a manner so that great numbers of prisoners would die or suffer severe injuries. Each person accused took a vigorous and active part in the execution of this plan. (See appendix.)

————————

The defense is headed by Lt. Col. Douglas T. Bates, who makes a motion in which the defense raises a plea to the jurisdiction of the court, and in support makes three arguments:

1. the accused are not described as enemy nationals and the indictment discloses no offense that the court is competent to try,
2. neither the names and nationalities of the victims nor whether the nations of the victims were at war with Germany at the material time have been disclosed, and
3. the accused are prisoners of war.

Colonel Bates is vociferous in making the motions. The court denies the motion and summarizes to the effect that:
- the accused have admitted to being enemy nationals,
- none of the victims was an American, and

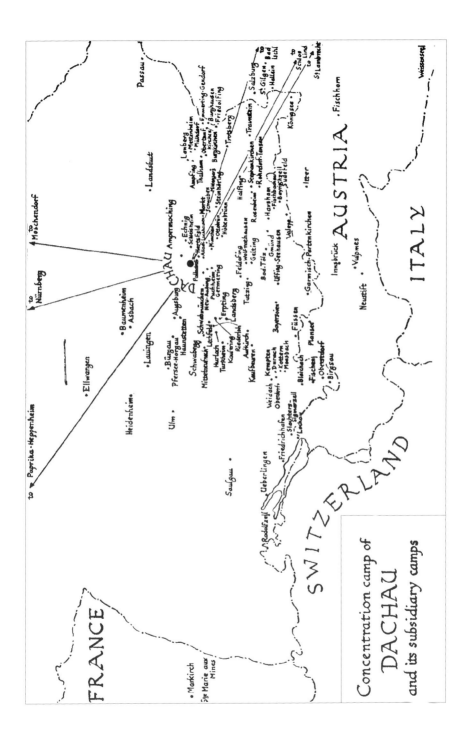

Concentration camp of
DACHAU
and its subsidiary camps

- a sentence may be pronounced against a prisoner of war for an offense committed while a prisoner of war and not while he is a combatant.

Colonel Bates also argues for the defense that:
- the indictment is so vague that it fails to inform each accused with sufficient certainty of the case he will have to answer, and
- the charges are bad for duplicity of each of the accused, and the charges should be particularized sufficiently to identify the place, time, and subject matter of the alleged offense.

Colonel Denson for the prosecution states in effect that:
- the charges are of a continuing nature and that common design in which the accused willingly participated clearly apprised in what they are called upon to defend, and
- the charges allege their participation in the running of the camp, pursuant to a common design, which included the subjection of described persons to stated wrongful acts at stated treatment places. (See appendix.)

The defense also makes a motion for severance of charges, based upon calling codefendants as witnesses, because the antagonistic testimony offered by some of them could prejudice all of the accused. The prosecution answers this by stating that the charges allege that all of the accused participated willingly and that the defenses of each of them could not be antagonistic.

Colonel Denson states that the charges allege the accused acted in pursuance of a common design. The charges thus allege that *all* accused acted in a common design to ill-treat the prisoners. This is a question of substantive law.

The court denies the motion for the severance of charges.

Colonel Denson adds that in Hitler's dictatorship there can be no agreement as in a conspiracy, and ultimately the defense of superior orders is not applicable because in that case only Hitler himself could be found guilty. Hence, the basic charge is that of common design in which all the accused willingly participated.

Once all the turkey plumage is plucked from the motions and arguments of the defense, nothing is left but the carcass of a hummingbird.

The defendants grow more sober as the trial moves forward.

The author works into the dusk at Dachau.

Chapter 14

I work nights to handle the pileup of papers on my desk concerning evidence for trial of the other three concentration-camp cases. The determination of which detainees to prosecute requires my review of the work of lawyers, officers, and staff, as well as of other resources.

I continue to talk with Hitler's recorders. The five gather at my living quarters after lunch on Saturday.

"Our discussions ended with Hitler appointed chancellor by President Paul von Hindenburg in January 1933. I would like to carry on from there if that is okay with you."

"That will be fine. We are through with most of our work for the trial, and this is a good time for us," says Krieger.

"Good. Who wants to start?"

Reynitz volunteers: "It becomes more vivid to me in retrospect that Hitler started with milder, then moved toward stronger actions.

He was testing the people, step by step, to see how far they would let him go. He became bolder each year. He was attuned to the feeling of Germany and other countries as well. He seemed to know how far he could go before a backlash might occur."

"What things did Hitler change after being appointed chancellor?"

Reynitz replies: "He started in 1933 by outlawing the labor unions and raiding their offices. I was not surprised by this because, before coming to power, he called unions 'Marxist organizations led by Communists and Jews.' His action pleased the large industrialists, who openly supported him with money."

"What happened to the unions?" I keep looking at Reynitz, who sits on the edge of his chair. The others look on approvingly.

"The unions were replaced by the 'Labor Front' headed by [Nazi leader] Robert Ley. Later, leaders of other organizations, including professional groups, were replaced. Hitler's appointees became the leaders of national groups—representing lawyers, journalists, doctors, architects, engineers, and so on. He obviously wanted no independent groups in the country."

Robert Ley

"That is a good statement, true to fact," Krieger approves. The others nod their consent.

"What did he do to accomplish that?" I look at Jonuschat, who leans forward, stroking his chin.

"He started to take away the independence of the separate states and later appointed his own men as state governors. This was a bold move. The governors eventually appointed local officials and judges. Power was becoming centralized in Hitler's hands."

"Good observation. Wish I had as good a memory. Nice going."

"These events are indelibly fixed in my mind. You would remember them too, if they had the effect of changing the government so radically."

"What about the Communists?" I ask Jonuschat again.

"Hermann Goering raided the Communist headquarters early in 1933 and publicly stated that he had uncovered a plot for a national revolution. All the Communists who could be found were arrested, and soon they disappeared. They were put in concentration camps, as I discovered later. Their seats in the Reichstag were immediately vacant," Jonuschat concludes.

Marinus Van der Lubbe

Reynitz picks up the thread. Relaxed, he says confidently, "In late February, less than a month after Hitler gained power, the Reichstag building was set on fire, and blame was put on the Communists. A young man, Marinus Van der Lubbe, a Hollander and admitted Communist, was charged and put on trial with a few other Communists for setting the fire. Goering testified that he found documents stating that this was the beginning of violent overthrow of the government. I was one of the court reporters.

"The day after the fire, Hitler issued a decree suspending constitutional rights—including free speech, free press, and free assembly. The search for Communists was stepped up. Now there appeared to be a legal right to arrest Communists and to deprive them of their seats in the Reichstag," Reynitz continues. I decide not to interrupt him. He has a terrific memory.

"At the trial, Van der Lubbe said that he alone decided to set the fire, contradicting Goering's testimony. While the trial dragged on for weeks, there was more and more street talk that Nazis had helped to set the fire, at many places in the large building. Van der Lubbe testified that he had used only his shirt to start the fire in one place. The jury convicted Van der Lubbe and set the other defendants free."

"Anything more about the Communists?" I ask Krieger. He seems ready to answer, and he usually has something important to say.

"The trial increased concern about Communist activities. There was growing pressure by the Nazis in the Reichstag for action on the issue. The pressure was intensified by Hitler's followers. Mobs of them gathered repeatedly outside the building. Included were uniformed troopers and civilians wearing swastika armbands and bearing flags. It was an intimidating demonstration."

"What happened then?"

"This was the atmosphere in which the Reichstag adopted, by the necessary two-thirds vote, the Enabling Act that suspended its legislative authority. The Enabling Act recessed the Reichstag and gave Hitler the right to govern by decree until 1937. This was later extended for another four years, but in fact it became moot after the war against Poland. Hitler was now an absolute dictator, answerable to nobody but himself. He moved quickly to centralize the government."

So the fire had two purposes—to get rid of the Communists and to help pass the Enabling Act. "That was a quite a stroke," I offer, eager to learn more. Turning to Reynitz, I ask, "What did he do about the Weimar Republic's constitution?"

He is quick to answer: "I learned later that Goering, pragmatic as usual, talked Hitler into recessing instead of dissolving the Reichstag. Besides making it easier to pass the Enabling Act, the Reichstag could be useful. Hitler could call it into session for important pronouncements, to get the attention of the German people and other nations."

"Hitler was smart to take Goering's advice. Could you go on?"

"Goering reminded Hitler of this later, when I was present at war headquarters. He said, 'I told you it would be useful to keep the Stenographic Office of the Reichstag. Those men are here now to help you.'

"To keep the Reichstag subject to his call, Hitler had to keep the constitution of the Weimar Republic. He never tried to set aside the constitution. With the Reichstag suspended, my position continued, with little for me to do. Occasionally I found outside work for lawyers and the courts," concludes Reynitz modestly.

"That was a good dissertation, I must say. You have fine recall." I compliment Reynitz.

"Thank you. But all that is burned into my mind."

I turn to Jonuschat: "What did Hitler do about the Jewish question? This was the overriding issue for him, I take it."

"Yes. When the Enabling Act was passed in March 1933, Hitler had his Nazis everywhere in Germany organize a campaign to boycott places owned by Jews. They carried banners on the sidewalks, in effect saying, 'Jews own this place—stay away.' I noticed that many civilians ignored the banners and went into these places. The Nazis usually did nothing to stop them, coming or going."

"Then how did he carry out this policy?"

"After a short time, Hitler issued his first decree against Jews, calling for a national, one-day boycott against their shops, businesses, and professional practices. This was the start—the first step in forcing Jews to leave Germany. I noticed that some Jews left, but the poorer Jews lacked the means to leave. Hitler said publicly, 'Jews are not Germans.'" Jonuschat concludes and relaxes into the davenport.

I turn to Reynitz and ask, "What happened next?"

He moves forward, pulls his ear, and begins: "In May 1933, Hitler dissolved all political parties but his own. He outlawed strikes of any kind. He talked openly about exterminating all his opponents and frequently mentioned Jews, Gypsies, and Communists. That word, *exterminating,* is closest to the German word meaning 'take out by the roots.' I was shocked at his use of that word applied to human beings.

"I was also shocked when Hitler openly stated, 'We will never get some old bucks into our party, but that doesn't matter for we will take their children.' If 'old bucks,' by their education and moral beliefs, were openly opposed to him, they were taken away, probably to concentration camps." Reynitz warms to his subject. I do not interrupt.

"He took the children by forming them into organizations—the Jungvolk when they entered school, the Hitlerjugend when they reached 14 years. They marched, drilled, and greeted each other with a raised right arm and a proud 'Heil Hitler.' They were in uniform, and the ambitious ones advanced in rank as in the military. These youth groups were formed before 1933; and now they grew in importance." Reynitz is attentive to detail.

"Did he take any action regarding education?" I ask Krieger.

Krieger answers with care: "One of Hitler's first acts in 1933 was to take over the educational system. The emphasis was on ideology—teaching students to think as Hitler did. In some Catholic schools, Hitler's portrait was hung on the wall next to the crucifix."

"How effective were the new schools?"

"This new schooling was so powerful that students would sometimes inform on parents or relatives who spoke against Hitler or the Nazis. German civilians had as much to fear from Hitlerjugend as they did from the Gestapo and SS. No matter who did the informing, any reported criticism meant confinement in a concentration camp without a trial. Now that Hitler was in power, his opponents became practically silent," Krieger concludes.

I ask, "Did the ministers and priests complain about this?"

"Some ministers and priests protested some of Hitler's actions from the pulpit, and they eventually disappeared, probably to concentration camps. Germany was half Protestant—mostly Lutheran—and half Catholic. The Lutherans were split and had no strong leader, especially after the official Reich Church was decreed in 1933 under a new constitution drafted by the Nazis for all Protestants," Jonuschat replies.

"This is important," I think. "What about the Catholics?" I stand, then pace.

"The Catholics were another matter. A concordat was negotiated with the pope in 1933. Hitler sent his emissary, Franz von Papen, to make a treaty with Vatican

Franz von Papen

163

Secretary of State Eugenio Pacelli, in early 1933. (Incidentally, Pacelli became Pope Pius XII in 1939.) The concordat was signed about three months later. The essence of it was to say, 'You leave us alone, and we will leave you alone.' You know that Hitler was brought up as a Catholic," Jonuschat answers.

"How did the concordat work?"

"The word went down from the pope to all ranks of the church to the effect, 'Do not criticize Hitler or the Nazis—this is best for the church.' I cannot tell you how much the concordat strengthened Hitler, but I believe it was the greatest single thing he accomplished up to that time. People were saying, 'Even the church is on Hitler's side,'" Jonuschat ends. I am surprised at his answer.

"Why do you think the pope agreed to that?" I ask Krieger.

"I think the pope agreed because he saw two alternatives and chose the least harmful to the church. On one hand were the Communists. After the 1917 Russian revolution, Stalin imposed his will on the people by purges, killing millions. Russia was atheistic and had an expansionist policy.

"On the other hand, the Nazis at that time were not atheistic and seemed to have limited goals—to stop Communism, to increase jobs, to regain German land lost after World War I, and to end reparations. I believe the pope thought Hitler would eventually go away, while the Communists, believing in world domination, were a permanent force of evil," Krieger states with conviction.

I rise to open the window a bit. "What about the officers from World War I? How did they take to Hitler?" I address Krieger again.

"Some World War I generals and colonels were critical of Hitler. They were pensioned, and their uniforms were taken away. This was a lesson to other military officers," he replies. "But obviously Hitler could not carry on without military experts. Many of the World War I officers supported him."

"Naturally, they would. They seem to have liked the war, the bang-bang of it," I respond, and the recorders all laugh. "What then?"

"Hitler was condemned by the League of Nations for his treatment of the Jews. A few months later, he withdrew Germany from the disarmament conference and the League and ordered a plebiscite. These actions were approved by over 90 percent of the vote. It was not reported who counted the vote," Reynitz answers.

"Where did you get this information?"

"I read British newspapers almost every day for several years, learning more from them than from the controlled press and radio in Germany. There were also other publications available in Berlin. I suspect that these newspapers were an important source of information for Hitler, telling him what other countries knew about his actions and how they felt about them. Apparently sales of English papers were not considered important because so few Germans could read them—less than 1 percent, I would guess," Reynitz continues.

"I should mention the peace pact signed in the summer of 1933. It was made by France, Britain, Italy, and Germany to maintain peace in Europe. As it turned out, this pact was meaningless. But it showed again how Hitler operated. He took actions like this to assure other nations he would not resort to war."

"What did Hitler do next?" I turn to Jonuschat, hoping he will have something to add.

"He was secretly building his military machine. Some armament factories were starting to appear. It would take some time—this was only his first year in power—but he was smart enough to plan for his most likely potential enemies, France and Britain, to lessen their guard."

"You certainly kept well-informed," I tell Jonuschat. I am pleased the recorders are being so open and so frank.

Jonuschat leans back in his wing chair, runs his hand through his hair, and continues: "Hitler made a speech, which I recorded, in the Reichstag on January 30, 1934, to report on his first full year as chancellor. It was, of course, broadcast on radio. I remember it was highly acclaimed by most Germans, who felt by now he was providing the leadership the nation needed. Looking back now, I see that the events I have mentioned, taken together, caused radical changes in German society and government. They were unprecedented in the history of the country."

"This is a good place to stop," I say. "It's getting near dinner time, and I know you want to go. I must say that Hitler had an eventful, if horrible, first year. I've learned so much and want to express my appreciation for your good memories and straightforward discussion. I can't thank you enough."

"We are glad to give all the information you want," Reynitz answers.

The man is fast becoming my favorite of the recorders. Tall and thin, his back straight, Reynitz leads the recorders back to quarters with a long stride. He is uniquely qualified to answer my questions. With a keen and analytical mind, honed by an excellent education and anchored in common sense, he earned a doctorate in economics from the University of Berlin in 1929. His skill as an observer has been developed from the perspective of one on center stage, just out of the spotlight's full glare. For me, he has been the right man at the right place at the right time, an eye-and-ear witness to Hitler's rise and fall.

Liberation at Dachau, April 28–29, 1945.

An American GI gives the last of his cigarettes to liberated prisoners.

Chapter 15

The Dachau Trial Continued, November 15, 1945

The main trial of Dachau starts today and will not end until December 13, 1945. The main Nuremberg trial will start November 20, 1945, and end on August 31, 1946. Both courts will try subsequent cases.

Sitting against the wall behind the prosecution table, I have a good view of the court on its high bench, and the defense table on the other side of the bench in front of the defendants. The translators and reporters are in the center.

The 40 defendants are a surly, defiant lot; they sit stiffly in four stepped-up rows of chairs, their defense lawyers, headed by Colonel Bates, at a large table in front of them. Each defendant is asked in turn by the court whether he understands the charges and is ready for trial. Each says "yes," pleading "not guilty" in a firm voice. When asked their nationality, they shout "Deutsch!" with obvious pride.

Behind a railing are 300 seats for the spectators, mostly from nearby towns. We want as many as possible to hear the facts. We make a detailed record so that no one can say the story is a fabrication.

I listen to most of the testimony, expecting that the first witness will prompt a sober response from the well-fed defendants. Instead, the only visible reaction is a defiant, "so-what?" expression. Nevertheless, all the testimony in this trial, the record of which reaches 1,900 pages, is horrifying.

The stories of several selected witnesses* are illustrative of the crimes committed at Dachau. Col. Lawrence C. Ball, an American army physician, describes the camp soon after it was liberated, noting the dead and dying prisoners strewn about the camp. In response to Colonel Denson's questions, Ball says:

First, outside the camp we saw a train . . . of about 40 cars . . . and open and closed boxcars. Those had in them 10 or 20 corpses . . . thinly clad. Many of them had their pants down as if they had dysentery. Some used other corpses as pillows.

Inside the camp, the crematorium had large piles of [nude] corpses stacked about it. They had a corpse smell which was rather prominent. There were large piles of clothing nearby.

They were extremely emaciated . . . their muscles had wasted. The fat had disappeared and their skin was leathery. Malnutrition [starvation] was extreme.

* For ease of reading, the answers are quoted without the questions, which are repetitive.

GIs view the bodies in 40-some open boxcars at Dachau, April 29, 1945.

Clothing from prisoners and remains from the crematory, April 29, 1945.

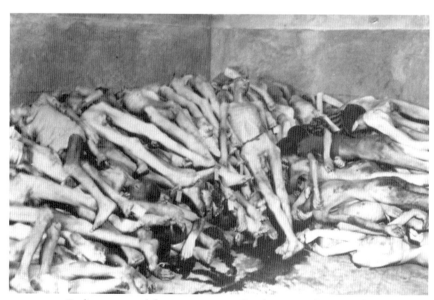

Bodies prepared for cremation at Dachau, April 29, 1945.

We also visited the inner camp [and] the hospital in the company of Dr. Blaha, a prisoner doctor from Czechoslovakia . . . in charge of the hospital [which] was extremely crowded. They had wards with three-decker beds . . . placed together so that three could sleep in them instead of two. A few had a blanket, most of them a sheet. A majority of the cases in the hospital were typhus, dysentery, phlegmon, erysipelas, tuberculosis, and general medical and surgical illnesses. Relatively well prisoners slept with those having these diseases.

I would judge about 4,500 were treated in the . . . four hospitals in Dachau [compound] and two [American] evacuation hospitals. [Another] 1,000 were treated in the SS hospital . . . A majority [died] from causes acquired before [liberation in] April 1945 . . . The population of the prison should have been decreased [before that time], and septicides used, and sanitation, bathing, and sterilization of clothing. [While I was there] the principal causes of death [were] typhus fever, dysentery, and malnutrition.

When we arrived . . . they didn't have . . . remedial equipment . . . the medicine . . . the insecticides . . . the vaccines available to the American army.

Colonel Denson also questions Dr. Franz Blaha, 49, on medical treatment of prisoners during his four years as a prisoner-physician. A 1920 graduate of the University of Prague, Blaha had specialized in surgery and pathology. Arrested and held by the Gestapo in 1939 for his anti-Nazi views, he was sent in 1941 to Dachau, where he was put to work first at menial tasks, then as a nurse, then as head of the prison hospital and pathologist at the morgue. His pertinent testimony relates to the starvation of prisoners:

> The daily average per-person food intake in 1942 was 1,200 calories, which a working prisoner received . . . in 1944, less than 1,000, between 1,000 and 800 . . . it should have been 3,000 calories . . . The working time for the majority of the work details was 11½ hours. [Actually, the workers were under orders for about 17 hours every day.]
>
> The prisoners got up at 4:00 A.M.—4:30 in winter . . . breakfast consisted of three-quarters of a cup of black [ersatz] coffee or tea; twice a week it was soup. Everybody received a piece of bread for a whole day; at first it was a quarter . . . and [at the end] an eighth of a loaf of bread. They began to put less flour in it and more potatoes, and beside that, sawdust.

Questioned about the cause of death in the hundreds of autopsies he performed at Dachau, Dr. Blaha testifies:

> Besides the epidemics, typhus and typhoid, most [deaths] were due to tuberculosis, from the phlegmon and the sepsis, dysentery and malnutrition, and sickness caused by malnutrition. In many cases the sole reason was malnutrition. We called it hunger typhus. Those deaths took place in the years from 1942 through [liberation] . . . The ones who died solely from malnutrition were Italians, Russians, and Frenchmen.

Dr. Blaha explains that thousands dropped dead at work. Many transports carried away from Dachau those too weak to work:

In 1943 instead of the small transports, there were big transports prepared; they were sent to Auschwitz, Lublin, Linz, and there were often 200 people at a time . . . This was known all over the camp . . . as 'the Heavenly Transport' . . . These people were sent to their death.

Another witness is Norbert Fried, 32, who has a doctorate and is from Prague. He was a prisoner-worker in subcamp Kaufering. He was transferred from Auschwitz in October 1944 (when the Russians were advancing toward Poland) to work at Dachau until its liberation. He tells much the same story:

We lived in so-called earth huts—a trench covered with a roof. There was one window and one door . . . 50 prisoners in each hut . . . 12 meters long and less than two meters wide. We slept on the wooden floor, one blanket but no pillow. We put our head on our shoes . . . [which] being of priceless value, were often stolen . . . there were only three latrines for 3,000 prisoners . . . always overflowing with filth . . . we had to walk through that filth, go back and put the shoes again under our heads . . . anyone who would lose his shoes would get the penalty of death.

In the morning, when we had to get up at 4:30, we got black water, no coffee, no sugar in it . . . at work we got three-quarters of a liter of thin soup water with dried vegetables in it . . . after returning from work [in an underground Messerschmitt airplane assembly plant] about 8:00 P.M. or as late as 10:00 P.M., we got the soup of the camp . . . made of unpeeled potatoes, about two halves in a liter, and sometimes of cabbage. After the soup we got our bread . . . in the beginning one-fourth loaf . . . and later one-eighth . . . about as much as two slices. At the camp there were 400 dishes [bowls] for 3,000 . . . so we waited our turn at the kitchen. Some were too weak to wait.

Of the 600 Jews who came to Dachau with me, not as many as 60 are alive.

Kaufering Camp Number Four near Landsberg became a sick camp, and Fried was made its record clerk. He says:

There was a special work detail . . . to bury [up to] 30 corpses a day. The naked bodies were put on a handcart, the gold teeth already removed. That was a special duty of one of the prisoners—a dentist under the supervision of the SS men.

Evacuation of the Kaufering camp, holding 3,000 prisoners, started on April 25, 1945, at noon. Some marched out and trains took out those too weak to walk. The earth huts were burned [and the invalids with them]. I ran away before the last train left . . . and I was hidden in the woods [until April 29] and then I found the Americans there.

Oscar Muller, an anti-Nazi German civilian prisoner in the main Dachau compound, testifies:

In November 1944 a transport came into camp . . . from Hungary. This transport was very much lousy. I was put in charge of delousing—to prevent the typhus epidemic in the camp.

There were always new transports coming into the camp, and that was the reason the typhus epidemic became worse . . . the population of the camp grew. They were clothed in the well-known striped suits . . . they often didn't receive any long drawers, and the largest number had no over-coats in the winter. They were exposed to the cold.

When I first arrived, Dachau had about 22,000 prisoners. In April 1945 there were about 33,000. The camp was suit-able under normal conditions for about 8,000 [not including the subcamps]. Underwear was not washed for up to 12 weeks. Some fell apart because they were not changed.

Bodies stacked outside one of the Dachau crematory, April 29, 1945.

Colonel Denson questions prosecution witness Prince Leopold of Prussia.

Some members of royalty also knew life in Dachau. One prisoner is Friedrich Leopold, Prince of Prussia, 50. He testifies:

I was arrested on May 25, 1944, at Bad Gestein . . . I was taken to Dachau in October 1944.

In the morning we got some so-called coffee, but it was black water, and a piece of bread, and sometimes a little bit of marmalade. For lunch we got some water soup. In there was some cabbage or some pieces of carrots and some peels of potatoes . . . [at the hospital] I received sometimes a little bit of some stuff cooked in milk. My normal weight was 155 pounds and [it dropped] to 95 pounds . . . I saw bodies . . . starved to death . . . only bones, which were covered with skin . . . some people had to undress in the open air . . . it was terribly cold . . . they had to line up in front of the dispensary . . . and some of them dropped to the ground.

I worked at the SS canteen where the SS men had their meals. I worked in the cellar . . . I washed dishes. In the cellar I unpacked boxes, which arrived with wine, champagne, and brandy. The SS men had good food, potatoes, vegetables, and very often meat.

A bronze bust of Hitler, above, and a leather Nazi notebook given to the author by one of Hitler's five non-Nazi war-conference recorders.

Chapter 16

November 1945

As the trial progresses, I continue to meet with Hitler's recorders after working hours and on weekends. One Sunday, beginning about 11:00 A.M., they arrive at my living quarters. We sit down in the overstuffed chairs, and everyone seems relaxed.

"In our last discussion, we left off where Hitler had completed his first year. I would like to go on from there," I say.

"I'll start," volunteers Krieger, and he slowly begins. "Starting in 1934, Hitler demanded arms equality with other nations, mainly Britain and France, who were traditional enemies. He spoke on the radio for all nations to hear. He said the German people could not be denied that right. He said nothing of restrictive World War I treaties."

Krieger is intelligent and to the point. He goes on: "That demand was appealing to Germans who were unemployed and had no skills. For many of them, their last jobs were as soldiers in World War I.

They wanted to be soldiers again, as they supported Hitler. The military buildup could be seen in construction of new factory and barracks buildings."

"What happened next?" I look at Jonuschat. He seems ready to talk.

"Hitler ordered purges of the SA leadership in June 1934. In the dead of night, SS troops went to the SA headquarters and shot Ernst Roehm, chief of the SA, along with a large number of SA officers and some innocent civilians. It was widely publicized, and Hitler reported the purge in a major radio speech.

"Hitler said that Roehm was plotting to overthrow him, even trying to have army units join the SA's four million in uniform. It was necessary to resort to the purge of the SA leadership to 'maintain order and defend the nation.' He also said the SS killed under a hundred SAs, but later reports by others said the total was much higher." Jonuschat pauses.

Jonuschat is obviously a well-educated man. He tells me he was born in 1901 in East Prussia, then moved to Berlin, graduated from high school, and earned a doctorate in political science in 1926. He entered the Stenographic Office of the Reichstag, served in the German army in 1941, and in September 1942 was recruited to Hitler's headquarters. He adds much to our discussions.

"In the United States, it was broadcast that this killing of Roehm and his henchmen showed Hitler's lust for power," I interject.

"May I say something?" asks Reynitz, sitting on the edge of his chair. "This purge was an example of his nihilist view of the value of man. The SA quickly dropped to about one-fourth of its highest membership. Some SA members, who were physically fit and true to the Nazi ideology, were permitted to join the SS, which was still a voluntary organization under Heinrich Himmler. Some units of the SA continued under new leaders to be used for dirty work, like persecuting Jews, Gypsies, and Communists."

"Good observation, Reynitz. Couldn't have said it better. Then what?" I ask.

"Shortly after the SA purge, President Hindenburg died, on August 2, 1934. I remember this date well. Hitler quickly combined the offices of president and chancellor and seized complete power as the head of government and the armed forces," Reynitz continues.

"Hitler called for a plebiscite when he took full power. Almost 90 percent of the people voted in favor. I don't know who counted the vote, but I feel sure Hitler would not have called for a vote unless he was sure of the outcome. He wanted to show Germans and those in neighboring countries that 'I have the people behind me.'"

"You certainly have a grasp of the facts. That is tremendously important. Please go on." The others eye him approvingly.

"In March 1935, compulsory military training was announced— 'to take the necessary measure to protect the Reich,' Hitler said. Those who had military experience volunteered, enlisted without waiting to be drafted, in the hope of early promotions. Most others were not complaining. They were accustomed to military duties. Some did object, like a tailor in my neighborhood in Berlin. He printed handbills and put them in letterboxes. The handbills stated that Hitler was preparing for war and everyone should stop him before it was too late. He was arrested and put to work as a tailor in a concentration camp, making uniforms," Reynitz remembers. He is a master of the facts, and I encourage him to continue.

"Almost immediately after the draft order, France and Britain denounced unilateral violations of World War I treaties. The League of Nations also objected. I read this in English newspapers. Hitler responded by saying that Germany wanted peace and that another world war would be a frightful upheaval. This was typical of Hitler—saying the opposite of what he intended. He was preparing for war." Reynitz leans back in his chair and relaxes.

The others nod in agreement.

"How was he able to finance the preparation? He was in debt: how could he find the money?" I look at Jonuschat, who has a good memory.

"He had Hjalmar Schacht, president of the Reichsbank. He was made finance minister and, among other things, he invented the 'Mefo Bills' backed by armament companies and the government, good for five years. They were merely promises to pay in the future, strange for Germans, who were accustomed to buying something only when the money was in hand. These certificates were used by factories to buy supplies and soon were being circulated like money."

"That is important. Was that the first time that happened?" I ask Jonuschat.

"Yes," he replies, as he slumps into the davenport again.

"What happened next?" I inquire of Krieger.

He scratches his head and says, "As we've said, Hitler did everything step by step, testing the people and also other countries. And he was being successful. In September 1935 he issued a decree called the 'Nuremberg Laws.' It took from Jews almost all rights of citizenship and prohibited them from marrying Germans. There was no economic or national security reason for those laws. They came from

Hitler's hatred of Jews as a boy in Austria. Jews were victims of his propaganda from the time he came into public view until his last days."

I look at my watch—it's 1:00 P.M. "Let's break for lunch," I say. "I'll take you to the officers' club, where they permit us to have guests."

The recorders put on their topcoats and follow me to the club.

"This is the first time I've been to the officers' club," says Thoet.

"I hope you will like it," I reply.

At the club, the maitre'd, who is dressed in a tuxedo, says, "Table for six? Right this way." He seats us by a window and asks, "Would you like some wine?"

I order two bottles of Liebfraumilch.

The club is huge and well furnished. The waiters wear short black jackets, black bow ties, and black trousers. We look at the menu, and the waiter tells us the specialty of the day is rack of venison, with small potatoes, gravy, and mixed vegetables.

"That sounds good," says Reynitz. "I'll try it."

The others, including me, order the same.

The waiter brings the wine, which is delicious. The meal is more so. The deer in the Alps near Munich are small, about two-thirds the size of the whitetails in the United States.

"This is great," I say, and the others readily agree. "This is the most tender meat I've ever eaten."

When we finish, they thank me profusely.

"Shall we continue where we left off?" I ask.

185

"We are quite willing," says Krieger. I am glad to hear that.

We saunter back to my quarters, about two blocks away. It is a cool day. At my residence, we all take the seats we had before.

"I'm grateful to you all," I say.

"We're grateful to you for the outstanding lunch." Krieger pats his stomach, and the others nod.

"The club always has a special on Sundays." Then after settling down, I ask, "Who would like to start?"

"I will," says Jonuschat. "Hitler invaded the Rhineland in March 1936. This was his first major military action. It was a bold move, even though France had withdrawn from the area some time before."

"How big is the Rhineland? Why was it important to Hitler?"

"It is quite large, lying just north of Austria, with the Rhine River and Stuttgart at its center. The area was important to Germany's economy because of its coal, industry, and barging," Jonuschat continues. "It had been granted to France by the Versailles Treaty, and Hitler was not yet prepared for full-blown war. He ordered withdrawal if France fought back."

"Then it really was a bold move." I continue to look at Jonuschat.

"When the invasion occurred, Hitler said, 'The area belongs to Germany, and my action is merely symbolic. Our territorial claims have now been satisfied.' While foreign countries complained, they did nothing, just as Hitler had surmised. They were drained economically from World War I and had no stomach for war. The German people were ecstatic, hailing this first military action as bloodless."

"How did Hitler advise his countrymen?"

Jonuschat continues: "Even as his troops were occupying the Rhineland, Hitler called the Reichstag into session to announce his action and, of course, to get worldwide attention. It was two years before the next bold move occurred. Meanwhile, he was building his military forces.

"The Germans rejoiced, but there was some fear that France would retaliate and perhaps start another war. Hitler gained much in prestige because not a shot was fired. All of this was freely and gleefully discussed in Germany." Jonuschat concludes his narration and relaxes.

Then Reynitz says, "Other countries did nothing except to denounce violations of the treaties. The British press made statements to the effect that, 'The Germans are only going back into their own country.' Foreign reaction, I and others thought, was mild, probably because no country, including Germany, wanted war. I would guess none was prepared for war.

"All European countries were practically disarmed after World War I. On reflection, I think the gap until World War II was a recess. World War I had damaged the economies of all participants, and the treaties following it bore the seeds for World War II, brought to fruition in the person of Hitler," Reynitz says, scratching his head.

Then he recalls: "He ordered fortifications along the long border from Switzerland to the Netherlands. It was later called the Siegfried Line, after a hero in German mythology. It was also called the Westwall, at least the northern extension of it. It was reported that the economy in the Rhineland had come to life, putting people to work."

"What next?" I ask Jonuschat. Sitting on the edge of his chair, he seems ready to speak.

"I read reports of the Spanish Civil War in the British newspapers, which carried views of other countries as well. In Germany, nothing was reported by the controlled press and radio. Nothing was said about killed or wounded Germans," he recollects.

"The secret was out when wounded Germans were brought home. Meanwhile, there were jokes making fun of Spain. A man going to the bathroom would say, 'Permit me, I have to go to Spain.' Or if a friend wasn't seen for a while, a remark would be made that, 'He is probably in Spain.'" Jonuschat leans back, satisfied with his recollection.

I look at Reynitz: "What went on in Spain?"

"Soon it was openly revealed that German planes and tanks were supporting General Francisco Franco's rebels. Spain was the testing ground for a technique called *Blitzkrieg* [lightning war], as we learned later. When Hitler's conquests started, there was wide publicity on how the Blitzkrieg worked. It was a combination of planes, tanks, and motorized troops moving forward as fast as possible.

"When Franco won, Hitler ordered victory celebrations in Germany. There were large parades in Berlin, hailing the victory. Government workers and others had the day off. Many used the time for visits and family picnics." Reynitz has a fantastic memory. He sits erect, pulls his earlobe, and continues:

"In 1937, reports in the world press were telling of purges in Russia, of opponents of the Red regime, and of hundreds of military officers considered by Stalin to be unreliable. Yet Stalin had no greater admirer than Hitler. At war headquarters, I remember his saying several times: 'I cannot allow myself to thoroughly purge the army as Stalin did, to relieve it of the damned intelligentsia.'"

Jonuschat picks it up: "Hitler had a great ego and always tried to be popular with his countrymen. This would restrain him from large army purges. Yet, the two leaders were alike in many ways. They both wore simple uniforms. Each permitted only one political party. They got rid of their political opponents by use of concentration camps. Both were dictators, Hitler probably more so than Stalin, who had to answer to party bodies. Both believed the ends justified any means. Both banned any type of people's organization. Both indoctrinated school children. Both believed in spreading their own ideologies into other countries. Both ruled the military forces. The goal of both was to dominate the world."

Then Reynitz says, "I could say the same for Mussolini, dictator of Italy since 1920. Hitler originally admired him."

Krieger finishes it up: "In November 1937, Germany, Italy, and Japan signed the Anti-Comintern Pact [Anti-Communist International Pact]. It was widely publicized. The announcements said the Communist International was a danger in both East and West and a threat to peace and order. The world press said this pact was disturbing in that it showed a potential for military adventures. I read these reports from many countries in the British papers.

"You will remember that Japan started its expansion by invading Manchuria and China in 1931 and that Italy invaded Ethiopia in 1935. So, in 1937, when the three expansionist-minded dictators joined hands, many countries were concerned." The others are amazed at Reynitz's recall. They look at him with astonishment and pride.

"I think this is a good place to end our discussion. Your information is terrific. I really appreciate your taking the time to share it with me," I say.

"Auf Wiedersehen," says Krieger, and they leave with broad smiles.

Victims identify defendants Wilhelm Wagner, above, and Christof Knoll, below.

Chapter 17

The Dachau Trial Continued, November 1945

In the courtroom, I sit behind the audience to determine how well the citizens can hear the testimony and see the exhibits. They can hear and see just fine. Today a crew from Munich is shooting movies, and the witnesses and defendants are instructed to speak slowly and loudly so everything they say will be picked up by the recording equipment. Klieg lights glare, and three cameras quietly grind away in strategic spots, lending a little action to the grim proceedings.

We hear from many witnesses about the torture of prisoners at Dachau by German guards. Among them is Chaim Sendowski, a tailor from Poland, 38. He came from Auschwitz to Dachau in October 1944. His detail was sorting rocks in a ditch. He testifies:

Six of us were throwing rocks through a screen, so we would only get the small rock. [SS defendant Wilhelm Tempel] said,

"If you bend the wire [of the screen], I'm going to beat you."
But we had to throw rocks against it, so naturally we had to
bend the wire. So he beat us and we had to work. My comrade
said maybe we should ask how we are supposed to do it without bending it. We were always afraid to ask . . . then my
friend said, "I will ask him." He said, "Mr. Rapportfuehrer,
please show us how to do it."

He used a [rubber-coated] cable and beat that man terribly, and later on . . . he also kicked him. And he beat the man
until he didn't have any strength to get up, and the blood was
just pouring from his head. He said, "Take this dirt away." I
took him to the hospital, and he was very ill, and his arm was
broken. And on the next morning . . . I went to see how he
was doing. I brought him some soup. I couldn't give him the
soup because he was already dead.

Then there is Rudolf Wolf, a German engraver from Freiberg, 35.
He was a prisoner in Dachau from September 1942 until its liberation
in April 1945. He tells more about the tortures:

I saw [SS defendant Friedrich Ruppert] beating someone very
often . . . He kicked the prisoners and also hit them with a
whip . . . so hard that the men became unconscious. He was
such a man who could beat people without changing expression. Just like a blacksmith striking cold iron.

The prisoner had to stand at attention in front of him,
then [SS defendant Franz Trenkle] . . . would use the outer
edge of his shoes and kick him in the lower part of his legs. He

did that to me personally, so that the blood would run. He scraped the skin off.

Whipping was done publicly at the formation place [gathering area]. The block was about the same height as this table. On the front part there were straps attached and [at the back end] a box. The prisoner had to step into the box and then had to lay across the block . . . Particularly strong prisoners . . . had to do the beating . . . one prisoner, Herman Folger, refused to do the beating . . . Trenkle walked over to him and [with a] cat-o-nine tails . . . hit him across the face twice, then did the beating himself . . . And then they had to go to the hospital, and across the posterior, which was mostly broken open, they received iodine. The men I saw beaten were Russian and Frenchmen. [They] received ten or 25 lashes according to orders. [Some] had to be carried to the hospital.

Next Riva Levy, 29, an office worker from Poland, testifies to the mistreatment of women prisoners:

[SS defendant Otto Foerschner] was very bad with food, [one] of the women did not work, so . . . we did not receive any food all day, and we were supposed to stand at attention from 6:00 A.M. to 2:00 P.M. And from 2:00 P.M. to 6:00 P.M., we worked at the carting of stone. Some of the women did not have any strength left for carrying stones, and they put a little less in that contraption for carrying the stones, and [for that] he beat them.

Franz Blaha testifies again, about the standing bunker, a cell used for punishment:

> The standing bunker was of such dimensions that one could not sit down in it, but could just stand up. One could just possibly bend the knees a little.
>
> I was not punished in the standing bunker, but I brought the dead bodies out of the bunkers several times. [They were] mostly Russians and Poles—during 1944 and 1945.

In a pretrial statement, defendant Emil Mahl backed Blaha: "Imprisonment in the standing cell [meant] eight to ten hours during the night, in several cases two to three nights without food or drink."

Blaha also describes wrist-hanging, another common torture:

> For instance, like in my case for not working properly, [prisoners] were hung up on a post . . . with their hands tied behind their backs . . . with a chain or sometimes a rope. They were hoisted up on a hook so their toes couldn't touch the ground . . . sometimes one, two, three, sometimes even more hours. I was hung there for an hour—with a chain.
>
> We couldn't move [our] hands for at least three days, and we couldn't work. I had blood clots on the hands, then swollen feet and great pain.

The Catholic priests who were anti-Nazi were also prisoners. Theodore Koch, a Polish priest since 1932 and Dachau prisoner from October 1941 to April 1945, testifies about punishment exercises:

There were jumps, knee-bends, and we had to do other gymnastics; that is, running on the knees. From Palm Sunday until Easter Sunday, we had to go through exercises on the formation place from 6:00 A.M. until 7:00 P.M. except for dinner. [During that week] many priests died during and after the exercises.

He also testifies about threats that prisoners would be made to leave camp on the invalid transports: "[This was considered a form of punishment] because it was the opinion that all of those who went on the invalid transport were to go to a gas chamber."

The witnesses continue along these lines, establishing a clear pattern of sadistic torture in the main camp and subcamps.

The defendants who choose to testify, upon cross-examination by Colonel Denson, admit only to occasional handslaps to the faces of some prisoners. When reminded of their voluntary and signed pretrial statements about beatings, they become evasive, saying they were mistaken in making the statements. They say these incidents could not have occurred at the stated times or places. A few say the handslaps were to remind the prisoners of rule violations.

And two defendants testify to beatings of prisoners by other defendants, apparently to gain leniency.

Hitler's Appeal to the German People to Repel Polish Terrorization.

Reichstag Speech on the 1st of Septembre 1939

Members of the German Reichstag!

For months we have been tormented by a problem once set us by the dictated Treaty of Versailles and which has now assumed such a character as to become utterly intolerable.

Danzig was and is a German city!

The Corridor was and is German!

All these districts owe their cultural development exclusively to the German people, without whom absolute barbarism would prevail in these eastern tracts of country.

Danzig was separated from us! The Corridor was annexed by Poland! The German minorities living there were ill-treated in the most appalling manner! More than a million persons with German blood in their veins were compelled to leave their homes as early as 1919/1920.

~~Here, as always, I have attempted to change this~~ tolerable condition of things by means of peaceful proposals for a revision. It is a lie when the world alleges that we always used pressure in attempting to carry out any revision. There was ample opportunity for fifteen years before National Socialism assumed power to carry through revisions by means of a peaceful understanding. This was not done! I myself then took the initiative in every single case, not only once, but many times, to bring forward proposals for the revision of absolutely intolerable conditions. As you know, all these proposals have been rejected. I need not enumerate them in detail: those proposals for a limitation of armaments, if necessary even for the abolition of armaments, those for restrictions on methods of warfare, those for eliminating methods of modern warfare, which in my opinion, are scarcely compatible with International Law. You know the proposals which I made as to the necessity of restoring German sovereign rights in certain territories of the Reich, those countless attempts I made to bring about a peaceful solution of the Austrian problem, and later on that of the Sudetenland, Bohemia and Moravia. It was all in vain!

One thing, however, is impossible: to demand that a peaceful revision should be made of an intolerable state of affairs — and then obstinately refuse such a peaceful revision!

And it is just impossible to assert that in such a situation to act on one's own initiative in making a revision is to violate a law. To Germans the dictated Treaty of Versailles is not a law! It won't do to blackmail a person at the point of a pistol with the threat of starvation for millions of people into signing a document and afterwards proclaim that this document with its forced signature was a solemn law!

In the case of Danzig and the Corridor I have again tried to solve the problems by means of peaceful proposals suggesting a discussion. One thing was obvious: they had to be solved!

That the date of this solution may perhaps be of little interest to the Western Powers is conceivable. But this date is not a matter of indifference to us. First and foremost, however, it was not and could not be a matter of indifference to the suffering victims.

In conversations with Polish statesmen, I have discussed the ideas which you have heard me express here in my last speech to the Reichstag. No one can maintain that this was an unjust procedure or even unreasonable pressure. I then had the German proposals clearly formulated and I feel bound to repeat once more that nothing could be fairer or more modest than those proposals submitted by me. And I now wish to declare to ~~the whole world that I, and I alone, was in a position to~~ make such proposals. For I know quite definitely that I was thereby acting contrary to the opinion of millions of Germans. Those proposals were rejected! But more than that! They were replied to by mobilization, increased terrorism, intensified pressure on the German minorities in those areas and by a gradual economic and political strangulation of the Free City of Danzig which, during the past few weeks, found its expression in military measures and traffic restrictions. Poland virtually began a war against the Free City of Danzig. Furthermore it was not prepared to settle the problem of the Corridor in a fair manner satisfying the interests of both parties. And lastly, Poland has never been willing to fulfill her obligations with regard to the minorities.

In this connection I feel it necessary to state that Germany has fulfilled her obligations in this respect! Minorities domiciled in Germany are not subjected to persecution. Dare any Frenchman get up and declare that French citizens living in the Saar territory are oppressed, ill-treated or deprived of their rights? No one can make such an assertion!

For four months I have watched these developments without taking actions but not without issuing repeated warnings. Recently I have made these warnings more and more emphatic. Over three weeks ago the Polish Ambassador was, at my request, informed that if Poland persisted in sending further notes in the nature of an ultimatum to Danzig and in further oppressing the German minorities, or if attempts were made to bring about the economic ruin of Danzig by means of customs restrictions, Germany would no longer stand aside and remain inactive.

196

Chapter 18

November 1945

The five recorders meet at 7:30 P.M. in my office. "You know that I have brought you together to proceed with your recollections. I am interested only in the major events." I pour the wine.

Reynitz says, "I understand and will keep my comments to those events. Hope you don't mind my starting first."

"Certainly not."

"As an official recorder for the Reichstag, I took down Hitler's speech to the Reichstag in February 1938," says Reynitz, sitting very straight. "Hitler said, in brief, 'It is intolerable that across our border, in Austria and Sudetenland [northern Czechoslovakia], live millions of our countrymen who want to be part of Germany. I demand their right of self-determination.' He had convened the Reichstag to make this announcement for all the world to hear."

"This was Hitler's first military action since the Rhineland invasion two years before, right?" I ask.

"Yes, it was," Reynitz continues. "Hitler used a combination of tactics to occupy Austria: a buildup of pro-Nazis there, blunt diplomacy, and a show of force at the Austrian border. A subdued Austrian chancellor could do nothing and so was replaced by a pro-Nazi in March 1938. I remember that month. German forces marched into Austria and occupied the country with little opposition. This was called *Anschluss* [annexation]. Briefly, that was what happened."

Reynitz goes on: "I remember that Hitler convened the Reichstag afterward, confirming his action and calling for a plebiscite, which produced over 98 percent in favor. There was also a plebiscite in Austria, with the same result. No one knows who counted the votes."

"What was the reaction of the German people you knew?" I ask.

Nazi roundup of Jews in Vienna—110,000 Austrians, 60,000 of them Jews, died in concentrations camps. Only 600 of 89,000 Jews remained in Vienna.

Krieger picks up on this: "They said it was like a miracle that Hitler could do again what he did in the Rhineland—bloodless occupation. They viewed him as a strong, decisive leader who made his actions seem legal.

"In the fall of 1938, Hitler made a speech at the Sportpalast in Berlin that the Sudetenland was his last territorial claim in Europe. This speech was carried worldwide by press and radio. It was followed by a meeting in Munich of the leaders of France, Britain, Italy, and Germany. It resulted in the Munich Pact, which allowed Hitler's troops to occupy the area.

"This was another bloodless takeover with the appearance of legality. It was supported by the German people I knew because Germans lived there," Krieger concludes and rests in his chair.

Then the recorders and I discuss the British prime minister, Neville Chamberlain, who returned to Britain in triumph and made a speech to Parliament declaring achievement in Europe of "peace in our time." I tell them about the news coverage of the event in the United States, which reported the Munich Pact as the appeasement of Hitler. I remember many press photos of Chamberlain in formal dress, with tall silk hat and the ever-present umbrella in one hand. He became a symbol of appeasement.

"I can't imagine anyone being as gullible as Chamberlain. He was a fool," I think to myself, as Jonuschat picks up our earlier discussion.

"Outside the Sudetenland, the rest of Czechoslovakia was then surrounded by German forces on the north, west, and south. Hitler wasted no time and forced that country to capitulate in March 1939. It was quickly occupied. We know now that Hitler threatened invasion beforehand, and there was little pretense of legality in that move."

"I'll say. There wasn't a pretext. Hitler was on the march." Then I ask Jonuschat about Hitler's next move.

"Hitler's press and radio stated that there would be an uprising of Germans in Memel, Lithuania. English newspapers reported that Lithuania was defenseless and that its leaders had signed a surrender agreement in advance of the occupation by German naval forces. Again, it was a bloodless action, but it was the last one.

"Hitler made a speech before a cheering crowd in Prague and a week later made a repeat performance in Memel. There was wide reporting of these events, followed by a few months of no military action," Jonuschat ends his statement. The recorders watch him with pride.

"About Jews, what did Hitler do next?" I look at Buchholz.

Buchholz is ready as this is one of his pet subjects: "Hitler's action against the Jews went step by step—with milder, then with stronger actions—always to see how far the German people would let him go."

"Give me some examples."

"First were the decrees. Next, stronger decrees forcing Jews to display the Star of David on their clothing. Changing their first names so all females would be called Sarah and all males, Israel. Cutting their rations in half and barring Jews from public transportation and the civil service. Almost everything possible was being done to force the Jews to leave Germany voluntarily," Buchholz recalls.

I ask him to continue.

"Then came the violence of Krystalnacht [Night of Crystal, or Shattered Glass], named after a night of breaking windows in Jewish shops and synagogues all over Germany in November 1938. Hitler's order came after the reported killing by a Jew of a minor German foreign officer in Paris. The order, as we now know, included instructions to arrest thousands of Jews and to take things of value from the synagogues. The Jews were arrested 'for their own protection.' They were sent to concentration camps, I was told."

"Go on." I notice that all the other recorders are looking at Buchholz. He seems to have a lot to say.

"A friend of mine said his two young children participated in looting a Jewish shop the night before. He was ashamed of what his children did and scolded them. Their reply was, 'Everyone else was doing it. The police just watched and did nothing.'" Buchholz finishes.

"That's revealing," I say. (See appendix.)

"This was carried further," recalls Reynitz. "About a week later, Goering called a meeting of gauleiters and kreisleiters from all over Germany. These were the chiefs of key areas in the structure of the Nazi party [not the local or state government]. *Gau* is a major area around a big city. *Kreis* is a cluster of small towns. *Leiter* means leader. The meeting was held at the new Luftwaffe Ministry compound, and I was one of the recorders.

"Goering said it was decided to impose a fine of a thousand million marks on all Jews in Germany. He said, in brief, 'You have seen how the people feel. [There was no significant objection in Germany, although most Germans didn't understand its purpose.] We have decided they deserve to be fined. Besides, we can use the money, starting with money from insurance claims for the damage [of Krystalnacht], which will be paid in foreign currency. Then you must see that money, valuables, and businesses will be taken from Jews in each locality, wherever found, to help pay this fine. Bank accounts, jewelry, automobiles, everything of value.'"

"How in the world could Hitler get by with all this?" I wonder. "Was Goering furious at that meeting?" I look again at Reynitz.

"Goering was firm but not furious. He was stronger when he complained that plate glass for stores was expensive and that some of it could be bought only in other countries at higher prices. He thought like Hitler, so he carried out his orders, all coming out of Hitler's hostility toward the Jews. Of course, many Nazis, too, hated Jews because of their wealth or status. I am speaking of Nazis who had little or nothing of their own. They were quite willing to carry out Hitler's orders against the Jews."

Reynitz goes on: "At another meeting Goering discussed repayment of the debt for rearmament. He had a simple answer: 'It will not be Germans who will pay. It will be the losers. So, why worry about it?'"

"What about unemployment?" I question Thoet. He hasn't said a word so far today. I note that he is a small man, most often a colleague of Reynitz. Born in 1906, he became a verbatim reporter for several states of Germany, then for the Reichstag. After a short military service, he was chosen by Krieger, in September 1942, as one of the best recorders to serve at Hitler's military conferences. No wonder—utmost detail is his habit, and he has a keen memory. The other recorders watch him as he prepares to speak.

"Employment was getting better. Millions went back to work in factories and other places or were busy in Nazi organizations or the military. The autobahns [super highways] were being built. They were said to be important for military and civilian needs. The plans for the autobahns were drawn years before Hitler gained power, but until the money could be found, they were gathering dust."

"I wondered how the autobahns could be designed and built so fast. Now, I know. Thank you very much. That was wonderful information. I didn't know that the plans for the autobahns had been drawn years before Hitler," confesses Krieger.

"Neither did I," adds Reynitz.

"How was the general economy going?" I ask Thoet.

"In 1939, between Hitler's military buildup and Hjalmar Schacht's genius for financing it, the whole economy picked up quickly. I must also tell you that Schacht had a falling out with Hitler and was relieved of his position. Schacht thought there was too much spending on armaments and had made a negative remark about Krystalnacht," Thoet recalls.

"What else did Hitler do?" I look at Buchholz and turn a page in my notebook.

"Church leaders began to speak out from their pulpits against the gassing of retarded people as ordered by Hitler. A highly respected bishop in Berlin gave a strong sermon against the killing of mentally incompetent people and called it murder. Public reaction was also strong. This practice ended, but there was no official response to the protests. It was just quietly stopped," Buchholz remembers.

"Why do you suppose Hitler did this?" Everyone is looking at Buchholz.

"I can only surmise it was done as a part of Hitler's goal to get rid of more undesirables—another attempt to reach the stronger German society he envisioned. Also, I suppose, taking care of mental illness was expensive and revenues were short. I should add that earlier those with chronic illnesses were sterilized, and there was no public protest about that."

"Did Hitler do anything remarkable regarding children or unwed mothers?" I remember, during my war-crimes investigations in the summer of 1945, seeing a large hospital in middle Germany. The occupation troops called it a "baby farm" because it had handled many unmarried maternity cases. An American officer-nurse there had worked with German nurses who told her that many of the maternity patients were single women whose babies were signed over to orphanages before admission. She said German women in that town outnumbered local men almost three to one and there had been what amounted to "free love," with government encouragement.

Now Thoet tells me, "Girls, usually members of the Nazi party, would have children by other members of the party or the SS. Each girl was required to sign a document giving up any control of the child. Each child was placed in an orphanage controlled by the party. There the children were indoctrinated in Hitler's philosophy like any other children. The employer of each girl was required to pay her for several weeks before and after birth. She went back to work and remained single. Neither parent was allowed to see the child."

"Can you imagine? Weren't there any laws against this?"

"There were paternity laws, but they were not used in these kinds of cases. The employer and the government paid all costs. And the practice was kept as secret as possible. Remember, Hitler wanted as many Germanic-type children as possible. So there was no discouragement of the practice.

"I didn't hear any protests from the churches or the public. Maybe that was because payment of expenses was kept so secret," Thoet concludes and leans back in his chair.

"How about the Rev. Martin Niemoeller?" I ask Reynitz about a famous inmate of Dachau. "He has received a lot of publicity in the foreign press and radio, I notice."

"Hitler ordered a constitution for the new 'Reich Church' for all Protestants soon after he became chancellor. Reverend Niemoeller was a popular Lutheran minister, and he objected from his pulpit to the state takeover of the Protestant churches," Reynitz tells me. "He was arrested and tried in 1937, but the jury acquitted him. He was arrested again in 1938 for offenses against the state.

"I was one of the reporters at his second trial before a Nazi special court. A Lutheran myself, I was particularly interested in the trial," Reynitz continues. "Gestapo men testified against him, saying they attended his services where he spoke from the pulpit against Nazi actions and especially about mistreatment of the Jews. Niemoeller testified firmly in his own defense about people being put in concentration camps without a trial, among other things.

"Thoet and I agreed during a recess that if the jury acquitted him, Niemoeller would go to a concentration camp. That's exactly what happened," Reynitz concludes.

"What occurred then?" I ask, looking at Krieger.

He says calmly, "In April 1939, I heard Hitler's speech at the Reichstag. He said the reports that he was planning to attack Poland were an invention of the international press. This was typical of him.

"It was the same pattern of diplomacy and promises. Up to that time each bloodless invasion came after promises, even signed treaties, assuring no invasion. Between invasions there was a space of time—a cooling-off period—before starting the next. Between times Hitler was clever in using the fear of war and Communism to frustrate and confuse those who might oppose his next move, in or out of Germany.

"Hitler had openly demanded the return of the Polish corridor, including return of the 'Free City of Danzig' [*Gdansk* in Polish], which was set up by World War I treaties. Poland refused. This area was important to Hitler's plans because it divided the large German state of Prussia," Krieger finishes on a distraught note.

"Did you get any feeling of how the German people viewed this?" I glance at Reynitz, who seems serious and ready to talk.

"The German people were nervous about these demands. They understood Hitler's pattern of demanding the return of lost territories where Germans lived, but they could feel the possibility of war. There was open discussion about this because Allied countries were making pleas to Hitler not to start war.

"Then came the *big surprise*," Reynitz continues. "Hitler announced late in August 1939 a nonaggression pact with Russia. Hitler's radio and press stated that neither Germany nor Russia would attack the other and that each would remain neutral in case either country became involved in war with a third power.

"We learned later that there were secret agreements in the pact dividing up much of eastern Europe. Russia would get eastern Poland, Estonia, and Latvia and would be free to take Finland. Germany would get the western part of Poland and Lithuania."

"Remarkable. It is difficult to imagine," I say and look at Jonuschat. He is solemn.

"How did the people of Germany take this?"

"The people I knew expressed astonishment. They were stunned. Up to that time they were always told that the Bolsheviks were our real enemies. Then, all of a sudden, without any preparation, there was a treaty with Russia. The people couldn't grasp the idea. They talked about it on the streets and in their homes." Jonuschat answers so quickly, it startles me.

"That must have been quite a blow to the Communists." I get up from my chair and look out the window. A few lights flicker in nearby windows.

"Nothing was heard from the Communists until much later. I suppose they were waiting for the party line. Finally, they made a public statement to the effect that Stalin made the pact to prevent Hitler from going farther east."

"A lame excuse," I think, as Jonuschat continues.

"I read the English newspaper, which quoted other nations. I bought the paper at a kiosk in Berlin. They were also in the dark until the announcement. All countries reported great surprise. Japan called it a 'pact with Satan' and renounced the Anti-Comintern Pact," Jonuschat recalls.

"That's quite a surprise," I say. "What did Hitler do to protect himself against revolt in Germany?" I look at Buchholz. This is a serious question. Dictators are more apprehensive about their own people than anyone else.

"Delayed news was typical of Hitler. He always waited until an event happened before announcing it. It was always the same, starting with his occupation of the Rhineland," Buchholz recalls. "My guess is that he did this for two reasons. First, he apparently didn't want to give anyone time to prepare for protests in Germany. Second, I think he felt that when Germany and neighboring countries were faced with a *fait accompli,* it would be too late for them to do anything about it. Looking back, I see that all of the protests from other countries were only verbal."

Reynitz recalls, "I remember reading in *Mein Kampf*—Hitler noted that 'an alliance with Russia embodies a plan for the next war.'"

"What happened next?" I look at Karl Thoet, who sits up straight, apparently eager to contribute.

"Hitler addressed the Reichstag on September 1, 1939, and I was assigned to record his speech. He said that Polish troops had started firing on Germans along the frontier that very day and that he ordered a return of fire to remove any element of insecurity.

"Hitler immediately hit Poland with his blitzkrieg, capturing western Poland up to the agreed-upon dividing line, and Stalin's forces moved westward to the dividing line, so that Poland no longer existed. In hindsight, one can see that if Britain and France interfered with Hitler's forces, at least Russia would not. Also that Hitler's use of the blitzkrieg would conquer Poland so fast that Britain and France would not have time to interfere. It took a little longer than expected."

"How did German civilians react?" I again ask Thoet.

"I did not talk with many people, and everyone was careful to speak very little about the invasion of Poland. But I did hear several remarks from civilians about the 'Sitzkrieg' in the west. I mean France and Britain did not react immediately."

"Why didn't the Germans talk about it much?"

"Because of fear of the Gestapo and other informers. There were no public protests, and I gathered that many Germans felt this was Hitler's way of regaining the Polish corridor and uniting Prussia. There certainly was an atmosphere of fear that Hitler had gone too far, especially, when two days later Britain, France, and others declared war on Germany," Thoet grimly recalls.

Then I tell the recorders that the pact with Russia and Hitler's invasion of Poland a week later were heavily reported by the newspapers and radio in the United States: "The stunning effect of the blitzkrieg was described in bits and pieces but finally summarized as a completely new type of warfare. This included advance planes bombing and strafing, followed by tanks and slow-flying Stuka planes bombing and strafing in cooperation with tank fire, followed by armored vehicles carrying troops with rifles, grenades, machine guns, mortars, and ammunition. Finally came the foot soldiers to mop up and occupy the invaded area. Poland's resistance was knocked out in a relatively short time. It startled most of the Americans I talked with.

"After a period of silence, we heard that the Communists were saying that Stalin could now show his might in stopping the Fascists from moving farther east. In America, the Communists came off as tightrope walkers," I say, realizing our discussion must end for the day. "This has been quite a session. I've learned so much about the beginning of the war."

"We enjoyed telling it to you—it is so clear in our minds," Krieger answers, and the others nod.

"Certainly, we enjoy reminiscing," says Reynitz. "But you know, we are not members of the Nazi party, and we disliked everything Hitler did. We enjoy hearing about the feelings in the United States, too."

"Thank you, and have a good night." With that, they go to the closet for their topcoats and leave.

A victim points out tormentor Josef Jarolin, above; and Jarolin takes the stand, right.

Chapter 19

The Dachau Trial Continued, Mid-November 1945

Sitting next to the wall behind the prosecutors' table gives me the best view of the proceedings. As we learned earlier, on-the-spot SS-guard beatings of prisoners were impulsive and brutal. Now we hear that when the gas chamber at Dachau failed to work because of sabotage by the prisoners building it, other means to kill were found.

Otto Edward Jendrian, a German prisoner, testifies:

I saw [SS defendant Sylvester Filleboeck] with a machine-pistol under his arm [also defendant Moll and crematorium head Bongartz] with pistols. They fired at naked bodies and [after the shootings I discovered] the victims were French officers up to the rank of general. I saw bodies lying on the ground and just at that time a new group of naked people arrived . . . They had to kneel down, hands tied behind back, and the reports [of the guns] sounded, and these naked bodies collapsed. They were shot in the back of the neck.

Dr. Franz Blaha and several others testify about the shooting of 90 or more Russian officers at the crematory:

We heard single shots fired. Afterward I went inside and saw the bodies [of the] Russian officers . . . many of whom I knew personally . . . They had shots in the neck, and [the guards] had taken out the gold teeth from them.

Additional testimony describes the efficiency of a method of killing often used in the camps. The victim was stripped naked (to keep blood away from reusable clothing), forced to his knees, head bent. A single shot in the back of the neck toward the brain brought instant death.

Gabriel Brzustovskj, 27, a prisoner from Poland, testifies:

I saw [SS defendant Vinzenz Shoettl] shoot a man . . . One shot to his cheek. The second one was a head shot . . . The man got out of the line because he wanted to get a drink of water.

A still cleaner method—hanging—was also used. Another German prisoner, Rudolf Wolf, testifies:

I saw across the street from the entrance of the hospital a group of prisoners. I walked over and joined them to see what was going on. There at the gate [defendant] Mahl and Bongartz were standing. In the middle of this group . . . was a young Russian . . . 18 or 20 years old. I saw Mahl put the noose of the rope, which was tied to the gate, around the neck of the young Russian. Then the stool under [his] feet was kicked away . . . I saw how Mahl was grabbing the Russian by the legs and pulling downward like a professional hangman; and as such he was known in the camp.

Then Helmut Opitz, a German textile worker and prisoner at Dachau, describes how SS defendant Josef Jarolin beat prisoners while they were hanging:

Jarolin pushed hanging men [so] they swung to and fro [then] beat these prisoners . . . with a bull's penis that was twisted and dried hard . . . on their faces and their backs, in front and on their shoulders. The prisoners were bleeding. They were Germans, foreigners, all nationalities . . . [This happened] throughout his tour of duty . . . from 1942 until 1943 when Jarolin was transferred from here.

The women prisoners were also subject to killings. Riva Levy testifies again, about impulsive hangings by defendant Emil Mahl:

Five prisoners made foot coverings from a blanket and [for that] were hanged . . . in camp number one on the formation ground [at Landsberg/Kaufering subcamps]. A hangman came from Dachau.

Another method used for deliberate execution was lethal injection. Ludwig Woehrl, from Munich, was a nurse while a prisoner at Dachau. He testifies about injections at the prison hospital:

I saw there that [SS defendant Anton Endres] made an injection into the veins [of] a Polish clergyman. I saw him a short while later over in the morgue. He was dead.

Then we hear from a German tailor, Eugene Seybold, 41, a prisoner in Dachau from 1942 to 1945, who worked at the crematory. He testifies to executions by injection by SS chief camp physician Fritz Hintermayer and by shooting and hangings at or near the crematory by Hintermayer, who made the death certificates. Seybold testifies that he was present when this doctor injected two pregnant women prisoners. Hintermayer's voluntary pretrial statement reads:

[There was an order for] the hanging of two pregnant Russian women. [A superior] demanded that I should kill the women by an injection instead. Though I did not know for sure whether [he] had the right to change the mode of death . . . I injected the two women . . . out of humanity, the more so since I knew that it is the usual custom of civilized nations not to execute pregnant women before delivery.

After Seybold testifies, Hintermayer changes his story:

I gave 1.5 grams of [evapanatrium, a narcotic] and ten cubic centimeters of distilled water. It was an intravenous injection

. . . into the arm. The sleep, or the anesthesia, comes in about
ten minutes . . . I returned to the crematory after the air-raid
alarm that had been called in between . . . The women had
shots through their heads. They were dead.

Heinrich Stoehr, 41, a former general hospital administrator and
Dachau prisoner for five years, worked in the prison hospital. He says:

I was a nurse in the septic surgical department . . . I saw with
my own eyes when the patients were sent into the shower
room. There they were injected . . . in the presence of a doctor
and after a few minutes the dead people started coming [were
carried] out.

Capo [prisoner block chief] Heiden under the pretense of
anesthesia often sent people into the hereafter. He gave injections . . . frequently . . . [SS defendant Anton Endres] never
stopped Capo Heiden from carrying out his terrible operations without anesthesia. Instead he assisted him.

The testimony about deliberate executions is overwhelming. Further testimony shows that those who died from executions, beatings,
and torture were generally cremated. Those dying from diseases often
were buried in mass graves. The crematory ran day and night, still not
enough to dispose of all the bodies. A large addition for more ovens
was built with the labor of Catholic priests, by order of the SS. The
priests were forced to dig their own graves, so to speak.

The defendants testify again that executions were carried out by
"superior orders." They deny any personal responsibility.

215

A 1939 magazine published this oil portrait of Adolf Hitler.

Chapter 20

Later November 1945

I meet again with the recorders at my living quarters. They all arrive at 7:00 P.M.

"Who wants to begin?" I ask. "We left last time with the conquering of Poland."

"I will." Reynitz raises himself and puts his wine glass on a side table. Pulling himself forward, he says, "Hitler had written in *Mein Kampf* that Russia would provide 'new territory.' He had spoken often of this and, as a step in that direction, had made the Anti-Comintern Pact with Japan and Italy.

"This was mentioned later at war headquarters. I learned there had been arguments between Hitler and his military chiefs about this question. On one side, the military chiefs contended that attacking Russia first, with the greatest military strength of the German forces, would assure success, while attacking Holland, Belgium, and France first

217

would diminish strength. Also, Britain and France could be counted on to do little but complain about an attack on Russia, as they did when Poland was struck.

"The other chiefs had argued that military history proved attacks cannot be successful if one's rear is exposed. Also, Britain and France had declared war on Germany two days after the invasion of Poland.

"As usual, Hitler had given public assurances to the world, after the Polish invasion, that his goals were satisfied. This was his usual statement, to make Britain and France keep their guard down." Reynitz recalls.

"Then what happened?" I ask Thoet, who sits on the edge of his chair.

"Denmark and Norway were taken over in early March 1940. There was no advance warning. When it happened, Hitler announced there was documentary proof that Britain and France had decided to carry out their joint flanking actions through those northern states, by force if necessary. Hitler said that his move was a friendly occupation." Thoet stretches, clasping his hands behind his head.

I ask Krieger, "What was the feeling of the people you knew in Germany?"

"Generally, I think those German civilians believed Hitler's reasons for taking Denmark and Norway. After Britain and France declared war on Germany, it seemed a reasonable move to them. However, we were nervous about the widening aggression. We were more concerned when it was announced in mid-March that our troops had struck through Belgium, the Netherlands, and Luxembourg.

"Hitler, as usual, announced this move after it happened. His propaganda told about proof, mainly by documents, that Britain and

France and others were preparing to strike at Germany through the same route. This happened quickly, and British, Canadian, and Belgian forces were trapped at Dunkirk." Krieger leans back in his chair.

Thoet wants to contribute. "What happened at Dunkirk?" I ask.

Thoet runs his stubby fingers through his thick hair and begins: "As I learned later, Hitler had considered attacking the Allied troops surrounding Dunkirk, but he left the attack to the planes alone, without ground support. He dallied for two days because he wanted to keep up the momentum of the blitzkrieg into France and was reorganizing his troops. The dalliance was a huge mistake."

"Why was it a mistake?"

"Because in those two days more than 300,000 Allied troops were evacuated across the English Channel into Britain. When Hitler finally decided to send in his troops to capture the Allies, it was too late. He had been too busy reorganizing his troops. The Allies had already been rescued. I learned this at German war headquarters."

I am reminded of the 1942 movie *Mrs. Miniver,* starring Greer Garson and showing Allied fighter planes providing cover for thousands of boats— from small motorboats and larger workboats to yachts and destroyers. I tell the recorders about how the British, French, and Belgian soldiers waded into the water and were pulled

Greer Garson, left, as Mrs. Miniver

aboard the boats, which quickly moved from the beach. The British Spitfire fighter planes drove away the German planes, permitting the evacuation to continue. Hitler had miscalculated in thinking planes alone could hold the enemy troops.

The recorders nod, and I continue: "Then, Winston Churchill was made prime minister of Britain when Chamberlain resigned on May 10, 1940. Churchill said, 'I have nothing to offer but blood, toil, tears, and sweat.' He started the air bombing of Germany almost immediately, demonstrating the determination of the British. I admire Churchill and have followed his career."

Winston Churchill

I open a window as the room feels a bit stuffy. "Then what happened?" I ask Reynitz.

He sits up straight: "I was worried about the expansion of the war and what might happen to my family in Berlin. I lived in an apartment there with my wife and two young daughters while I continued to work in the Reichstag, although there was little work to do.

"About the same time as the invasion of the Benelux countries—Belgium, the Netherlands, and Luxembourg—British planes started to bomb German towns. As soon as possible, I moved my family to a smaller town, 45 miles from Berlin," Reynitz concludes.

I think of Churchill's speech to the House of Commons and excuse myself. I go to rummage through some papers in my bedroom to find an issue of *Stars and Stripes*, then return to my seat. "Prime Minister Winston Churchill's media speech after the evacuation of Dunkirk in mid-March 1940, was anything but humble:

We shall not flag or fail. We shall fight on the beaches, we shall fight on the landing ground. We shall fight in the fields and in the streets, we shall fight in the hills. We shall never surrender.

"Dunkirk was a blunder on Hitler's part, and it probably made him lose the war. It was a great victory for the Allies. But let's continue. How did Hitler attack France?" I inquire of Thoet.

He leans forward before speaking: "From Dunkirk, Hitler sent his troops on the English Channel to Calais, Verdun, Sedan, and Belfort, near the Maginot Line. He encircled Alsace and Lorraine with Panzer tanks and poured through the line. The French guns there pointed eastward and could not swing around. The French had abandoned them a few days before."

Thoet continues: "Finally—after the railroad yards and some industries were bombed by the Germans—the French declared Paris an open city."

Then I tell the recorders, "Premier Paul Reynault of France radioed a plea for America to help him 'before it was too late.' A few days later he again appealed to America to 'send clouds of planes to crush the evil force that dominates Europe.' Hearing this frightened me because if Hitler took France, the only Allied force left in Europe would be Britain. Do you know whether the German people were told about this?"

Buchholz stands, stretches, and says: "Germans were informed about the war in France only when the fighting was over. The Reichstag was called into session, and I was among those assigned to record his speech. Hitler repeated that he had proof that the French were about to strike at Germany through Holland and Belgium, so German forces had to prevent this."

"Again Hitler made an excuse for his aggression. He was good at that," I comment.

"Yes, but who believed it?" says Buchholz.

"Would you carry on?"

"He spoke some time, glorifying himself. He was bragging about the quick success in conquering France, thus overcoming a longtime enemy of Germany," Buchholz recalls, then stretches, and sits down.

Jonuschat and Krieger stretch in their chairs. I watch them relax as I turn the page. Finally, everyone settles down.

"What brought the invasion of France to an end?" I look at Jonuschat.

"France and Germany signed a peace agreement at Compiègne on June 21, 1940, in the same railway car Germany had surrendered in 22 years before. Hitler was there to witness the humiliation of the enemy. I remember the date because it was so important."

"What did the German civilians think of it?"

"There were doubts in the minds of many of the people I was in contact with—about whether the attack on France was justified or reasonable. But we were told only of quick successes with few casualties. Everyone was relieved that it had been mastered in such a quick and decisive way. I learned later at war headquarters that there were many losses on our side but more on the French side," Jonuschat concludes.

"I understand Marshal Henri Petain at Vichy, in mid-France, was put in charge of the French government, but only for domestic affairs. The Germans kept military affairs in Paris. Is that right?" I ask Buchholz.

"Yes, and that was when air bombing of Britain began in earnest. Then came the heavy bombing raid on Berlin, where I lived, in August 1940. I was surprised because Hermann Goering, chief of the Luftwaffe, assured the German population in several speeches that no enemy flier would appear over German territory. If any did, he said people could call him 'Meier,' a common name in Germany."

"Can you tell me what Hitler was planning next?" I ask Reynitz.

"Perhaps I can because of personal experience," Reynitz recalls. "There was sly talk of invading Britain. I recall a meeting. I was assigned for duty at the Ministry of Propaganda. There the press people were told what *had* to be published and what could *not* be published."

"Did the press follow those instructions?"

"Yes, of course—it was controlled by the government."

"Did you hear anything else?"

"There were several briefings at these meetings. At one of them the leading man, the director of this conference, said, 'We are expecting something, but I can't tell you where or when it will happen, just that there's something in the air.' It was revealed at a military conference later that Hitler had planned to invade Britain."

"Did Hitler actually talk about Britain?"

"There were questions and answers about Hitler's earlier offer to Britain to make peace and join with him if there should be war with Russia. I thought to myself, after Hitler had told so many lies about *not* invading neighboring countries, who could believe him? I must add that invasion of Britain wouldn't shock our population because it would stop the bombing of Germany," Reynitz finishes.

I ask Thoet, "What was said about the bombing in Germany?"

"The Germans were told by radio that British bombers were killing innocent women and children, a most inhuman thing to do. This was repeated many times. Even Josef Goebbels made strong speeches on the radio to that effect."

"What was said about the bombing of Britain?" I ask. "It seems to me that with each bombing the other, something must have been said."

"Nothing was said about bombing Britain, but in November 1940, Goering spoke on the radio and told how Coventry, England, was hit by a heavy Luftwaffe air raid. And he went on to say that other cities in Britain would be bombed. I felt fortunate that my family was out of Berlin," Thoet recollects.

I can see everyone is getting tired and suggest we take a break.

A Frenchman wept when German troops marched into Paris, June 14, 1940.

Hitler

Chapter 21

Later November 1945

After a 15-minute break, we come back together and continue. I tell the recorders about movie-theater newsreels in America of what was then called the "Battle of Britain," starting in the spring of 1940. One newsreel that I saw showed high flames from burning buildings and the wailing of sirens. While the bombing of Britain continued, the Royal Air Force bombed more German targets.

I also tell the recorders that I remember when Hitler's blitzkrieg hit France: "The press and radio in the United States reported the invasion and the Maginot Line mentality of the French. They appeared content that their fortification on the border facing Germany was adequate. The line consisted mostly of tank traps and artillery protected by steel and concrete fortifications:

"Hitler's blitzkrieg struck at the northern end of the Maginot Line and poured into France. Such a maneuver was like an end run in a football game. I read that the Maginot Line was useless because its artillery could be aimed only eastward and that it was abandoned by the French.

"During the year of intense bombings of Britain, the American press reported that an equally important 'Battle of the Atlantic' was becoming even more intense. German submarines working in 'wolf-packs' seriously interrupted merchant shipping from many countries. American cargo ships were being hit as well. Pleas for help came from Churchill. All these events were heavily publicized in the United States," I continue.

"After his election to a third term in November 1940, President Roosevelt announced his Lend Lease program. He made a major radio address in late 1940, saying that helping Britain would help the United States keep its own democracy. He used a simple illustration: 'A neighbor's house is on fire, and he needs to use my water hose. Should I lend it to him or hold out for the price I paid for it? No. All I want is my hose back after he has put out the fire.' He said he would send destroyers to Britain, using the term 'Arsenal of Democracy' to describe the role of the United States. The other side of the bargain was that the United States would get the use of British islands in Newfoundland, Bermuda, the Caribbean, and British Guiana for common defense of the hemisphere. Congress passed the Lend Lease Act in April 1941.

"Well, I've said my piece. Now, who would like to carry on?"

"I'll try," says Reynitz. "Another event during the Battle of Britain was the Italian invasion of Africa. I remember this as a kind of side war, with Mussolini apparently wanting a piece of the pie. When the British forces drove the Italians back, Hitler came to Mussolini's aid, sending Gen. Erwin Rommel and his Afrika Korps and quickly regaining the area the Italians had lost.

"In late 1940, Mussolini sent troops into Albania and Greece. The Greeks soundly beat the Italians and drove them back into Albania."

"What happened next?" I turn to Buchholz.

"Rudolf Hess, who was the third-ranking German, behind Hitler and Goering, made a stunning parachute drop into Scotland in May 1941. His purpose was to make a peace treaty with the British, believing that they would join Germany in fighting Russia. He was arrested, and after the war he was tried as a war criminal. He was sentenced to life instead of execution because of his attempt at peace with Britain," says Buchholz.

Mussolini and Hitler

I remember Hess is now at the Landsberg prison. "Then what?"

"Hitler was massing his troops along the Russian border in early 1941. He was preparing for invasion of Russia. He had more than 3,000,000 troops, 600,000 vehicles, 750,000 horses, 3,600 tanks, and 1,800 planes. I have it here in my notes, as I expected this would be asked," says Reynitz.

"Why so many horses? This was blitzkrieg, wasn't it?"

"Yes, but I understand the terrain was too rough in places for mechanized forces to get through. Russia also uses horses, but the Germans who rode horses had rapid-firing weapons. There may have been other reasons, but this was all I heard."

"How did the attack begin?"

"At 3:00 A.M., for example, when the guard was being changed at Brest on the Russian border, the Germans gunned them down instead of saluting them. A three-pronged attack was directed north to south at Leningrad, Moscow, and Kiev. Hitler wanted to have it over with before winter because his troops had only summer clothing."

"Wishful thinking! Can you continue?" I ask Reynitz.

"Hitler announced the attack, but only after it started. I heard Hitler's speech on the radio. He said he needed more land for Lebensraum," Reynitz continues.

"On that day everybody was silent, wondering when the war would end. In a fortnight, the trains came from Russia with wounded German soldiers. Nobody could expect anymore that the blitzkrieg would bring the war to an end quickly as in France, because the Russian front—from the North Cape to the Black Sea—was 1,700 miles," Reynitz recalls.

I see Krieger move forward, a quizzical look on his face. "How do you figure 1,700 miles?"

"Well, 100 miles equals 161 kilometers, so 1,700 miles equals about 2,900 kilometers. It's a long stretch," replies Reynitz.

"I see you're about right," Krieger allows.

"Let me tell you this," I put in. "While German forces were still advancing in the fall of 1941, I made a trip to Washington, D.C., on legal business. I called a good friend from St. Paul to invite him to lunch. Instead, he insisted I have lunch with him at the Press Club, where he was a member.

"After lunch and an interesting talk by a popular columnist, the crowd of nearly 300 left in a hurry. My friend and I relaxed and stayed to avoid the crunch at the three elevators. When we finally rose to leave, my friend introduced me to a tall, courtly man who was the resident head of Tass, the Russian news agency. He was sitting at the next table. I couldn't resist asking him about Hitler's invasion of his country. At that time American news reports were telling of Hitler's swift attacks into Russia.

"I asked the Tass chief how the war was going, thinking I would get a shrug or a noncommittal comment. Instead, he was open and talkative. He said, 'We have a large country. We know it better, and this gives us the time we need.' I asked him, 'How will you be able to stop the huge forces of the Germans?' His reply was, 'We will let them sink farther into our large featherbed, then smother them.'" I conclude the aside, then return to Krieger's topic: "Please go on."

"The goal was to take Leningrad, Moscow, and Kiev before winter started. The plan failed in November 1941 because the German soldiers and their equipment were not prepared for deep-freeze weather."

"No wonder. This alone illustrates that Hitler didn't know how to direct a war. But he seemed bent on taking Russia as he had written he would in *Mein Kampf.*" I glance at Krieger.

He says calmly: "An amazing thing happened. The Russians removed the machinery from many factories and moved it farther to the east. They got it all out ahead of the German forces, I discovered later at headquarters. It was often mentioned that the Russian counterattacks were furious and constant, starting at Moscow.

"When Hitler's attacks failed, he made a broadcast speech at a big rally at the Sportpalast. He said, as I recall, 'Russia is already broken and will never rise again.' He was very confident of victory in Russia."

Then Krieger stands: "It was like a thunderbolt to hear on December 7, 1941, that Japan struck the U.S. fleet at Pearl Harbor in Hawaii. The fleet was almost destroyed. Four days later Hitler declared war on the United States."

"Why did he do that?" I wonder.

Krieger goes on, all eyes upon him. "I learned later at war headquarters that there was an agreement between Germany and Japan. Only a month before, about a dozen countries, including Japan, renewed the Anti-Comintern Pact. Before that, Hitler had congratulated Japan on conquering Manchuria. I would not be surprised if Germany and Japan had agreed to a declaration of war by Germany on the United States should Japan strike first."

I explain to the recorders that evidence of this is being adduced at the Nuremberg trial. Then, "What did the German people think of all this?" I address Jonuschat.

He moves forward in his chair. "Most of us wondered what was the use of it all. As I told you before, Hitler's goal of Lebensraum did not move Germans much because they did not see a need for more territory. They certainly wouldn't move to live and work in Russia."

"That would be something," I say. "Germans working in Russia. It would be like ants living among anteaters."

"Or sheep living among wolves," says Reynitz. Everyone laughs.

Changing the subject, I ask, "What did the German people think of the Communists?"

"Most Germans were fearful. But those I knew and talked with did not feel it necessary to attack Russia to contain them. Most felt taking Czechoslovakia and regaining the Polish Corridor by an agreement with Russia, followed by the war in Poland, went far enough."

He is right, of course, and I ask, "Did the German people think the invasion of Russia was justified?"

Krieger begins: "On the whole, Germans were nervous and bewildered by the attack on Russia. Personally, I felt that with the long front going into Russia, it would be impossible, geographically, to win. The invasion, with all the problems of constantly attacking and keeping up supply for those massive forces, could never succeed, I felt, though I am no military expert by any means.

"Hitler did not trust his 'old-school' generals, who occasionally retreated when confronted by heavy Russian counterattacks. He dismissed two older generals who had retreated and replaced them with younger officers he trusted. Hitler promoted colonels to generals."

"What was going on in the Russian war?" I glance toward Reynitz, who clasps his hands inside out, making his knuckles crack.

"There was fierce fighting southeast of Kiev in the Caucasus toward the oil fields. When his troops were losing ground, Hitler sometimes would say, 'If we lose that place, the war is over.' Then, when the place was lost, he would order an attack at another place as though the recent defeat never happened," Reynitz goes on.

"Though he often overruled the advice of his military chiefs, they did not argue against him. They would not dare. The only exception I remember was when he consented to retreat from some mountains of the Caucasus," concludes Reynitz.

"Why wouldn't they dare?" I ask Buchholz.

"If a general tried to argue against him, Hitler would go into a rage and talk, talk, talk. Hitler knew his greatest strength was in making speeches, and he used them to control his generals. Only two generals, Alfred Jodl and Erwin Rommel, tried to argue with him after he gave his orders, and after his speech they were soon silent," Buchholz verifies what has been said earlier.

"Hitler's blitzkrieg had failed. It was now the bitter winter of 1941–42. What was the reaction among the people in Germany?" I ask Thoet, who holds his chin.

"It became apparent during the winter that the German armies had been stalled. The Russians continued counterattacking

Gen. Erwin Rommel

fiercely. There was general discussion as to when the war in Russia would end. German soldiers were returning to Germany with severe cases of frostbite. Among those with whom I had contact, there was simply bewilderment."

"What did you do during that winter?" I ask Jonuschat.

"I was still in the Wehrmacht, doing mostly guard duty, but I was often called to do my usual work at the Reichstag while wearing my army uniform. I was able to visit occasionally with my family near Berlin," he replies while stretching once more.

"Was there any favorable news?"

"The only favorable news for Hitler in 1942 was that General Rommel's Afrika Korps was winning out over the British and threatening Egypt. Hitler's U-boats [submarines] were sinking British and American ships in record numbers. Hitler now held a big portion of Russia, as well as western Europe. This was probably the highest point in Hitler's conquests. He occupied more territory than Napoleon ever did," Jonuschat recalls.

We are getting weary, I think. I've run out of questions momentarily, and there is complete silence. Then Reynitz begins to sing:

> Show me the way to go home
> I'm tired and want to go to bed
> I had a little wine about an hour ago
> and it went right to my head.

Laughter. "Where did you learn that song?"

"From the Americans at Berchtesgaden."

I look at my watch. "Good heavens, it's past 11:00. The time has gone fast. I can't tell you how much I appreciate this. So much happened, and your memories are just great."

"We have told you the main parts, not the details," says Krieger.

They go to the closet for their topcoats. Then all shake hands with me and depart.

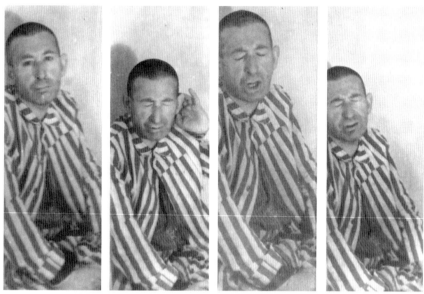

The Nazis recorded the results of air-pressure experiments on Dachau inmates. Though custom dictated the release of prisoners who survived such experiments, this subject appears to be the same one pictured in the experiment on page 241.

Chapter 22

The Dachau Trial Continued, Later November 1945

I remain in my seat behind the prosecutors' table as we hear witnesses testify to the use of healthy prisoners for medical experiments at Dachau.

Franz Blaha, the prisoner physician, describes the freezing-water experiments done for the Luftwaffe:

The prisoners were put into a big basin of cold water without clothing, and they were kept there up to 38 hours. By means of a thermometer in the rectum, the temperature was measured and noted on a clipboard. Every time the body temperature dropped ten degrees, blood was taken from an artery at the throat, and it was examined in the laboratory, usually first as to sugar content, calcium, and nonprotein nitrates. At 25 degrees Centigrade [80 degrees Fahrenheit], the people usually died, but one of them could stand it to 19 degrees [68 degrees Fahrenheit].

Sometimes the experiment was interrupted to warm the subject before proceeding again. They did this either with heat apparatus or animal heat. There were two women [camp prostitutes] in a bed, and they took the frozen person in between them, and they had to warm him up. Reichfuehrer Heinrich Himmler was present at one of these experiments.

Mostly Polish and Czech Jews, then the Russians, were used. Very, very many died . . . of calcification [freezing].

Asked when this took place, Blaha answers:

[The years] 1942 and 1943. All these bodies were dissected in the presence of [SS Dr. Sigmund Rascher] and the organs were taken out immediately, sometimes while they were still in the living condition. They were dispatched immediately to Munich to the Pathological Institute.

Some prisoners were kept from four to six hours, some 24 to 26 hours, in the cold water. Almost everyone died, and their time in the freezing water was noted on a clipboard by Dr. Rascher. Other evidence shows that these experiments were carried out for the Luftwaffe, to find ways to revive bailed-out fliers rescued from the ocean. Sometimes different types of clothing were used on the subjects.

One of the lucky subjects, Mizyla Tzepla, also testifies. He was in the prison hospital 42 days after the experiment. He says: "I had a colleague, a male nurse there. He told me, 'You are real lucky. They selected 300 and only ten could stand it. You are one of those."

According to Martin G. Weiss, SS camp kommandant, Reichfuehrer Heinrich Himmler took direct charge of medical experiments at Dachau. This information is partially corroborated in copies of letters by Dr. Rascher to Himmler.

Weiss testifies in his own defense that Himmler went directly to the experimental station and called for him:

Himmler received me immediately. When I opened the door of the experimental station, he was very angry. Probably the staff physician, Dr. Rascher, had complained about me because I didn't follow all of his wishes. Himmler received me with the following words, since he had never known me before: 'Well, you are the man Weiss.' Then he didn't let me speak, but he immediately explained to me that I was to give no orders to staff physician Dr. Rascher, that he was not under my supervision . . . [but that he] was under the personal protection of the Reichfuehrer [Himmler].

SS Dr. Sigmund Rascher

He further stated that I had to comply with every wish of Dr. Rascher, whether Dr. Rascher demanded cognac or coffee, no matter what. Upon my saying that these things were restricted, the Reichfuehrer explained to me that it was my duty to get these things. If Dr. Rascher expressed a wish to me, it was as if he, the Reichfuehrer, were to give me that order. This discussion took place in the presence of prisoners in the experimental station.

We learn that SS camp doctor Fritz Hintermayer directed saltwater experiments at Dachau, to determine whether a bailed-out German could survive on ocean water. Blaha testifies:

About 50 to 60 persons from Room One of Bloc One did not get anything to eat but only received salt, that is, ocean water [for five days] and . . . their urine, blood, and excrements were examined.

During these experiments, there was a revolt. The prisoners, who were starved, beat the male nurses who took care of them . . . but none of the prisoners died, because they received food from other prisoners illegally . . . For this experiment they specifically used Gypsies and Hungarians.

An air-pressure experiment was done, also for the Luftwaffe. Blaha testifies about a "bell-like" compartment:

Twenty or 25 prisoners were locked up in one of them, then by means of machines, the air pressure was raised and lowered suddenly. Many were dead, and some of them died shortly after that. Some of them had hemorrhages, for in-

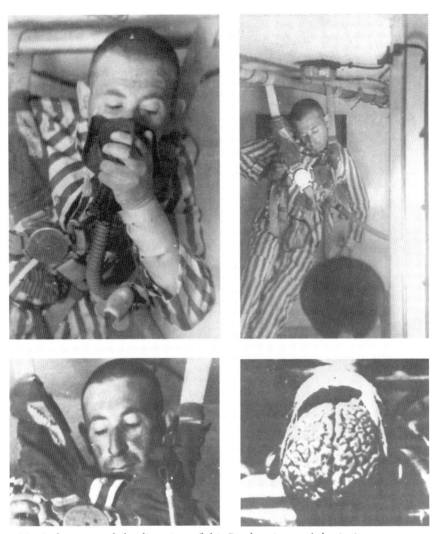

Nazis documented the dissection of this Dachau inmate's brain in an attempt to determine altitudes at which flight crews could survive without oxygen.

stance, to the ear or to the nose. All of these dead ones were dissected. Most died of brain hemorrhages or of embolisms or infarctions of the heart and lungs. [The subjects were] Czechs, Poles, and Russians. I think more than 100 died.

Then there were liver-puncture experiments:

That was done by Dr. Branto [a camp physician]. He made a series of liver punctures [to obtain pieces of liver for examination] on ill people, on healthy people, people who had stomach diseases, and people who had gall diseases.

The liver punctures were performed "by a needle" on live prisoners without anesthesia: "The procedures were painful because they were done in a series of several punctures, and the subjects died as a result of that. They were Poles, Russians, Czechs, and also Germans."

Blaha also describes phlegmon experiments conducted with healthy prisoners. He says:

Forty healthy men were used at a time—20 received intramuscular and 20 received intravenous injections of pus from diseased persons. All treatment was forbidden for three days, by which time serious inflammation, and in many cases general blood poisoning, had occurred.

Then each group was divided again into groups of ten. Half were given chemical treatment with liquid and special pills every ten minutes for 24 hours. The rest were treated with sulfanilamide and surgery. In some cases all of the limbs were amputated.

My autopsies also showed that the chemical treatment had been harmful and had even caused perforations of the stomach wall. For these experiments Polish, Czech, and Dutch priests were ordinarily used. Pain was intense in such experiments.

Most of the 600 to 800 prisoners . . . used finally died. Most of the others became permanent invalids and later were killed.

Heinrich Stoehr, nurse at the prison hospital, also testifies:

[Phlegmon experiments were supposed to prove] that the worst diseases could be treated with biochemical methods. Thereupon, it was the task of Schulz, the chief doctor of the SS hospital, to produce the worst of all diseases. The main task was not to produce phlegmon, but the sepsis. For this purpose, pus was injected not only into the muscles but also into the veins . . . They were entirely healthy people . . . the last series consisted of Polish and Czech priests.

The sepsis was supposed to be produced by the pus, and then it was tried to fight this disease with biochemical and also with allopathic means.

Dr. B. W. Glick of the American army is questioned about taking pus from a person with diseased blood (pleghmon) and injecting it into the body of a healthy person. He says:

Yes sir, I believe you can infect anybody; it does not matter what their health is . . . Well, the treatment as we have it today in the American army would not only include the local treatment of dressings or surgical treatment but kinio-therapy, the sulfa drugs, and penicillin.

A GI enters Dachau subcamp Landsberg after Nazis set fire to trench barracks filled with Jewish slave laborers too emaciated to escape, April 29–30, 1945.

Chapter 23

The recorders gather at 1:00 P.M. on Saturday at my living quarters.

"I'd like to know a little more about what was happening to the Jewish people," I say.

Reynitz shows interest at once: "You will have to remember that they were Germans first and Jews second. They were decent people. I had several friends who were Jews, and my doctor was one."

"What did Hitler do next about the Jews?" I ask Reynitz.

"The pressure on Jews to leave Germany continued, by all the means we talked about before. In December 1941, Hitler issued a decree, the *Nacht und Nebel Erlass* [Night and Fog Decree]. The effect was to legalize the action of Nazi organizations in taking remaining Jews from their homes at night, whole families, and putting them on transportation to move them out of Germany. The decree merely formalized what had been going on for some time. I had noticed myself that a Jewish family would be at home on one day, and the next day they were gone. Mostly to Poland, I learned later." Reynitz stands.

"How were they restricted in their activities in Germany?"

"They had been forbidden to leave their residences without police permit to buy clothes, to shop at any time except between 4:00 and 5:00 P.M., to smoke tobacco, to use pubic telephones, to keep pets, to have their hair cut by an Aryan barber, or to own any electric appliances, record players, typewriters, or bicycles," Reynitz recalls and sits.

"Why was that done? It seems rather silly." I turn a page in my notebook. Reynitz still sits erect.

"Hitler's hatred for the Jews was unbounded. He tried to drive them out of Germany by all kinds of incredible decrees. When he acquired territory outside of Germany, like Poland, he put them in concentration camps such as Treblinka and Auschwitz."

"What else?"

"The Final Solution—extermination of the Jews—begun late in 1941, was made official in 1942. Hitler's prediction of this action, stated in *Mein Kampf* 16 years earlier, became reality," Reynitz recalls. The others look at him with admiration.

"Were there any exceptions to death?" I ask Jonuschat.

"The exception was the use of able-bodied Jewish men and women in forced labor, for making armaments. When they became too weak to work, they were taken to the gas chamber, supposedly for delousing and showers, then to the crematory. We learned all this later from witnesses who were transferred from eastern camps when the Russians were advancing westward. Pregnant women were killed at once. The same fate befell children not fit for work."

Still smoking trench barracks and the awful result of the Nazis' intentional fires.

"What was the point of Final Solution?" I stand to ask.

"Hitler said in *Mein Kampf* that there would be no Jews left in Europe. He was a murderer, plain and simple. Killing never bothered

The American army calls on the help of German civilians in the nearby town of Landsberg to remove the burned bodies of Jewish prisoners for decent burial.

him. I don't know how else to put it," he answers. The other recorders all watch him, finding no fault with what he says.

"Can you go on?"

"This short description does not include the beatings, starvation, torture, and killing of Jews in the camps by the SS guards or the use of hundreds of Jews for medical experiments in several camps. But the gas-and-burn method became the way to exterminate more Jews quickly and with less debris—clothing and bodies—for disposal.

"Hitler also ordered extermination of the Polish intelligentsia, nobility, and clergy, I learned later . . . I have the feeling that Hitler's two wars—the senseless genocide of Jews and his military conquests—were inconsistent. Neither supported the other." Jonuschat leans back in his chair and clasps his hands behind his head. The others approve.

"Did he say anything about this publicly?" I inquire of Thoet.

He replies: "Concerning the Jews, Hitler said, in effect, at a military conference, 'They rightfully hate us, just as much as we hate them. When the war is over they will be uprooted from Europe.' However, Germans were not informed about the systematic genocide, and no foreign newspapers were permitted in Germany after the war started in Poland in 1939."

"Did Hitler meet with anyone about the Jews?" I sit down again, listening to Thoet.

"Starting in December 1942, when he was at war headquarters, the chief of the SS, Himmler, had private, unrecorded meetings with Hitler before or after the military conferences," concludes Thoet.

"This may be a good place to end this discussion. It is almost time for dinner. I want to thank all of you for sharing your memories."

With that our meeting closes.

Wilhelm Keitel, Hermann Goering, Adolf Hitler, and Martin Bormann, walking abreast at Wolfsschanze. Count Claus Schenk Graf von Stauffenberg, later involved in a plot to kill Hitler, walks behind (far left).

Chapter 24

December 1945

The five German recorders meet with me again at my quarters at 7:00 P.M.

"Now to get on with all of you being assigned to Hitler's head-quarters. I'd like to hear more about that." I look at Krieger, who was directed by Goering to recruit the "best obtainable recorders in the country" to record statements made at Hitler's twice-daily military-situation conferences.

"I selected the men, and we all went to Hitler's headquarters," Krieger says. "We all had about the same experience. We arrived between September and December 1942. At first there were six, then eight of us. All of us had been civil-service officials in the Stenographic Office of the Reichstag.

"I reported to a building in an isolated place outside the town of Vinnitsa in Ukrania, southwest of Kiev. This was the command post

251

for the war in Russia. The code name for the place was 'Werewolf,'" Krieger recalls.

"What happened when you arrived there?"

Krieger goes on: "The adjutant took the first three of us to a room where we met Martin Bormann. He was in his Nazi uniform, decorated as befitted the head of the Nazi party, under Hitler, of course. He was a short, heavy man with a round face and a grim expression. We were introduced, and we shook hands. I then sat at a table where he handed me a paper and said, 'Read it and sign it.'"

"Did you see Hitler?"

Krieger continues: "I was reading the paper when Hitler came into the room and half-sat on the edge of a desk nearby. He said nothing. I saw that he had on a plain army uniform with no decorations except an Iron Cross. He was awarded the medal for combat as a private in World War I."

"What did the paper say?"

"The paper had several paragraphs, each beginning: 'The party member agrees to . . .' As a matter of fact, none of we three were party members. I thought of telling Bormann, but on second thought I realized he might say, 'Then it is certainly high time to alter that.' But there was no time to worry about that. Hitler himself told us: 'Whoever will give away anything he has seen or heard here will lose his head.' And that settled it. The pledge was signed by all three of us," Krieger recalls.

"Bormann took the paper and put it in a file. Later I learned that two SS clerks of the party's offices in Munich had been trying to take notes at the military-situation conferences, but they could not keep up. Hitler wanted every word spoken to be recorded without error."

"How did you work?" I look at Buchholz.

"It was arranged that two of us would work together, one at each end of the long conference table, so not a word would be missed. We would then dictate from our stenograms to one of several female typists who would type while listening. What one of us missed, the other would catch, so we could verify the verbatim transcript as it was being typed."

"What happened to the transcript?" I glance at Buchholz.

"The transcript consisted of an original and two copies," he replies. "The original was retained for Hitler's use, a copy went to the Wehrmacht historian Brig. Gen. Walter Scherff, and a copy was placed in storage in care of the SS men.

"Hitler wanted the transcripts within 48 hours of the end of each conference. Normally, there were two conferences each day—one after noon and the other after dinner—with staff officers and others on the military situation. We rotated in pairs so we could hear everything and make sure the transcripts were finished in time. We were free to go as we chose after being questioned separately by the counterintellegence corps. This gave us the chance to exchange what each of us found out at the military conferences, so when we finished each of us knew what the total facts were," concludes Buchholz.

"Why did Hitler want verbatim transcripts?"

Buchholz replies: "In the course of time we learned that Hitler had reasons for these verbatim transcripts. He said, 'As a man of destiny I want them for history, even if they fall into enemy hands.' He especially wanted a correct record of what his military leaders said at each conference, and the 'exact orders' he gave them, so he could refer to the transcripts if anyone claimed a misunderstanding, intentional or otherwise."

"That's interesting. And what else were you told?" I look at Thoet as do the others.

"All of us were warned several times not to discuss, amongst ourselves or with the typists or anyone else there or elsewhere, anything said by anyone at the conferences," says Thoet.

"He certainly was secretive," I say. "What occurred next?"

"We were shown to our living quarters. Each of us had a private room. The typists were housed at another place, two in a room. We had a common lounge at headquarters where we could rest and talk about anything except the conferences." Thoet remembers the details.

"What happened in the lounge?" I ask Thoet.

"Hitler made infrequent visits to the lay staff in the lounge. There was no conversation. Hitler did all the talking—his monologue lasted almost a half-hour sometimes," Thoet finishes.

"Were you in uniform?"

Buchholz is ready: "A few days after I arrived, my colleagues and I were issued plain gray civil-service uniforms, with no insignia or decoration of any kind. One day at a conference, Goering saw our uniforms for the first time and said loudly, 'You call those uniforms?' As chief of the Luftwaffe, he had many medals and decorations, quite a contrast with Hitler's plain uniform—and ours."

"What was the average day like, would you say?" I notice Krieger with a paper clip. He tries to straighten it as he listens to Reynitz.

"Hitler was in the conference room first, and we came next, one of us sitting down at each end of the table, with our pens, pencils, and notebooks. The generals, admirals, and others were in an anteroom where there were refreshments. They waited there until Hitler gave the order for them to come in," Reynitz recalls.

"The conference started with briefings by the chief officers on the military situations. They made short statements of what the combat generals under their command in the field had most recently reported by radio, pointing to marked maps. The field marshal doing the briefing would sometimes say, 'If this and that happens, we should do this,' and so on. Other times he would describe the situation and simply say what he intended to do with his forces. Then came the briefing by the navy and lastly by the air force."

"With all three branches reporting to him, Hitler had rather complete information on the military situation, didn't he?" I continue to question Reynitz

"Yes," says Reynitz.

"Did Hitler look at the maps?" I glance at Jonuschat.

"Hitler, with spectacles on because his eyesight was poor, would look carefully at the maps on the conference table. He also used a magnifying glass, which he kept in his pocket, even though the maps were large and detailed. I have noticed that pictures of him show no spectacles. I'm sure he didn't want outsiders to know about his poor eyes," says Jonuschat.

"How long would these conferences last?"

Jonuschat stands to stretch: "The first conference, near noon, would last from two to 2½ hours. Sometimes the evening meetings were shorter. But there were many exceptions. More and longer sessions were held when the military situations were bad.

"Usually from ten to 20 or more attended a conference. Besides the military chiefs and their adjutants, there were sometimes field commanders, SS representatives, whoever Hitler wanted there."

"What was the atmosphere at these conferences?"

Reynitz still sits straight in his wing chair: "The atmosphere was very grim because the Russians were counterattacking with great effect. No one smiled or made any jokes. Hitler was serious to the extreme. There was no geniality. There was pressure on everyone."

"How did Hitler act at these conferences?"

Krieger picks at his fingernail with the straightened paper clip as Jonuschat prepares to answer.

"Hitler listened to his military chiefs, asked questions, and made comments, but at the end he stated his orders for combat moves. He almost always overruled his staff chiefs, who recommended retreating and regrouping. He ordered them to hold their positions, even if they had to fight to the last man."

"Overruling his field marshals was a gutsy thing to do."

"He didn't like to hear bad news and would usually disregard it. He improvised tactics on the spot. He seemed to believe he was infallible," Jonuschat answers.

"How long were you in Ukrania?" I ask Thoet. He seems relaxed. Reynitz, too, has his long legs stretched out, his head resting on the back of his chair.

"To the end of October 1942, when Russian artillery shells were exploding about 60 miles from headquarters. Hitler then ordered headquarters moved to Wolfsschanze—a hidden place near Rastenburg in East Prussia. The battle at Stalingrad was then nearing its peak. A hell of a fight," says Thoet with conviction.

He continues: "The Sixth Army, the largest and best equipped, was surrounded by the Russians at Stalingrad. The generals told Hitler that if they could not break out and retreat, there would be a terrible loss. Hitler was firm and said again, 'There will be no retreat. I will try to get some more tanks there, and Goering will drop supplies by air to the troops, and we will have victory.'"

"What happened then?" I inquire, looking at Reynitz. He straightens in his chair.

"None of these things worked. The Russians kept on counterattacking until finally, near the end of December 1942, that large battle at Stalingrad was lost. The commander, Field Marshal Friedrich Paulus, surrendered. Hitler blamed Paulus for the defeat of his prized Sixth Army, which was encircled by the Russians, and said, 'He should have shot himself.' But it was obvious to me that Stalingrad was lost because of Hitler's orders to stand and fight to the last man. Everything was captured—tanks, trucks, ammunition, and many thousand men. Everything. I learned that the prior attacks against Moscow, then Leningrad, carried the same orders," Reynitz answers. The others watch him with interest and approval.

"Did Hitler say anything publicly about Stalingrad?"

"Hitler publicly stated that the sacrifices of the Wehrmacht were not in vain and that it was still the main force in eastern Europe. He ordered a period of three days of mourning in Germany, and all nonessential activities were to close down during those three days. But, at that time, the Russians were advancing all along the front. I believe the heavy loss at Stalingrad was the turning point on the eastern front," Reynitz ends, relaxing into his chair.

"Why would his top commanders obey his orders?" I ask.

Jonuschat answers, "They were strictly trained to obey orders of the highest in command. Remember, they took oaths to obey Hitler as Der Fuehrer. For that reason they probably were afraid of each other. They also were afraid of being reported if they talked about Hitler out of his hearing."

"A good reason," I think. "How did Hitler find out whether his field generals failed to obey his orders?" I ask Reynitz.

He repeats what Buchholz said earlier: "Hitler had two spy systems in the staffs of his field generals. Reports of Nazi party spies came to Martin Bormann. SS spy reports came to the SS liaison officer in headquarters, appointed by Himmler. If a frontline general spoke against an order of Hitler's or retreated instead of fighting to the last man, Hitler found out these things by secret radio or telephone. The generals had no way of knowing who was a party member or SS man."

"What happened to a general who failed to obey Hitler's orders?" I look at Reynitz.

"When his orders were not followed, the next day he would say to the general reporting to his conferences, 'You failed to obey my orders.' These generals would not be seen at headquarters again."

"Did heavy combat losses bother Hitler?"

Buchholz sits on the edge of his chair: "If they did, he never showed it. He was convinced he could conquer Russia somehow, always relying on his intuition. He told his generals that his orders were based on his intuition and that they knew nothing of politics."

"Relied on his intuition, did he? That's no way to direct a war. What did he do about bad news?"

Buchholz continues: "Hitler never wanted to hear any bad news. He listened but soon switched the subject. When he read a report, a letter, or memo, he skipped over the bad news. It was evident that he read only the parts that were agreeable to his thinking."

"What happened next?" I ask. Jonuschat looks at me expectantly, and I nod.

"The Balkans were being threatened as the Russians moved westward from Stalingrad, and the war in Africa was going badly. The forces under General Rommel were being pushed back. In March 1943, Rommel was ordered out of Africa and, as I recall, he was sent to inspect the front at Greece," Jonuschat answers.

Gen. Erwin Rommel

"Did anyone try to kill Hitler at this time?"

"About that time, as I learned later, there were two attempts on Hitler's life that failed because the bombs didn't go off or Hitler did not arrive at the place. I was told that one bomb was placed in an airplane carrying Hitler, but the fuse failed to function. Another time I was told a bomb was carried in some new uniforms that Hitler was to inspect, but Hitler did not attend this inspection."

"Did Hitler blame others for defeats?"

"He always blamed the field marshals for defeats, for not fighting to the last man. In North Africa it was Rommel, as it was Paulus at

Stalingrad. Sometimes he would talk at length, in a continuous monologue, about generals giving ground when there were still unwounded troops to fight. Sometimes Hitler's angry speeches would last for a half-hour, and no one at the conference would say anything afterward," Jonuschat replies.

"Did Hitler pay any attention to what other countries were thinking?" I look at Thoet.

"Hitler had special offices in headquarters where men listened to foreign radio broadcasts. They would type the important parts, and these reports would be submitted to Hitler first thing in the morning. If there was something very important, he would open the morning conference by saying, 'Did you hear about [such and such]?'"

"Hitler was secretive to the extreme," I say as Thoet continues.

"I noticed that he would announce those reports that fitted in with his own thinking. For example, if Stalin, Churchill, or Roosevelt was quoted in a way that confirmed what Hitler had been saying at his conferences, he would announce that but keep everything else secret. He often said that the British were stubborn people. When Churchill said they would never surrender, Hitler announced that as confirming what he said previously. And when he had reinforced his troops in the Balkans and Greece, he announced that Churchill had said the best 'second front' for the Allies would be the 'soft underbelly of Europe.' There actually was a southern front," says Thoet.

"That special office also received information by telegraph, telephone, and messenger. Hitler always knew what his enemies and others were saying," Thoet concludes.

Two, then three, of the others stand up and stretch. One walks to the window and stands looking out for a few seconds before he returns to his seat.

"Did Hitler know that the Allies cracked the Ultra Secret [a system for scrambling and unscrambling radio messages] with the Enigma decoding machine learned from a Polish soldier?" I address Reynitz, who likes such subjects.

"I never heard that at headquarters. But Hitler often said at military conferences, 'What we say here today is known in London tomorrow.' He said he suspected there were traitors in headquarters. That could not be true, of course, as the security was so tight."

"What happened later in 1943?" I ask Krieger.

"In the summer, Mussolini was overthrown, and this was discussed at the conference—also that desertions in the Italian army followed. Mussolini was replaced by Marshal Pietro Badoglio."

"Then what?"

"Hitler ordered German forces into Italy, to hold what he called the southern front. When it was reported at the conferences that the Allies had taken Sicily, Hitler ordered SS Col. Otto Skorzeny to rescue Mussolini, who was held captive in northern Italy. It was reported later that Skorzeny was successful in a spectacular raid by his special SS unit."

"What happened at Rome?" I ask Krieger.

"There was discussion at headquarters about what should be done with the Vatican when German troops entered Rome. Hitler said, in effect, 'It would not embarrass me to go in there and kick out all the swine and seize all the traitorous documents.' He always hated the pope and the church. He could not stand to see any strong organization function independently. Of course, he would not go so far as to invade the Vatican. He knew that half the population of Germany was Catholic, and he was an adroit politician.

"About the same time that fall, the Allies invaded a beach south of Rome, and there was much discussion about the crucial battles in Italy that lasted many months," Krieger recalls.

"Was there any discussion about the meeting of Churchill, Roosevelt, and Stalin at Teheran in Iran later in 1943?"

Jonuschat is ready: "Undoubtedly his press office advised him about this in a daily report, but he would not tell all that he received. I only assume that this was bad news that he did not wish to announce to the military conference. We know now, of course, that one subject of the conference of these leaders was the invasion of Europe. But if the subject matter of the conference was in the daily report, Hitler did not report it. The meeting of these three leaders for the first time could only mean bad news. It had already been reported several times at conferences that Stalin was urging the Allies to open a 'second front' to relieve his forces."

"Was there any discussion about an invasion by the Allies?"

Jonuschat recalls these events easily: "There were several discussions in military conferences about the certainty of an invasion. Support from Britain would seem necessary, so Hitler thought the invasion would be into northern France. Hitler and his inner circle were sure of that."

"What did Hitler do?" I think Jonuschat will know.

"In December 1943, Hitler announced at a conference that General Rommel was appointed commander of German forces to defend the coast of northern France against an attack across the English

Channel. I would guess that Hitler appointed Rommel because he was still a hero in Germany, even though he lost in Africa," Jonuschat concludes.

"This is a good time to end our conversation. It's time to get to bed."

"So long," says Krieger, and the others get their coats.

Col. Douglas Bates examines Dr. Klaus Schilling.

Chapter 25

I am a bit late. The seats at the prosecution table are all occupied, and I find myself in a chair at the back of the room. Filming with four cameras adds life to the proceedings.

We hear of malaria experiments conducted at Dachau by defendant Dr. Klaus Schilling, 74, from 1942 to 1945. He testifies that in 1899 he started malaria research in Africa, returning there four times, then continuing his research in Italy. There he met two doctors, who took him to Germany to meet Himmler in December 1941. Schilling says:

Himmler himself gave me the order to continue my studies in Dachau . . . the sole purpose was to find a vaccination against malaria. The mosquitoes were put into a cage ten centimeters wide and ten centimeters long and just as high. These cages were covered by mosquito gauze. Such a cage was then put in between the legs, or the arm was put on top of the cage. Then the mosquitoes bit through the gauze. The majority of the subjects were used for reinfection . . . injected repeatedly . . . to step up their immunity.

The Rev. Theodore Koch, a Catholic priest, was one subject of Schilling's malaria experiments. He testifies that he was on his last legs and put in the prison hospital. On release, still weak, he was sent to Schilling's experimental station:

For two days, I didn't eat and I was very tired, so for two days, and two nights almost, I slept . . . On the next day, not only I, but also the others who were in the same room with me, were sent to another room where pestilent mosquitoes were in little boxes . . . Each . . . received a small box, with a mosquito, and we had to hold our hands over that box, which was covered with a towel. That lasted a half-hour or an hour a day for almost one week. Also a male nurse . . . brought us another box with mosquitoes and it was put in the bed, between our legs for either a half-hour or an hour . . . Then each morning the blood smear was taken from the ear . . . my temperature was taken during the day and also at night.

Father Koch goes on to testify that he was released after 17 days and then had malaria attacks: "Malaria recurred precisely every three weeks for six months. The symptoms were high fever and chills, and there were pains in the joints."

The Rev. Frederick Hoffman, a German priest and prisoner in Dachau from 1941 to liberation in 1945, testifies that approximately 200 priests were used in the malaria experiments.

Then Schilling testifies in his own defense about the effects of malaria:

> The brain is the main organ with respect to acute malaria. Of course, the brain will also suffer under the anemia of chronic malaria, but the most important changes are in the brain. The smallest capillaries of the brain will be plugged and blocked, because the malaria parasites will cling to the walls of the blood vessels.

Schilling is asked a crucial question: "Were the prisoners volunteers for the experiments?"

> This question was considered only with a very few patients. There were only about four or five patients who refused to be immunized. I talked to these four or five patients, and I explained to them that the vaccination would not be dangerous to them and that these experiments were of such a great importance that they could cause a great scientific discovery. Then these patients did not offer any more resistance . . . I told my assistants repeatedly that they should only give me patients that did not suffer from hidden diseases.

Dr. Franz Blaha testifies in contradiction: "None of them volunteered for it, and many we saved from these experiments."

Blaha identifies Exhibit No. 38:

It is a request for new prisoners for the malaria experiments which was directed to the Kommandant Weiss and also signed by Professor Schilling . . . The subjects were given physical examinations before being used for malaria experiments . . . To see if those people [were healthy enough to] be used for that purpose.

Defendant SS Kommandant Weiss, when confronted by Denson about Schilling's requisitions, admits he approved them, as he did requisitions for other medical experiments. His initials are plainly marked on these papers.

Questioned about autopsy findings, Schilling testifies: "Blaha simply kept these dissections secret from me."

Asked on cross-examination whether he knew that those receiving the last doses of pyramidon (an experimental chemical) died, Schilling says: "Dr. Blaha did not notify me about the new-born cases of pyramidon poison. If he had, I would have stopped the experiments immediately. The cases are Dr. Blaha's fault."

Dr. Blaha contradicts his testimony:

The subjects were treated in different ways . . . with quinine, neosalvarsan, atipyrin, pyradium, and dye 2516, with several combinations. All the people who died of malaria and consequences, I dissected [with Schilling present or receiving the vital organs]. The causes were severe intoxication . . . and other diseases . . . the intoxication of neosalvarsan in the year 1943

Colonel Bates questions a witness.

and then of pyramidon in 1945 . . . through big doses . . . the people could not tolerate . . . and which acted as poisons on them . . . First, three died on the same day and that was a big sensation in the entire hospital.

Blaha also testifies about dosages:

Perhaps 1.5 or two grams for a few days, but not too long because the poisonous action of the pyramidon becomes dangerous when it acts for a long time . . . After three days, signs of poisoning would show up in vomiting, and so forth.

Confronted with more exhibits found at Dachau by American troops after the liberation in April 1945, Schilling testifies: "This is one of the usual card file cards. I assumed they were burned—they were not burned. They were put aside so that they could be used as evidence against me."

We also learn that a "skin and bone museum" was maintained at Dachau. Dr. Blaha describes how human skin was removed at the morgue, then treated:

We took the [tattooed] skin from the chest and the back. We had to use chemicals and treat the skin with them. Then these skins were placed outside in the sun and parts were cut out according to drawings given to us by the SS men. They were for saddles or riding breeches, for gloves, for house slippers and ladies' handbags.

[That] was done in the masses . . . in 1942 . . . Especially the Russians were used for that . . . also Poles and other inmates . . . It was forbidden to cut out the skin of Germans. This skin had to be from healthy prisoners and free from defects. Sometimes we did not have enough bodies with good skin and [SS defendant Dr. Rascher] would say, 'All right, you will get the bodies.' The next day we would receive 20 or 30 bodies of young people. They would have been shot in the neck or struck in the head so that the skin would be uninjured.

And Dr. Blaha describes how skulls were prepared: "They were cut off, and then they were boiled. All the soft parts were removed and bleached in concentrated peroxide, dried, and then put together again."

He also tells of filling orders for complete skeletons: "The last time a request came through [SS defendant Dr. Hintermayer] was in February 1945—that was for two skulls and one skeleton."

In a pretrial affidavit, Dr. Blaha stated:

In the case of skulls, it was important to have a good set of teeth. When we got an order for skulls from Oranienburg [camp at Berlin], the SS men in camp would say, 'We will try to get you some with good teeth.' So it was dangerous [for a prisoner] to have a good skin or good teeth.

Some skulls were preserved at Dachau, some not.

The author, above, with German V-2 missiles; children in the rubble of Allied bombing, right; slave laborers making—and sometimes sabotaging —munitions, below.

Chapter 26

December 1945

The recorders meet with me again in my living quarters at
7:00 P.M.

"Greetings. How are you this evening?"

"Couldn't be better," says Krieger, "except for Thoet, who has a
bad cold."

"I'm anxious to get home to Berlin. I've had a letter from my wife,
brought here by a direct-flying plane. She and my two daughters are
having a hard time making it on the short rations card." Reynitz is
grim.

"I see. Wish I could help. The only thing I can think of is to get
you a ride on one of those direct-flying planes. I'll look into it. Let's
begin where we left off last. Who'll start?" I ask.

"I will," says Krieger, leaning forward in his chair and speaking
slowly. "Hitler's domain was shrinking. His forces were pounded with

greater intensity on all fronts. There was much bad news. Russians were advancing in Poland. The Allies made landings several places in Italy. The Allies were now united under the American general, Dwight Eisenhower. Almost all the news for Hitler was getting worse, especially from Russia," Krieger concludes.

"The tables were finally turning against Hitler, as well they should be. What about taking slave laborers from other countries? That is a violation of the Hague Treaty." I address Hans Jonuschat, who is the best on legal questions.

"In March 1944, the question came up about the Hague Treaty and that taking millions of foreign workers from occupied countries was in violation of the treaty. Hitler said he didn't care about the Hague Treaty. He had said the same thing several times before: 'Whatever you do—if you win—it's unimportant. Nobody will ask. I am right in putting these people to work, to give me manpower to replace those drafted into military service.'"

Fritz Saukel

Jonuschat goes on: "Gauleiter Fritz Saukel had been appointed directly by Hitler sometime before, and in 1944 he was ordered to speed up the drive to get able-bodied civilian workers from eastern Europe and Russia to do armament work in the concentration camps."

"Did Hitler say anything about concentration camps?" I ask.

Reynitz moves forward in his chair: "I feel sure Hitler did not know all of the mistreatment and killings that went on in the concentration camps down to the last detail. But he certainly knew these civilians from occupied areas were slave laborers and worked against their will. He had private conferences with Heinrich Himmler and Albert Speer many times. I recorded a conference between Hitler and Speer about these camps. He didn't care about details. He wanted to get the manpower to make armaments.

"This had been going on for two years, but in 1944 I'm sure it was stepped up considerably, as manpower became acute because of the heavy losses in Russia," Reynitz recollects.

"Heavy losses is putting it mildly. It was actually disastrous. What about Allied air bombings in Germany?" I ask him.

"Everything was worse than ever. Berlin was bombed several times. One time I went to Berlin on leave, and I saw a macadam street burning. The incendiary bombs were the worst. I also saw many that had not detonated.

"One of the typists had a letter from a relative in Frankfurt saying much of the city was in rubble," recalls Reynitz.

"I had leave for about eight or ten days about every six months. It gave me the opportunity to talk with my family and friends. They brought me up to date on what was going on inside Germany, especially from Allied air bombing," he says.

"What effect did the bombing in Germany have on the people you talked with?"

Reynitz, still erect in his chair, looks at me, and the others look at him. "The influence of the bombing on the population was astonishing. There was demoralization of the people. I suppose that was the aim of the Allies. But I think in many cases the influence was to the contrary. If a man lost everything, had no place to sleep and little food, he would say, 'Now there is nothing else to lose, and we must learn to fight better and to work harder.'"

"What did Hitler say about Allied bombings of Germany? It seems to me he would comment about this." I glance at Jonuschat.

"In several military conferences, Allied air raids on German cities were discussed. Hitler was angry and said, 'We can fight terror only with more terror. Why can't I find out what our bomber planes are doing to cities in Britain?'"

Jonuschat continues: "Hitler said in a conference that the V-1 missile was inaccurate, and he was upset that he could not find out what damage it did. He relied more on the V-2 rocket, which could be aimed more accurately, was supersonic, and could not be shot down by enemy fighters. Hitler still hoped to bomb the British into submission, to stop their bombing of German cities. But he was angry when told that no one could measure the damage in Britain." Jonuschat finishes and leans back in the davenport.

"Were any of your residences bombed?" I glance at Buchholz.

"Yes. One day my colleague and I were in the room with Hitler before the conference started. I told Hitler that Thoet's apartment building in Berlin was destroyed, and my apartment was severely damaged. His comment was: 'It will be rebuilt, and then it will be better than before.' He also said, 'I know the British. They are stubborn people. They will go on with that until the bitter end.'"

Buchholz goes on: "Later, in a military conference, he warned Goering not to neglect fighting against British bombers with his fighter planes. Goering complained that he did not have enough planes and that over 75 percent were on the Russian front. He said Allied bombs were falling on German homes, railroads, highways, and even in the fields. He called it 'area bombing.' Hitler made no reply.

"The apartment where I had lived was in a suburban residential quarters. There were some anti-aircraft barracks nearby, but they had few weapons. They couldn't do much to stop the bombing at night.

"At a conference one day, Goering described how aluminum foil was dropped from Allied planes to foul up the German radar," Buchholz concludes.

"Jonuschat, you told me about Hitler's avoidance of looking at physical destruction. Can you give me an example?"

"He refused to look at any destruction in Germany. If the headquarters railway train passed through rubble, the shades on the windows were pulled down by his order or that of an adjutant or Bormann, who knew Hitler's wishes."

Jonuschat continues: "One time—I think it was at Leipzig—the headquarters train, on its way to Berlin, stopped in a switchyard alongside a train from Russia that was evacuating wounded German soldiers. I was told Hitler became angry and ordered all the shades drawn on that side along the whole train."

"The next major event?"

Jonuschat sits erect and intense, his feet flat on the floor: "Hitler was told the Allied forces were strong and moving northward toward Rome. In June 1944, he said, 'Rome is such a historic city, and it should be saved from ruin by a major battle. I have ordered [Field Marshal Albert von] Kesselring to withdraw our troops from the city. If I didn't, he would probably do it on his own.' Kesselring was a famous and popular commander, and Hitler probably did not want a confrontation with him. But Hitler was probably thoughtful about saving Rome," Jonuschat recalls.

Then I tell the recorders about the Allied invasion of France, which occurred about the same time as the surrender of Rome: "The invasion of Normandy was a bloody event. The Allies lost many men and ships from German artillery, air bombing, and ground forces.

"A furious hurricane hit across the Cherbourgh peninsula after the invasion started in June 1944. For a four-day period, all ship landings and flying stopped. I learned this from *Stars and Stripes.*

"The media in America were critical of the effort, saying the Allies had gained only a toehold in France after seven weeks of assault. What they didn't understand was the difficulty of getting through the hedgerows. Tanks could not be used in the hedgerows, as their bellies would be exposed and their guns would be pointed skyward in the attempt to get across. The American press and radio continued to complain about the lack of progress. Some writers predicted our failure.

"But we broke through with the Saint Lô bombing, got through Mortrain, and finally, in August 1944, the Allied forces encircled the Germans. Capturing Port of Brest made a new path for the troops following. The American press obviously was wrong," I finish my monologue.

Then Reynitz says, "Not long after that, in September, I was summoned to Hitler's bedroom at about 11:00 P.M. I learned later that he had been ill in bed for two days with the onset of Parkinson's disease. He had only his shirt on. Gen. Alfred Jodl, chief of operations, was there, and Hitler was talking to him about his plan for the Ardennes Offensive. I took verbatim notes of their conversation, and it was clear that it was entirely Hitler's idea.

"Jodl kept saying there were not enough soldiers, equipment, and supplies for such a long drive, and that there was not enough gasoline for the tanks and other vehicles. Hitler bluntly said, 'You will get all you need when you take Antwerp, an Allied supply port.'"

"What a preposterous idea—you will get all you need when you reach Antwerp! Again, this shows that Hitler had no business directing the war. What was the plan, anyway?" I ask.

"Hitler said his plan was to split the Allied forces and deny the important seaport of Antwerp to them. I think he desperately needed some kind of victory after so many losses on all the fronts, especially in Russia," Reynitz recalls and goes on:

"He ordered Jodl to draw the plans for the offensive through the Ardennes forests and hills in Belgium. He ordered that the spearhead of the drive be manned by Waffen SS. He directed that SS Col. Otto Skorzeny assemble English-speaking troops dressed as American soldiers. They would be parachuted in ahead of the drive to create confusion by attacking American soldiers behind their front line and destroying their communications and ammunition dumps. Hitler said that after the plans were ready and the troops and equipment assembled, the attack would start in late fall. Then rain and fog would ground the American planes."

"You certainly have a fine memory, Dr. Reynitz. That was a good account of how Hitler operated," I say. He leans back and smiles.

"Who wants to carry on?" I ask. Thoet leans forward, and I nod.

"When Allied troops crossed the German border, Hitler ordered German units that had already been wiped out to push the Allies back. He said, 'If the Allies come farther into Germany, the war is lost.' He had said the same thing about situations occurring earlier. Then he would order another attack as if nothing had happened. He was following his old pattern of always being positive, never negative. After a serious defeat, he often ordered an attack at another place, saying, 'We will have victory.' He acted like a man waiting for a miracle."

"Carry on," I say as Thoet warms to the subject. The eyes of the other recorders are on him.

"When Allied troops were close to taking Aachen, Hitler said at a military conference, 'We cannot allow that to happen.' There was a discussion that Aachen was a city of 400,000, including its suburbs, and that its capture would demoralize the German people. It is a famous city, I think the most ancient in Germany. It was the seat of the revived Roman Empire, and Charlemagne was crowned emperor there in 800. His rule is called the First Reich; that of Chancellor Bismarck in the late 19th century, the Second Reich," Jonuschat concludes.

"Who wants to finish this up?" I ask, glancing at Buchholz. He has been unusually quiet, but he sits forward, now ready to talk. I nod.

"I think the major events were the advances made by the Allies into Germany and their very heavy air bombing of German cities. They crushed cities unmercifully, and the worst were those incendiary bombs that crashed through tile roofs and burned out the insides of homes and business buildings.

"It was awful. There was no pattern. Women and children were killed and buried in the rubble. I can't remember a worse year. We were all talking about it in Hitler's headquarters. The staff there were receiving letters from home telling about the horror of it all," Buchholz concludes.

"That is terrible," I say. Then looking at Krieger, I ask, "What about Russia?"

He replies slowly: "The Russians made huge advances in all the eastern countries—one after the other. They took countries such as Czechoslovakia, Hungary, and Romania.

"It seemed as if Hitler's forces were falling apart. There just was no stopping the Russians and Allies from closing in. And the worst thing of all was that Hitler himself was all bent over, his face was always red, his hands were always shaking, and he shuffled his feet instead of walking." Krieger recalls all this soberly. He relaxes into his chair with a sigh.

"That must have been quite an experience," I say.

"None of us thought it was more than Hitler deserved. It was the beginning of the end for him." Krieger is composed but unsmiling.

"Anything else?" I ask no one in particular.

Krieger picks up the ball again. "When the Ardennes Offensive started on December 16, 1944, Hitler's headquarters were near Bad Nauheim, about 30 kilometers north of Frankfurt. The attack started at several points and Hitler had ordered as many troops as possible into it. He seemed pleased when at first the offensive, moving rapidly toward Antwerp, was successful.

"He said nothing when told his offensive had been stopped half-way to Antwerp. What *could* he say? He ordered another attack at the north side of the Bulge. His conduct was the same as ever," Krieger concludes.

"I think it's time to stop," I say.

Each man shakes my hand, puts on his topcoat, and leaves.

Minister of armaments Albert Speer, right; master propagandist Joseph Goebbels, below; Luftwaffe commander in chief, president of Germany, and presumed successor to Hitler, Hermann Goering, below right.

Chapter 27

December 1945

The five recorders meet with me again in the evening at my living quarters.

"We left off last time with the failure of the Ardennes Offensive, which Allied forces called the Battle of the Bulge. Who would like to start?" I ask.

"I'll do it," says Reynitz. "But first everyone should be aware that Hitler had a split personality. He lived in two worlds—reality and fantasy." Everyone looks at Reynitz.

"In the real world, Hitler dismissed from his mind military reverses. When I was on the headquarters train, he refused to look at bombed German cities or wounded German soldiers. As far as I know, he never saw a concentration camp. He usually shut his mind to anything unpleasant.

"In the fantasy world, Hitler predicted that if the Russians came too close, the Allies would certainly join his troops in the fight against the Russians because the Allies hated Communism as much as the Germans. If the Allies chose not to fight with us but fought the Russians directly, we would wait until they became exhausted, then come out of the National Redoubt in the Alps, to make victory ours. This was his constant hope. The hope was dashed when Himmler sent only half of the 80,000 SS troops he had ordered," Reynitz recalls.

"Hitler was a dreamer, wasn't he?"

"Yes, and worse than that, he was a liar," Reynitz continues.

"Goebbels was on the radio almost every day telling how the unconditional surrender demanded by the Allies would mean disaster. For example, he gave one illustration after another of how the advancing Russians raped women and killed captured German prisoners in Prussia—by the thousands. He stressed that every German should fight the Russians and Allies to the utmost; otherwise, half would be killed and the other half made slaves. Goebbels was Hitler's inventive mouthpiece.

"For the most part Germans believed this propaganda. Many willingly remained in the Volkssturm, but many of the elderly moved westward. They were desperate and afraid of capture by the Russians."

"Why should there be a Volkssturm?"

"Because the means for getting young men into the Wehrmacht were exhausted," Reynitz answers.

"Did Hitler give his usual anniversary speech?" I nod at Buchholz as he sits up straight.

"Yes, it was the 12th anniversary of his coming to power. Among other things he said, 'We may have lost the battle, but not the war.

We will arise like a phoenix out of the ashes, and final victory will be ours.'"

"Hitler never gave up, did he? It seems he was still dreaming. That, or he was plain nuts. Did he still talk of winning?"

"He made no direct comment about winning," says Buchholz. "He ordered a last stand at the Roer River. When the Allies crossed that and were moving to the Rhine River, Hitler ordered a last stand to protect the Ruhr area [Ruhr River valley] east of the Rhine."

"What is the Ruhr area?"

"This is the largest and most important coal mining and industrial area in Germany. Here are the large cities of Essen, Dortmund, Düsseldorf, Wuppertal, and Duisburg, where factories made armaments in large quantities. Hitler said as he had before, 'If we lose there, it is over.'"

"Why did he make such a statement?" I nod at Krieger, who is ready.

"He often did this. I think he was trying to jar his generals. When the Americans crossed the Rhine on a bridge at Remagen and helped the other Allies encircle the Ruhr area, Hitler ordered a court martial and sentence of death for the commander, a German colonel at Remagen, for not destroying that bridge.

"Hitler said little about the big loss of the Ruhr area. Instead, he ordered a new army to be built up near the Harz Mountains. He also said any German soldier who was not wounded and did not keep on fighting was a traitor. He ordered anyone who quit fighting to be hanged."

"What about the Russians?" I ask Jonuschat. The others watch him.

"The Russians were advancing toward Berlin and Hitler ordered the city defended by imaginary divisions. When his top staff told him those divisions didn't exist, he did not believe them."

"Where were Hitler's headquarters at that time?"

"Headquarters were still in the Chancellery in Berlin, since the last of December 1944," says Jonuschat. "The offices and conference room were above ground, and there were two bunkers deep underground, one for Hitler and his top staff, the other for the rest of us. When the air-raid warning came, we all went down into the bunkers."

"Where was your sleeping room?" I ask Reynitz, who sits up straight.

"My sleeping room was on the second floor. If the alarm sounded, I had to go to the ground level, then down the stairs to the bunker. The stairs were dangerous . . . partly destroyed by fire as a result of Russian bombing. Sometimes I was helped down the stairs, two staircases down, around 40 steps in all.

"When we were summoned to Hitler's bunker, an SS man or adjutant had to lead us. We could not find it alone."

"How was Hitler's health at that time?" I nod to Krieger, who proceeds slowly.

"Hitler's health became visibly worse in the spring of 1945. His face became red, he shuffled slowly, his hands trembled, and his head hung down. He stopped making angry monologues at the conferences every time a field general retreated rather than fighting to the last man, as Hitler had ordered. He talked less. His routine at the conferences remained the same, but he would swing from hope to despair."

Krieger goes on: "He was attended by Dr. Theo Morrell, who was usually at headquarters. We thought he was giving Hitler too many drugs. Once Dr. Morrell came to my room when I was sick in bed with influenza. He injected me with a syringe that I thought was big enough for a horse. Since that time I have been allergic to sulfanilamide. He said he was the inventor of the drug and owner of a factory in Germany that produced great quantities, and that he had another factory in Romania."

"Did Hitler complain about his health?" I ask Krieger while he is still on that subject.

"Hitler did not complain about his health, only about never having any pleasure. Once in a while, before that time, the headquarters would be moved to his favorite place, his home, called Berghof, at Berchtesgaden, for a change. There he would see his favorites: Eva Braun and his dog, Blondi. The dog was always with him there."

"What did Hitler think of the people of his inner circle?" I nod to Jonuschat. He stands to stretch his legs.

"Hitler talked about Rudolf Hess in a fond way, but when he recalled Hess para-

Eva Braun

chuting into Scotland, in 1941, Hitler said, 'He must have gone mad.' He mentioned favorably Albert Speer, his minister of armaments. Speer came to headquarters occasionally, but only when summoned through Martin Bormann, who handled appointments and usually decided who could see Hitler. Hitler liked Speer but not as a friend. Hitler had no camaraderie with anyone.

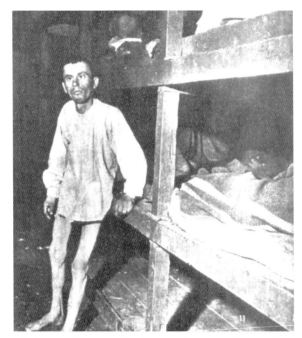

Prisoners found at Buchenwald, too weak to walk.

"Just before I left the headquarters, General Jodl said at a conference that with such a small corridor between the Russians and the Allies left for escape, it would be better to go to the Alps. Hitler ordered many generals to go to Berchtesgaden. He ordered the staff there too. I left with some others on April 20, 1945, which happened to be Hitler's 56th birthday."

"Had Hitler made up his mind on what to do?" I nod to Thoet.

"Hitler had not made up his mind whether to continue the war from the Alps or to stay in Berlin to the last. He was still saying, 'When the Russians and Americans meet, the Americans will join us in fighting the Russians. If not, they will fight themselves to exhaustion. Then we can move in from the Alps and victory will be ours.'"

"What were the conditions when you left Berlin?" I ask Reynitz.

"I was afraid I would be sent to combat with the Volkssturm. But I was more afraid of being shot because I knew too much. The evening before I left, I went to the railway station. I wanted to try to get on the train to reach my family, to see whether they were still alive. I came to the station just as the train was going out. The next evening I was lucky to be flown to Berchtesgaden. There was no way to reach my family. The Russians were about to encircle Berlin."

Then I recall: "On April 26, three days before the rapid advance of American troops, the SS ordered evacuation of the Dachau camp. Thousands of prisoners were forced to walk south toward Bavaria in an effort to carry out Himmler's order [according to the trial record] that no prisoners be allowed to fall into the hands of the enemy alive."

The room is very quiet for a moment

"We'll stop here. It's getting late."

And the five recorders put on their coats and leave.

*Below, the conference room at Hitler's Berghof,
near Berchtesgaden; right, SS chief Heinrich
Himmler.*

Chapter 28

We meet again the next evening. I cannot help but wonder why the recorders have been so open and frank with me. And rarely have they corrected or contradicted one another. At Berchtesgaden, they were interviewed separately and recited identical stories. Maybe they are simply meticulous reporters, who can tell only the truth. Perhaps it is because I'm a lawyer and ask questions appropriately. Whatever the case, they are not party members, and they didn't like Hitler. I believe what they say.

"Well, there's not much more to cover beyond what happened at Berchtesgaden during the summer before you came here. I think I'll start with you, Dr. Reynitz, as you are most familiar with the area from visiting your daughter in Munich. Am I right?"

"Yes, I think so." Reynitz looks to the others. They nod.

"You're elected. You might start with a description of the town."

"As you may know, Berchtesgaden, Germany, is a town of 5,000, only about ten miles from Salzburg, Austria," says Reynitz. "It is famous for its markets and winter sports. On a mountain near the town was Hitler's home, the Berghof. It had an underground bunker and served occasionally as his headquarters during the war. In late April 1945, our team of recorders was ordered by Hitler to go to the town and wait for him."

"Why did you wait for him?"

"When I left Berlin, Hitler still had not made up his mind whether to continue the war from the Alps or to stay in Berlin. He had ordered Himmler to send thousands of SS troops with full equipment and conceal themselves in the Alps.

"All of us stayed in a Berchtesgaden hotel and waited. The last two of our colleagues to arrive—Kurt Haagen and Gerhard Herrgesell—had recorded Hitler's final conference, at which he said he would stay in Berlin. They said Hitler learned that the trusted head of his SS, Heinrich Himmler, had sent only about half the number of SS troops ordered to the Alps and had tried to negotiate peace through Swedish leaders. Hitler called Himmler a traitor and refused to see him or talk with him on the telephone," Reynitz concludes.

"Members of the inner circle were beginning to leave Hitler, were they not?"

"Yes, and there were more of them, as we learned later." Reynitz still sits on the edge of his chair. The others are attentive.

"We waited in our hotel rooms, still apprehensive that we might be drafted into the Volkssturm and ordered into battle. We heard on the radio that Hitler was killed while defending Berlin. Then we heard that he had committed suicide on April 30."

"All eight of us recorders were quartered in the same hotel and had chats all summer about what occurred in all of Hitler's military-situation conferences. In that way we were able to learn the whole story," says Krieger, who speaks slowly.

"You see, two of us recorded each conference, then spent the next two days finishing the transcript. So usually each of us recorded conferences every third day. We were all interested in learning the main events we missed because Hitler gave us strict orders not to talk with each other about anything said at the conferences. That summer we were free to do so for the first time. We did, and all of us gained from the experience."

"Tell me more of that time in Berchtesgaden."

Hans Jonuschat says: "We all gathered, except our colleague Kurt Haagen, who did not wish to meet with us. But Gerhard Herrgesell told us that many of our documents, stenograms, and transcripts had been burned by SS troops at Hintersee, a village a few miles away."

Karl Thoet picks it up: "When the SS said they were going to burn all the documents, I went to one of our generals there and told him, 'Der Fuehrer wants all of his documents preserved for history, even if they fall into enemy hands.' He didn't seem to pay much attention, and as far as I could see, he did nothing. The SS was in charge of the area, and several regular army generals were just waiting for Hitler's instructions, as we were."

"Hitler had learned that Goering was planning to take his place as leader," says Heinz Buccholz. "Bormann convinced Hitler of this, and Hitler ordered the SS to arrest Goering."

I look at Krieger, who seems ready to speak. He says, "By radio in Berchtesgaden, we heard that Hitler had committed suicide along

Bormann gazes at Hitler.

with Eva Braun, by then Mrs. Hitler. Our wait was over on May 5, when American troops occupied the town of Berchtesgaden."

"How did you get along with the Americans?" I ask Jonuschat.

He sits straight up and runs his fingers through his sparse hair. "We were relieved because we knew the Americans were no threat to us. We told them who we were and offered to cooperate. The Americans realized we were in the civil service in the Reichstag before the war and not members of the Nazi party or SS. They told us we were free to go as we wished. Herrgesell, Peschel, and Haagen went elsewhere."

Reynitz continues the discussion: "The Americans questioned us separately about our histories before and during the war. We told our stories in great detail, and they told us our stories were exactly alike. That's why they cleared us.

"They were intensely interested in and asked us many questions about Hitler's conduct during the war. We told them about the verbatim records of Hitler's military conferences that the SS had burned in Hintersee, about four miles away," says Reynitz. "They immediately wanted our help in finding the records."

"What did you do?"

"Three of us went in a Jeep with an American official—Counterintelligence Corps agent George R. Allen of the 101st Airborne Division—to Hintersee. We looked around and found this pit with burned papers in it. He dug around deeper in the ashes until finally he found some envelopes that had not been completely burned. We recognized the stenograms and transcripts of Hitler's military-situation conferences that we or our colleagues had dictated to the typists.

"We took the papers back to Berchtesgaden. Agent Allen went back to the pit again twice in the next few days to recover all he could, around 800 pages. Altogether there were verbatim records, some partial, some complete, of around 50 of Hitler's military conferences. This amounted to about 1 percent of Hitler's documents originally stored there," concludes Reynitz.

"What made the SS burn those important papers?" I ask Thoet.

"I don't know. Hitler did want all of them preserved for history. That I know for sure."

Thoet continues: "Gerhard Herrgesell and Kurt Haagen were the last of Hitler's recorders to leave Berlin. They told us what happened in the last ten days before Hitler committed suicide on April 30, 1945. General Jodl stayed with Hitler almost to the end and said as he left, 'I don't

General Jodl

want to get killed in this mousetrap.' Hitler decided to stay in Berlin to the end. His last conference was with one person, his adjutant."

Krieger picks it up again: "Agent George R. Allen came to our hotel in the evenings, and we five would gather to chat in German. That was really fun. Sitting on beds or on the floor, we talked about many things besides Hitler and the war, things like history and philosophy and our families in Berlin."

"We couldn't get to Berlin and our families because of Russian occupation," Reynitz says. "We all stayed in the town and helped the Americans by translating to English the notes and transcripts found in the pit. [The papers are now kept at the University of Pennsylvania Library, in the original German language. They are fairly good illustrations of how Hitler conducted his military conferences.] We also helped all summer with the translation of voluminous other documents found elsewhere. We answered many questions about our observations at Hitler's headquarters during the war.

"We were advised by Allen that it would be dangerous to try to reach Berlin, as the Russians controlled the area west of there, and they were not noted for taking prisoners. We were told that before everything was cleared up between the Russians and the Allies, we should go to the Dachau camp, where our talents could be used. And that's what we five did, arriving here late in September 1945," Reynitz concludes.

"That brings us just about up to date. Anyway, it is time to adjourn. What do you think?"

Krieger glances at his wristwatch. "It is 10:30, time to hit the sack. I guess you're right." He looks at the others, who nod agreement.

As they go to the closet for their topcoats, I say, "This may be our last discussion all together, and I want to thank each one of your for your wonderful memory of the facts and the way you presented them. I'm grateful to all of you. You'll be hearing from me from time to time."

"It's been a pleasure," says Krieger. He shakes my hand. The others do, too, and show me their smiles for the last time.

———

Before they leave Dachau, Hitler's recorders give me memos detailing their impression of Der Fuehrer. All write that he often ignored reality and relied on his intuition.

Hans Jonuschat puts it this way: "One should think that he was blinded concerning the realities of power in Germany and in foreign countries, particularly with his enemies. He would overlook or treat in an offhand way such things as would not conform with his deductions . . . [He had] a demonic nature."

Karl Thoet writes: "Der Fuehrer was a very energetic and fanatical man. He was demonic, possessed by the idea to secure a happy future to the German people, not minding any resistance and using all his power to break it."

Ludwig Krieger also remembers that "Hitler's total will and actions were directed only by the idea to win the war. All things hindering himself and the army . . . ought to be exterminated and eliminated."

Heinz Buchholz tells of Hitler's consideration of a possible uprising in Germany: "At a special occasion, he said that he would order Himmler [if a riot should occur] to exterminate these elements before they could become dangerous."

Ewald Reynitz concludes, "Hitler was a maniac. He couldn't distinguish reality from fantasy."

———————

Not too long after my last meeting with the recorders, I reach the magical number of 92 service points. The right to go home is mine. About the same time comes an order from Munich that Colonel Cheever wants to see me there. I can't imagine what he wants from me.

On the way to see Cheever, I think about my situation. I am fed up to my eyebrows with war crimes. Two reasons: I am exhausted from working more than 60 hours a week for a long period, and the war crimes have filled me with disgust. I can't wait to be done with it.

When I arrive in Munich, I am ushered into Colonel Cheever's office. I salute him and stand at attention.

"At ease, Captain. Have a seat."

"Thank you." I take a chair.

The author before leaving Dachau and upon mustering out.

"I know you have the points necessary to return home, but I want to make you an offer. If you'll stay another two months, I can see that you are made a major."

"Sir, I have no interest in that and choose to return home. I want to start a law practice."

"I can understand that, but with being made a major, your pay will go up. Besides two months is a short time. We need you in your position until we can find a replacement who would have the respect of the lawyers there."

"Sir, I appreciate your offer, but I still choose to return home."

"I can't do any more, and it is obvious you have given your rights a lot of thought. I give you my warmest regards."

Standing up, I salute him, make a military about-face, and depart. On the way back to Dachau, I think of home. Oh, how good it will be to get back. I don't give a second thought to the colonel's offer.

An interpreter reading sentence to Kommandant Martin Weiss, above, and to Dr. Klaus Schilling, below.

Chapter 29

Sentencing, May 1946

I am not guilty. Please get it over with." These are the last words of Dr. Klaus Schilling at the gallows at Landsberg prison before his hanging on May 28, 1946.

The trial court's 36 death sentences have been reduced to 28 (all hangings) and commutations granted to some of the other eight, ranging from imprisonment for life to imprisonment for terms of seven to 20 years.

Schilling's execution and others occur after extensive consideration of petitions for clemency. The death sentences have been affirmed only after automatic review of the trial record, first by headquarters of the Third Army and finally by USFET (U.S. Forces, European Theater). The reviews have considered everything from the legalities of the charges to proof beyond a reasonable doubt to all the defendants' sentences, petitions for commutation, and mitigating factors. The defense of "superior orders" has been fully considered for all defendants.

There is no doubt that the reviewing authorities have used the "mitigating factor" rule in reducing some sentences. They affirm the trial court, however, in finding that all 40 defendants willingly participated in the common design at Dachau and its subcamps, in a totally criminal operation.

The reviewing authorities have commented in part:

• "International law is part of German law, and since a German court could have tried and punished the offenses [citing precedents], a Military Government Court, as successor to the jurisdiction of the German courts, may likewise do so." Denson says that the German criminal code as applied to its civilians could have been used against the defendants for such crimes as assault, mayhem, kidnapping, and murder.

• "It is a well-settled principle of law that where two or more persons combine to perform a criminal act, each may be liable criminally for all of his acts and of his confederates, done in furtherance of the common design.

• "That there was present and in full force a common design to commit certain acts unlawful by all the legal and humane standards of civilized nations was not seriously challenged by the defense.

• "The only serious issue presented is the effect to be accorded the defense of superior orders raised by each accused" [citing, for example, the German Military Penal Code]: 'If a provision of the criminal law is violated in course of the execution of an official order, the superior who issues such an order alone bears the responsibility for it. However, the subordinate who obeys shall suffer the penalty of an accomplice.'

- "Action in compliance with a superior order is not a defense to a crime against international law [citing authorities]. The court . . . considered that plea as a mitigating fact with respect to punishment of some of the accused."

My own view is that Germany as a signatory was, and still is, bound by the Rules of Land Warfare. No nation has yet asserted its right to withdraw from the treaties agreeing to them or to call for a convention to modify them, as they have a right to do under the treaties. My view is that the signatories have accepted the results of the war crimes trials at Dachau.

The prosecutions of the SS perpetrators were conducted not merely to punish them but also to make a record of their bestial conduct.

I became anti-Semitic. It is a good thing I am being executed.
I would have killed thousands of Jews.
— *Wilhelm Tempel,* SS guard at Kaufering subcamp,
Landsberg, before his execution for war crimes

SOUTHERN GERMANY EDITION

THE STARS AND STRIPES

Daily Newspaper of U.S. Armed Forces ... in the European Theater of Operations

The Weather
Today: Cloudy. Showers. Highest temperature 64 degrees.
Tomorrow: Partly cloudy.

Wednesday, July 4, 1945

Case of the Leaning Cop
PITTSBURGH, July 3—Patrolman Victor Grayser admitted drinking a "few" and "leaning on a doorway." The Police Trial-Board charged him with "leaning on a sidewalk."

Volume 1, Number 58

Truman Asked

Borneo Sniper Shoots At MacArthur, Misses

Old Glory Flies Over Germany

2nd Armd. Leads Allies In Parade Into Berlin
Joint Occupation

By JACK SULLIVAN, Staff Writer

U. S. 2nd Armd. Div., British and French troops today completing the joint occupation of Berlin, as a symbol of combined efforts in the defeat of Germany and their cooperation in peace. The 2nd Armd. (Hell on Wheels) rolling into Berlin shortly after noon yesterday, as beat upon the ruins made by U. S. Flying Fortresses, British Lancasters and Mosquitoes, and Soviet artillery.

Berliners stood under dripping trees and under the remains o streetcar sheds to watch the lon convoy of 16,000 men and 4,000 vehicles pass. The streets wer ... tered with signs saying: "Thi ... has no part in rac ... Red Army does ... of the

---

Army Talks

SPADEWORK FOR VICTORY

VOL. IV. N° 10   17 JULY 1945

So What!
By Paul Light

Horace Russell Hansen, assistant county attor. ... w fighting with the ... forces in Normandy. ... French native far ... underfed, down-at-the- ... begone individual he ... Horace finagled a ... itation recently. ... ating took three ... writes, "There were ...-soup, lamb, fresh ... arrots, warm bread ... then roast duck. ... ied potatoes and ... strawberries with ... n and Calvados (a ... k distilled from ... nally coffee, crack-

ragged, impenetrable profusion of thorny brush, weed, vines and odd-size trees grow along these walls.

"That," says Horace, "is the damned thing we call a hedge-row. It's almost impossible to crawl through one. The Germans burrow into these hedge-rows and make machine-gun emplacements. It takes artillery to blast them out."

Redistribution

Horace is proud of his foxhole de luxe. It's lined with heavy cardboard from ration boxes. His shelter tent covers it. His bathtub is a hole in the ground lined with his raincoat. He heats water in a German helmet.

RESTRICTED

Capt. HANSEN
WAR CRIMES BRANCH
HQ. THIRD US ARMY
JA SEC

...TARY GOVERNMENT
GERMANY

TECHNICAL MANUAL
FOR
LEGAL AND PRISON OFFICERS
2 EDITION

TM 27-251

WAR DEPARTMENT TECHNICAL MANUAL

TREATIES
GOVERNING
LAND WARFARE

Capt. H L Hauce
War Crimes Branch
Dachau
Col. Cheever, Third Army

WAR DEPARTMENT · 7 JANUARY 1944

Chapter 30

Finally persuaded to write of my experiences during and after World War II, I decide to look at the materials I have saved from that time. With amazement I examine the correspondence, memoranda, letters home, clippings, brochures, maps, photographs, issues of *Stars and Stripes, Yank* magazine, *Army Talks,* tapes of interviews, and the record of the Dachau trial. Letters to and from the National Archives in Washington, D.C., produce additional information.

Wishing to learn more from Hitler's recorders, I write all five at their last known addresses. Only one letter arrives in return—from Elizabeth Jonuschat, still in Berlin. She says three of the five, including her husband, Hans, are dead. Thoet is in a nursing home, unable to speak. The only one left is Ewald Reynitz, somewhere in Munich.

I ask Elizabeth Jonuschat to get me the address of Reynitz, and she does. Later she sends me letters from her dead husband, including photos of Hitler and his home, the Berghof at Berchtesgaden. In April I reach Reynitz on the telephone in Munich. Does he remember me?

"How could I forget you? You helped me so much."

I make arrangements to see him in Munich in May.

——— ———

May 1984

My wife, Ruth, and I have lunch with Reynitz the day after our arrival in Munich. Reynitz, 82, seems in good health and is happy to see us at our hotel. He orders a special kind of beer and, raising it, says with humor, "Here's to my friend who hasn't changed much in nearly 40 years, except for some baldness."

We drive him to his home a few blocks away, see him to his apartment, and agree to see him at midmorning the next day.

"I hope you don't forget," he says with a smile.

The next day Reynitz tells me that when his wife died two years ago, he moved from Berlin to Munich to be near his "middle" daughter. (He has three.)

After more small talk, I begin to ask him about Hitler, planning to continue for as many sessions as we have time for. On the second day of what turns out to be a two-week interview, however, Reynitz gives me a scare.

"What are the signs of a heart attack?" he says. "Yesterday, after you left, I was sweating a lot and had dizzy spells for a while. You must keep in mind that I haven't spoken or thought in English since I left Dachau early in 1946."

"How do you feel this morning?" I am beginning to think my trip to Munich might be in vain.

"So far, I feel okay," says Reynitz.

I decide to question Reynitz slowly about Hitler and do what I can to make our sessions easy. I record only his answers:

"The balance between reality and Hitler's intuition was tilted heavily in favor of his intuition. He had a zealot's faith in his own mysticism.

"When he spoke of his *intuition,* he often mentioned *politics* [what the German people would think], *foreign policy* [how other countries would react], and *morale* in the armed forces.

"For every decision, there never was a gray area, only black or white alternatives. I cannot emphasize this too much. Hitler was never in doubt about anything, even without having the facts. He said he was a man of destiny. He was certain he could *do* no wrong, much less *think* any wrong. Many of his military orders were those of a stubborn and irrational man. Two examples stand out: the fiasco at Stalingrad and the failure of the Ardennes Offensive. In both, he overruled his field marshals.

"Hitler never permitted much discussion of defeat. He thought that would be a sign of negative thinking and weakness. Instead, he would order a new attack, thinking that would show positive thinking and strong leadership.

"Hitler and his top followers kept repeating that Germany would have won World War I if not stabbed in the back by the 'November Criminals,' as he described 'the politicians prodded by Jews.' A politician on behalf of Germany signed the November 11, 1918, armistice ending the war.

"Hitler's constant propaganda urged that Germany avenge itself for the terrible consequences of that armistice—especially the heavy money reparations laid on Germany and its loss of many territories.

"In Hitler's view, his military moves were a continuation of World War I. His book, *Mein Kampf,* makes this abundantly clear.

"I think if Hitler had stopped at the end of 1938, he might have become a German hero. But, starting in September 1939, he began outright conquest without any pretense of legal basis. His only excuse for the conquests was his own policy of Lebensraum. His real target for Lebensraum was eastern Europe and Russia. To reach those goals, he decided to protect his rear by invading western Europe. Slavs and Marxists were his ultimate goals.

"There was no need for Lebensraum. Germany was exporting grain and factory goods and importing some items like metals and oil. It had land not being cultivated. Germans had no desire to live and work in another country. Each country has its own heritage, traditions, and culture which its people would like to keep alive. Even in Germany, those in the north would not like to be moved south to Bavaria or vice versa. Germans didn't take Hitler's theme of Lebensraum seriously. It was too far away. Only his promise of full employment was important.

"People in different countries with varying cultures do not want to be united under one government, so conquest is really useless. There are many examples of this in the world today."

———

During our last session for the trip, I show Reynitz a copy of a statement by SS Col. Erich Kempka.

He says, "I remember that well. I told the American intelligence agent, George R. Allen, at Berchtesgaden, that we recorders knew Kempka well enough to know he was not a clever man and couldn't possibly invent a story like that. I know he was telling the truth.

"Bormann was never seen again, and I'm sure I would have heard of it if he had been. I'm sure he was killed when the tank he was using for protection flew apart during an antitank strike from the Russians, as Kempka said."

Then we read together the pertinent parts of Kempka's statement:

In the days after 20.4.45 [April 20, 1945] I have still seen Hitler several times in his bunker in the Reichs Chancellery. He had not changed in his behavior and gave a quiet impression. Eva Braun stayed with the Fuehrer. After 28.4.1945 there were rumors in the Reichs Chancellery that the Fuehrer had been married during the night from 28 to 29.4.1945 to Eva Braun . . . Only on 1 May 1945 [state secretary in the German Ministry of Propaganda] Dr. Naumann confirmed the fact of the marriage of the Fuehrer . . . I spoke to the Fuehrer for the last time on 29 April 1945 . . .

On 30 April 1945 at 1430 hours [2:30 PM] SS Sturm-bannfuehrer Guensche telephoned me and asked me to come to the Fuehrer-bunker. Besides that I was to take care that five cans of gasoline, that is to say 200 [liters], were brought along. I at once took along two or three men carrying the cans. More men were following because it took some time to collect 200 liters of gasoline. By order of SS Sturmbannfuehrer Guensche the cans were brought by these men to the entrance of the Fuehrer-bunker located in the garden of the Reichs Chancellery, which was next to the so-called tower-home and about 20 meters beside the so-called Haus Kempka, my quarters . . . The men at once returned after putting down the cans. There was a sentry of the SD at the entrance of the bunker.

I then went into the antechamber of the briefing-room where I met Sturmbannfuehrer Guensche. Guensche told me that the Fuehrer was dead. He did not tell me any details about the death of the Fuehrer. He only explained he had got the order from the Fuehrer to burn him at once after his death so that he would not be exhibited at a Russian freak-show.

A short time after that SS Sturmbannfuehrer Linge [valet of the Fuehrer] and an orderly who I do not remember came from the private room of the Fuehrer carrying a corpse wrapped in an ordinary field-gray blanket. Based on the previous information from SS Obersturmbannfuehrer Guensche, I at once supposed that it was the corpse of the Fuehrer. One could only see the long black trousers and the black shoes which the Fuehrer usually wore with his field-gray uniform jacket. Under these circumstances there was no doubt that it was the corpse of the Fuehrer. I could not observe any spots of blood on the body wrapped in the blanket.

Thereupon came Reichsleiter Martin Bormann from the living room of the Fuehrer and carried in his arms the corpse of Mrs. Eva Hitler, nee Braun. He turned the corpse over to me. Mrs. Hitler wore a dark dress. I did not have the feeling that the corpse was still warm. I could not recognize any injuries on the body. The dress was slightly damp only in the region of the heart.

Behind Reichsleiter Bormann there came also Reichsminister Goebbels. SS Sturmbannfuehrer Linge and the orderly now went upstairs with the corpse of the Fuehrer to the bunker exit towards the garden of the Reichs Chancellery. I followed with the corpse of Mrs. Hitler. Behind me came Reichsleiter Bormann, Dr. Goebbels, and SS Sturmbann-fuehrer Guensche.

Reichsleiter Martin Bormann wore uniform. According to my recollection Dr. Goebbels also wore uniform. It was shortly before 1500 hours [3:00 P.M.), if I remember, that I received the first notice from Guensche at 1430 hours [2:30 P.M.] and needed five to 10 minutes to reach the Fuehrer-bunker. SS Sturmbannfuehrer Linge and the orderly carried the corpse of the Fuehrer from the westwardly directed bunker exit in the tower-house and put the wrapped corpse on the flat ground in a small depression which was about four to five meters distant from the bunker exit.

There was no lawn, rather bare sand; in the last period construction work was being done in the Reichs Chancellery. I put the corpse of Mrs. Hitler next to the Fuehrer's. Immediately . . . Guensche poured the complete contents of the five cans over the two corpses and ignited the fuel.

Reichsleiter Martin Bormann, Reichsminister Dr. Goeb-bels, SS Sturmbannfuehrer Guensche, SS Sturmbannfuehrer Linge, the orderly, and I stood in the bunker entrance, looked towards the fire, and all saluted with raised hands. The stay in the bunker exit lasted only a short time because the garden of the Reichs Chancellery was under heavy artillery fire. The short-lasting leaving [sic] of the bunker exit already meant a danger to our lives. The ground of the garden of the Reichs Chancellery was ploughed by shell holes . . .

In order to return to the garage I had to pass through the Fuehrer-bunker and wanted to look once more at the rooms in which the Fuehrer had lived last. I followed the personnel mentioned into the living room of the Fuehrer. Opposite the entrance of the room, the dimensions of which are only three by four meters, stood a narrow sofa. Before the right front leg of the sofa lay a Walther Pistol, 6.35 millimeters caliber, which, as I knew, belonged to Eva Braun. Also on the floor approximately before the middle of the sofa lay a Walther Pistol, 7.65 millimeters caliber. I supposed that this pistol belonged to the Fuehrer. I myself did not touch anything in the room, but silently stood there only for a few seconds. I did not put any questions, and no one else spoke to me. According to the situation it was clear to me that the Fuehrer and Eva Braun shot themselves. From the location of the two pistols I concluded that the Fuehrer sat about in the middle of the sofa before firing the shot and Eva Braun had sat on the right part of the sofa. After returning to the garage I notified my men that the Fuehrer was dead. A ceremonial was not held . . .

In the late afternoon of 1 May 1945, I received official notice from SS Sturmbannfuehrer Guensche, who was the kommandant of the Reichs Chancellery, that on the same evening at 2100 hours [9:00 P.M.] the break from the Chancellery was to take place . . .

The persons included in the break assembled at 2100 hours in the coal-bunker of the new Reichs Chancellery . . . The persons assembled there may have amounted to 500 to 700, among them a number of women. All available weapons, rifles, submachine guns, pistols, automatic carbines, light machine guns, and Panzerfauste were distributed . . . But ten or 20 meters behind the second roadblock we received strong machine-gun fire from all sides and had to retreat again. Further breakout attempts failed.

Later on, five or six (German) tanks and armored recognizance cars arrived which were manned by soldiers. It was decided that the tanks were to attempt the breakthrough and that the men who had broken out of the Reichs Chancellery were to advance under the protection of the tanks. Behind one tank state secretary Dr. Naumann went as the first in the top of the tank-turret, behind him Martin Bormann followed by SS Standartenfuehrer Dr. Stumpfegger. I went behind Dr. Stumpfegger. More men joined us. After the tank had gone about 30 to 40 meters, it received a direct hit with a Panzerfaust. The tank flew apart. I saw a short flash of lightning and flew to the ground, where I remained lying unconscious. My last impression was that Dr. Naumann, Bormann, and Dr. Stumpfegger fell together and remained lying . . .

"I firmly believe every bit of Kempka's statement is true. He couldn't invent any part of it," says Reynitz. He seems weary, and I decide to go.

"Auf Wiedersehen," I say. "Your memory and expression of events is phenomenal. It is great to see you after so many years." I thank him profusely and depart. But we will keep in touch over the next year.

The author with Hitler military-conference recorder Ewald Reynitz in 1985.

Chapter 31

Fall 1985

Starting to write about my experiences in Europe, I feel the need for clarification on some points. I telephone Reynitz in September 1985.

"Bitte," he answers in a soft voice.

"This is Horace Hansen. I would like to see you again in October, after Oktoberfest, naturally."

"Fine. I would enjoy seeing you. I presume you will bring Ruth with you?"

"Yes. We plan to see Vienna this time. We love the Alps, the best part of Europe, we think. We are planning about a month, and to spend half that time with you, before and after Vienna."

"Good. We'll have the same beer at the Wachau Hotel, if they have any left."

We meet Reynitz as planned—same place, same beer, and much reminiscing.

"I have read *Mein Kampf,* about 700 pages of the rambling mess. What do you think of it?"

"More than a mess, it is insane," Reynitz answers.

"But the leaders in France, Poland, and Russia should have read it and taken seriously his warnings of the war to come," I say.

"You're right, and did you notice that from beginning to end it is Jews, Jews, Jews—in international control of finances, control of the press, control of propaganda, mixed in with treachery of all kinds?"

"Yes, Jews dominated his thinking from the beginning to the very end of the war. He was consumed by the subject."

"Well, that can be the first subject tomorrow morning—if you don't forget," Reynitz concludes.

———————

The next day, we start talking about Hitler and the Jews. I record his answers, which expand upon the information I have already gathered:

Hitler's hatred of Jews started, he said, as a young man in Austria. His hatred grew into a policy of extermination, killing millions. He started with decrees to drive Jews out of Germany. He spaced his persecution by harsher decrees in Germany until Krystalnacht caused great disgust in most Germans. After that and the billion-mark fine, Hitler kept his actions secret. The Final Solution, systematic murder of Jews, started [officially] in 1942 outside Germany, particularly in Poland and Czechoslovakia.

Remember that Hitler was fighting two wars—a war of conquest and a war against the Jews in all of Europe. A war against Jews made his other war more difficult.

It was a paradox that there were skilled Jews in the management of the I. G. Farben chemical factories. Without Farben, Hitler would not have been able to adequately supply his military forces. The company made synthetic oil, gasoline, vehicle tires from coal, and other items critical to the operation of the war machine as well as the lethal and odorless poisonous gas used in the gas chambers at concentration camps, usually built next to the crematories.

The top executives of Farben were prosecuted at Nuremberg as war criminals for the use and murder of slave laborers from foreign countries in the Farben factories. Alfried Krupp, of the Krupp family-operated armament factories, was likewise prosecuted.

When the Russians counterattacked from Moscow in December 1941, it was a great shock to Hitler. From then on the counterattacks increased in fury. He knew then that the war was lost. But in January 1942, at the Wannsee Conference near Berlin, the Final Solution of the Jewish problem was organized. Hitler licked his lips. He was a mass murderer, and not only of Jews.

The two happenings were a month apart, and the third—declaring the war on America that sealed his doom—occurred four days after Pearl Harbor on December 11, 1941.

But the war on Jews continued unabated until the last. He said many times at war headquarters: "People will be eternally grateful that I have extinguished the Jews in Germany and Europe." In saying that, he presented himself as an internationalist, a benefactor of humanity, and worker for the Lord. Of course, he was dead wrong. Before Hitler, the Jews in Germany were integrated with society and were good Germans. They were actually Germans first, and Jews second.

An English writer and historian, David Irving, disputes Hitler's part in killing Jews, saying that Himmler did this on his own. This statement flies in the face of historical facts— Krystalnacht, the huge fine against Jews, Auschwitz, the Wannsee Conference, and [Hitler's own] statement that *he* had extinguished the Jews in Europe, to mention but a few.

Himmler was totally dedicated to Hitler and would not dare to carry out mass killing of Jews in Europe without direct orders. When the policy became known, it became a lingering embarrassment in West Germany. Konrad Adenauer became chancellor when the new government of West Germany was formed in Bonn in 1949. Adenauer had made several sympathetic speeches and arranged for aid to be given to the struggling new State of Israel.

About the concentration camps:

You realize that these [concentration] camps housed able-bodied men and women, and some Jews were taken by force from Hitler's conquered countries and made to work against their will. When reminded in a military conference that this was a violation of the Hague Treaty, Hitler said, in effect,

"What of the treaty? We win and who will ask?"

Hitler's lack of concern about what happened to millions of foreign workers [slave laborers] in these camps is another example of his nihilist view of the value of man. Remember that Hitler said, "If a camp is threatened, clear it out." And when Albert Speer said, "We don't have enough trucks." Hitler ordered, "Then march everyone out. If that doesn't work, kill the prisoners and bury them." (See pages 322-23.)

When I learned at Dachau in 1945 how the concentration camps were operated and how it produced armaments and war materials of all kinds, I was surprised at first. But when I saw evidence of the whole pattern, not much surprised me anymore. Hitler and his Nazis followed the principle that the ends justified the means. This is the principle generally used by total dictatorships everywhere.

On Hitler's penchant for secrecy:

If the German civilians knew about mass killings of Jewish families and the killing of non-Jews in the concentration camps, many would have protested. Thus, Hitler had to keep such actions secret. Secrecy was a fixation in Hitler's mind.

He repeated many times while I was in his military headquarters that "No one is to have knowledge of any more than is absolutely necessary for him to do his job" . . . Even General Jodl, chief of army operations staff, was surprised to hear about Buchenwald when American troops were advancing toward it. He didn't know about concentration camps.

The Nazis photographed this series to show the extermination of prisoners marched from a work camp in Romania. Here the prisoners line up, minus some items of clothing, in a mass grave they prepared for themselves.

After the Romanian prisoners have been shot, a Nazi officer tromps across them, instructing his soldiers to make sure all are dead.

On Hitler's "Nero order" to destroy all industry and communications:

> It was not a rational order. It reminded us of the Roman emperor Nero, who fiddled while Rome burned, hence the sobriquet. Hitler ordered destruction of the means for Germany to rebuild itself after losing the war simply because it did not deserve to survive. He was placing blame for losing the war on his countrymen. He never blamed any defeat on himself, even though he was the dictator and sole director of his war.

Finally Reynitz speaks of the Neo-Nazis:

> Here in Germany, they are not significant because they have no Hitler and, of course, there is not a deeply depressed economy. If those two ingredients come together again, we could have a repetition. No doubt the Neo-Nazis are operating in many countries and are spreading hatred. But as I said, the Neo-Nazis cannot get anywhere on hate alone. In the long run, education of youth on the truth about Hitlerism is the best answer for keeping peace and democracy.

What can be done now?

> I can only speak of Germany. Here the young people don't want to think about the time of Hitler. I think that young and old, in other countries as well, need to understand the early signs of a trend toward dictatorship. Only then will people have a chance to stop the trend.

*The last time the author saw
Ewald Reynitz, Munich, 1985.*

Nazism was the worst upheaval in the history of man. It changed the face of Europe and Asia. Its story must be repeated to each generation to keep the memory of its hatred, mass murders, and nihilism alive. Education is indispensable.

————————

Dr. Ewald Reynitz died on November 9, 1993, shortly after the death of Karl Thoet.

SIMPLE SIMON SMALL SIGN SHOP
ROBERT G. EGERMAN - Owner
2201 SIXTH STREET NORTH
ST. CLOUD, MINNESOTA
(612) 252-   , 0 92

MAY 16 '83

Truck Lettering - Signs - Plastic Letters & Changable Message Systems - Name Plates

SUPERINTENDENT OF SCHOOLS
WILLMAR MINN

DEAR SIR,

WITH DISGUST, I READ THE ARTICLE IN THE ST. CLOUD TIMES
ABOUT ONE OF YOUR TEACHERS TEACHING THE INOCENT STUDENTS ABOUT
THE "HOLOCAUST" IN THE HIGH SCHOOL CLASSES.

THIS TEACHER, AGE 40, WAS ONLY A FEW YEARS OLD DURING THE WAR.
WHAT DOES HE KNOW?

IF THERE ARE NO SYNAGOGUES IN WILLMAR & AS THE ARTICLE STATES ,
HE IS OF SCANDINAVIAN DESCENT HE HASN'T BEEN EXPOSED TO THE
POISONS OF HE JEW.

DID IT EVER OCCUR TO YOU THAT MAYBE AND I SAID "MAYBE" THAT
THE ONE ABOVE SENT HITLER TO THIS EARTH TO TAKE CARE OF THOSE
PEOPLE THAT REJECTED THE "SAVIOR" OVER 1980 YEARS AGO?

DOES MR. BORTH TELL HIS STUDENTS ABOUT THE BUTCHERY OF MENAKIN

COPY OF THIS LETTER AND THE ARTICLE IN THE PAPER IS BEING
THE NATIONAL ASS'N OF WHITE PEOPLE IN NEW ORLEANS AND
S ALSO BEING SENT TO MR. ROGERS IN LAKE WALES FLORIDA OF
LUX KLAN   I HOPE THEY PAY YOUR SCHOOL A VISIT.

Willmar's class about Holocaust draws hate mail

WILLMAR (AP) — A Willmar high school teacher who designed and teaches a course on the Holocaust says he is shocked by hate mail he received following publicity about the 13-week course on the extermination of Jews during World War II.

Bill Borth said local response to his course has been positive and that he has received favorable comment from other school systems and instructors across the country.

But he said hate mail has taken some of the joy from the praise. Borth said he received newsletters boosting white supremacy and anti-Semitism, along with notes accusing him of misinforming innocent students.

Hate letters also have gone to the school principal, the superintendent and the student council, he said.

One newsletter, "The Special Report," published in California, claims the Holocaust was a hoax. Jews were not exterminated, the newsletter contends; they died instead of a typhus epidemic. And the gases were used only for fumigating barracks.

"Why people go to such great lengths to distort history — that bothers me," Borth said of the publication.

Overall, Borth said, he found the hate mail interesting but shocking.

He believes the hate mail is all the more reason for the class to continue, to educate students about what hatred and prejudice can lead to.

The Willmar School Board agreed, also reacting with surprise that so much hatred exists.

HANSEN, DORDELL, BRADT, ODLAUG & BRADT
ATTORNEYS AT LAW
800 DEGREE OF HONOR BUILDING
SAINT PAUL, MINNESOTA 55101
(612) 227-6058

HORACE R. HANSEN
WAYNE P. DORDELL
GENE P. BRADT
DAVID J. ODLAUG
WILLIAM M. BRADT
DARRELL M. HART

J. MARK CATRON
MARK H. RUBY
THOMAS J. PETERSON
JOHN H. GUTHMANN
CRAIG D. PETERSON
RANDALL W. SAYERS
MARY KAY KOLAR

June 2, 1983

Mr. William Borth
c/o Willmar High School
Willmar MN

Dear Mr. Borth:

I hope that the "hate mail", as reported in the St. Paul Pioneer Press for May 31 (clipping enclosed) will not discourage you from continuing to teach the history of extermination of Jews by the Nazi Regime during World War II. The Holocaust is so thoroughly documented as to reassure you that your detractors are blinded by their bigotry. The lessons which all of the atrocities committed by the Nazis are so important for this and future generations to understand that it needs periodic revew. Perhaps efforts such as yours will contribute to preventing future wars.

Having been involved in the investigation and later the prosecution of war criminals at Dachau, I reviewed the evidence first hand. I have a set of the photographs taken by the Army Signal Corps when the concentration camp at Dachau was overrun by the Seventh Army. For example, these show that at a subcamp of Dachau, where Jews were held, the Nazis set fire to the barracks burning the Jews alive when it was certain that the camp would be taken by our forces. I have other materials which may be of interest to you. Should you find occasion to come by this way, let me know in advance if you are interested in seeing these materials. I will be happy to talk with you, and I encourage you to keep up your classes on this important history.

Sincerely yours,

Horace R. Hansen

HRH/smb
Enclosure

Appendix

Introduction, page 3, new paragraph 2:

See at left news clipping and example of hate mail that flooded Willmar, Minnesota, regarding William Borth's class about the Holocaust. Borth also received threats made by telephone to his home, prompting a report to the Federal Bureau of Investigation. The local school board named him "Teacher of the Year."

Introduction, page 3, new paragraph 3:

1. In regard to the powers of the president, the Constitution of the United States of America states: "The President shall be Commander in Chief of the Army and Navy of the United States, and of the Militia of the several States, when called into the actual Service of the United States."

2. In regard to regulation: The president or a person acting under him may draft a proposed regulation and publish it in the *Fed-*

eral Register with a period for comment by interested persons. The period varies depending on the nature of the regulation. After the period for comment, the executive issues the final regulation and publishes it in the *Federal Register*. It then becomes law until it is overturned by Congress or a court.

3.   In regard to executive order: An executive order is drafted by the president or upon his order. The regulations are codified in the United States Code—32 U.S.C. 501.1 and 501.2 state that action should be prompt and vigorous; 32 U.S.C. 501.2 states that the president shall determine what is top secret and lists almost everything; 32 C.F.R. 501.4 authorizes the president to declare martial law in event of civil disturbances; 32 C.F.R. 501.5 gives the president the authority to protect federal property and functions; 10 U.S.C. 502 states that each person enlisting in the armed forces shall take the following oath:

> I do solemnly swear (or affirm) that I will support and defend the Constitution of the United States against all enemies, foreign or domestic: that I will bear true faith and allegiance to the same; and that I will obey the orders of the President of the United States and the orders of the officers appointed over me, according to the regulation and the Uniform Code of Military Justice. So help me God.

Executive orders, which are practically limitless, can be overturned by Congress, but Congress is extremely reluctant to act (as in Desert Storm, for instance). Only Congress may declare war, but again this body is reluctant (something might go wrong), leaving the decision for military involvement to the president.

A court may overturn an executive order, but because of the long-standing presence of these orders and the large scope of many of them, a court would be extremely reluctant to act against the president.

Chapter 7, page 93, first text line:
According to Col. William D. Denson, chief trial judge advocate for the prosecution of the Dachau concentration-camp case:

"Heinrich Himmler, chief of the SS, assigned to one of his stalwarts, Theodor Eiche, the job of recruiting personnel for Dachau and the other camps. He wanted ruthless men to replace the initial Bavarian police guards. Eiche formed the Totenkopfverbaende (SS Death's Head Battalion). These units were recruited from the unemployed, off the streets of the cities like Berlin, Hamburg, and Munich. This scum, men known to have brutal natures, served as staff and guards in the concentration camps.

"These recruits, who couldn't make it in civilian life, were attracted by wages and the splendor of the black SS uniform. In their case, it was set off with a red fez with the design of a human skull beneath the swastika and a black silk tassel. The mentality of the group that administered these camps—down to the level of the guards and the functionaries who ran the work office and the secu-

rity office—bordered on pure bestiality, and it is inconceivable their conduct was necessary to maintain discipline.

"When these camps were first organized to make nonconformists into conformists to National Socialism, the emphasis was on discipline. The prisoners had to make their bunks and square the corners of their bedding, that sort of thing. And you had to be on time, you ran to this, you ran to that. No infraction of the rules was tolerated.

"Then the emphasis changed. It wasn't on discipline but on the need for armament work. So the Nazis set aside the concept of discipline to force the slave laborers taken from conquered countries to work. The guards had to and did exercise a certain dominance. Whenever you confine a man to work against his will, you need to exercise a certain amount of authority for him to appreciate that he's subject to your will—even to your whim and caprice. The result in the concentration camps was that brutality and sadism became the usual routine.

"It was routine brutality to tie a man spread-eagled to a table, called a whipping block, and beat his back with a stick and make him count his lashes in German, even if he was Polish or Hungarian and did not speak German. If the prisoner failed to count correctly, he was made to go back to one and start all over again. This was in many instances an execution because of the poor physical condition of the prisoners.

"The prisoner too weak from starvation and beatings to work was simply put to death by a bullet, then cremated in the ovens at Dachau or buried in mass graves. [The gas chamber at Dachau, built by prisoners, was sabotaged by prisoners during construction and was never operative.] Consequently, those who died at Dachau were executed by

Prisoners drag a body to the ovens at Dachau. See also next page.

other means or were transported to the gas chambers at Castle Hartheim, which served the Mauthausen concentration camp near Linz, Austria. The prisoners at Dachau called these transfers of prison-

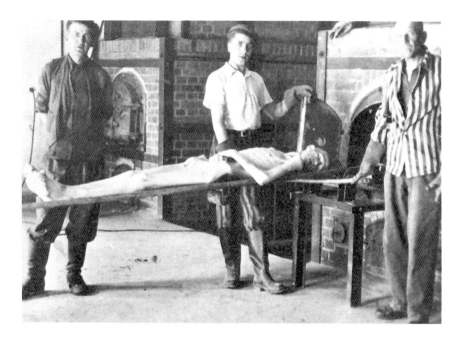

Dachau prisoners position the body of an emaciated comrade in the crematory.

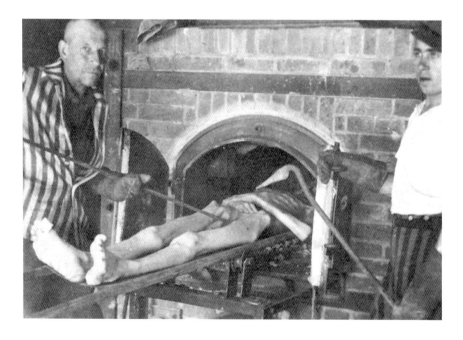

ers 'Heaven Transports.' The name came from the prisoners at Dachau who worked in the supply section. The Nazis received back the clothing and prosthetic devices, such as artificial legs and arms, of those prisoners who had left Dachau on these transports and who no longer had any use for these things because they were dead. These materials were recognized by the prisoners at Dachau when returned there for reuse. Both Buchenwald and Flossenburg camps had their own gas and cremation facilities."

Chapter 9, page 113, new paragraph 3:
According to Col. William D. Denson, chief trial judge advocate for the prosecution of the Dachau concentration-camp case:

"Guilt had to be established beyond reasonable doubt and to a moral certainty. This is the same standard used in the state and federal courts in the United States and in military government courts. We accorded the defendants the presumption of innocence, as in United States courts. That had not been afforded in German courts.

"I believe the way the military government courts handled these rules comported very favorably with our concept of providing due process. That is, each accused had a right to written charges, to a trial, a right to confrontation by his accusers, a right to be represented by legal counsel and a right to enter a plea of not guilty. If he did not plead, a plea of not guilty was entered for him. This automatically cast the burden on the prosecution to prove the offenses charged beyond a reasonable doubt and to a moral certainty.

"In the Dachau trial, all proceedings were conducted in both German and English as well as in the language of the witness then testifying, and the defendants had the right to cross-examine any witnesses against them. They also had the right to present evidence on their behalf and to testify themselves, or to remain silent. The defendants exercised these rights at the trial. The procedures were like those used in peacetime in any state or federal criminal court in the United States."

Chapter 9, page 116, new paragraph 1:
According to Col. William D. Denson, chief trial judge advocate for the prosecution of the Dachau concentration camp case:

"Karl Koch, kommandant at the Buchenwald camp, provided a flagrant example of how those in charge profiteered on human suffering. Tried, convicted in a German court late in the war for mistreating prisoners, and sentenced to be hanged, he was pardoned by SS chief Heinrich Himmler. Later he was tried, convicted, and executed for embezzling six million marks from the funds supplied to him for defraying the costs for maintenance of the camp, including food, clothing, and other needs of the prisoners. [Ilse Koch, Karl's wife, was notorious for making lampshades, gloves, and purses from tattooed human skin.]"

Chapter 13, pages 152, new paragraph 3, and 154, new paragraph 2:
According to Col. William D. Denson, chief trial judge advocate for the prosecution of the Dachau concentration camp case:

"The phrase *common design* derives from the common law of England. In order to justify receipt of evidence or testimony from witnesses who were there at various periods, but not at the same time nor continuously during that period of time, it was essential to have some mechanism that would permit receipt in evidence of that type of testi-

The author and Col. William D. Denson in New York, 1984.

mony. Also, the phrase is anathema to the superior-orders defense. In order to invoke the defense of superior orders, the act that is commanded must be of such nature, that if performed by the person to whom the order has been given, and is known to him to be illegal, he does not have to perform it. If he does such an illegal act, superior orders constitute no defense."

Chapter 18, page 201, new paragraph 3:
Col. William D. Denson, chief trial judge advocate for the prosecution of the Dachau concentration-camp case, said that learning to overlook brutality or even to become its perpetrator was the result for many of those who had to live and work in Hitler's Germany and in the camps:

"I recall an exceptional case in which a camp doctor came from a normal background. When he became a doctor he was sent with the German army to the Russian front, where he was wounded. Because of his wound, he was assigned to interior zone duty. He was sent to a medical unit in a concentration camp near Berlin—Oranienberg

[Sachsenhausen], I believe. There he was known as 'the angel of the camp.' Whenever a prisoner was really debilitated and absolutely worked down to a nub, this doctor would give him rest and rehabilitation, and the prisoner would be excused from going out on the work details. He did that for any prisoner, regardless of nationality or religion.

"Later, he was sent to Dachau, where he changed completely. He began to cuff prisoners around or report them to the guards for beatings. On one occasion he kept prisoners standing at the roll-call place for a number of days just after they had been brought into camp without having had any food or water. Many collapsed and died in their tracks.

"He was later transferred to the Buchenwald camp. That's where he started his butchering. If a man came to the hospital with an infection in his finger, the doctor wouldn't treat the infection; he just cut off the finger. If he saw a prisoner wearing a yellow triangle that had a black triangle superimposed on it [which meant Jew married to a Christian], he would say 'Kommen Sie hier' [come here]. If he felt like he wanted to increase his experience in the resection of a stomach, he would remove a part of the prisoner's stomach. If the prisoner lived, he was lucky. If he didn't, it made no difference. The change in the doctor's conduct was like a snowball rolling down a hill. The more he was exposed to the brutality prevalent in the camp, the more it rubbed off on him. He became a brute, despite his background. He was the son of a Lutheran minister and had been very compassionate in his early medical career.

"I suppose that change of conduct would happen to anyone, even you or me, if we lived in that kind of environment."

Glossary

AA. Anti-aircraft. Land-to-air missiles intended to disable or destroy enemy aircraft. Proximity to target aircraft triggers device.

Adjutant. Attendant to a commanding officer, used to accompany and help, in many ways.

Anti-Comintern Pact. Anti-Communist International Pact.

Antwerp, Belgium. The second seaport (after Normandy) used to supply Allied troops.

APO. Army Post Office.

Ardennes Offensive. Battle of the Bulge.

BBC. British Broadcasting Corporation. Principal radio voice for Allied forces.

Blitzkrieg. Literally lightning war, a sudden, all-out attack of such force as to assure victory.

Capo. A prisoner trusted to maintain order in the bloc (barracks) and to perform other duties assigned by a Death's Head guard in a concentration camp.

CO. Commanding Officer.

Commuted. Reduction of sentence for death or imprisonment.

C ration. A tin-can ration, usually of beef stew or beans with ham, carried by U.S. soldiers.

DP. Displaced person.

Dugouts. Large holes dug in the side of a hill or underground, heavily roofed or barricaded.

Engineerst. A special section of trained engineers, primarily building roads and bridges.

Flak. Fragments of an exploded cast-iron shell. Used in anti-aircraft, anti-personnel, and artillery shells.

Flares. A light attached to a small parachute, usually made of phosphorous.

Formation place or ground. Area of the concentration camp where prisoners line up or stand at attention, or report for roll call or duty.

Foxhole. Hole dug in ground to protect one or more soldiers from shrapnel and bullets.

Gauleiter. Leader of a *gau*, a larger division of the Nazi party. Usually centered in a large city.

Gear, normal. Backpack with blanket, underwear, toilet articles, and rifle.

Gestapo. Geheime Staatspolizei. Secret state police.

GI. Government Issue. Term applies to drafted U.S. soldiers. Nobody knows how it got started.

Hedgerows. Land boundaries developed by the Normans in the 11th century. Strips of trees and brush separate a pair of three-foot ditches dividing two-acre sections of land.

Heidelberg scar. A scar incurred in a fencing match.

Hitlerjugend. Hitler Youth.

HQs. Headquarters.

Ivans. Russian soldiers.

JAGD. Judge Advocate General's Department, a lawyer in command of a staff of lawyers and nonlawyers acting as clerks or typists.

Jeep. A "General Purpose" vehicle. The natural sound of GP.

Kreisleiter. Leader of a *kreis,* or district, a smaller division of the Nazi party. Sometimes a cluster of small towns, having one Burgomaster, one clerk, one vital recorders keeper, and so on.

Lebensraum. Living space for a greater Germany. Hitler's excuse for attempting to conquer Europe.

Maquis. French Resistance fighters.

MG. Military Government. A group on staff of a division, controlling civilians in conquered territory. Duties include maintenance of law and order, supervision of coasts, civilian supply, public health, money, banking, commerce, labor, education, records.

Mine. An explosive device, usually dug into the ground, close to the surface of the earth, intended to destroy tanks and other vehicles, or to cripple or kill soldiers. Triggered by pressure, slight when intended to blow off the foot of a soldier, greater when used to kill as in the case of a "Bouncing Betty."

MP. Military Police.

Napoleon, Bonaparte. French dictator who crowned himself emperor in 1804 and was defeated in his attempt to conquer Europe 1815, at Waterloo.

No Man's Land. The earth space between dug-in soldiers on both sides, usually mined.

NSDAP. Nationalsozialistische Deutsche Arbeiterpartei. National Socialist German Worker's Party. Nazi Party, for short.

Parade rest. A position with feet slightly apart, left arm at rest, and rifle held with right hand, muzzle up and butt at feet.

Phlegmon. Diseased blood.

Pontoon, steel. Airtight floating device with steel or wooden stringers on top, for use as a temporary bridge. Held by cables to either side of river. Strong enough to handle tanks, ducks, and other heavy vehicles.

POW camp. Prisoner of War camp. Place designed to detain captured enemy soldiers.

Pup tent. A tent made by connecting of two pieces of canvas, one carried by each soldier. Officers usually have a complete tent.

Redoubt, or National Redoubt. French word meaning secret place to conceal army and equipment. In text, meaning the Alps area abutting Bavaria.

Reichsleiter. Top-ranked person in Nazi party.

SA. Sturmabteilung. Stormtrooper units, also called brown shirts.

SD. Sicherheitsdienst. Security Service. Often worked with Waffen (armed) SS, mostly capturing individuals disloyal to Naziism.

Sepsis. A form of blood poisoning.

Siegfried Line. A line of fortifications, usually protecting a national border from invasion; or protection of a river from crossing. Named after a figure in German mythology.

Slave laborers. Persons taken from conquered territory by Germans and forced to work against their will in concentration camps in Germany and elsewhere. Used as replacements for German draftees, in direct violation of Hague Treaty.

Spitfire. British fighter plane.

SS Schutzstaffel. Guard detachment, containing the following:

1. Allgemein. Civilian SS. Diplomats, industrialists, doctors, law-yers,state employees, etc.

2. RSHA. National Security Office. Most important bureaus were Bureau III, the SD (Sicherheitsdienst, Security Service inside the Reich); Bureau IV, the Gestapo; and Bureau VI, Foreign Intelligence.

3. Waffen-SS. Armed SS.

4. Death's Head Battalion. Wore skull-and-crossbones on fez and black SS uniforms. Concentration camp guards.

Star of David. A six-point star used to identify person as Jewish.

Stars and Stripes. U.S. Army tabloid, usually of eight or more pages, giving information on U.S. troops and commanders, movements of the army including maps, and news from the States.

Static defense. Situation in which both sides of a conflict occupy trenches so that neither side may advance.

Strafe. Bullets fired in a stream, usually from an airplane. About every tenth bullet is a red tracer, enabling the pilot to see the direction of bullets.

Subcamps. Small camps housing slave laborers. Strung along a rail-road, highway or river, in woods, making parts to be assembled at a "mother" concentration camp, like Dachau. Designed to avoid Allied air bombing and artillery.

Ultra Secret. An American system for scrambling Allied radio mes-sages and unscrambling German messages. The Germans used the Enigma machine, a device that used three wheels set in like positions and changed daily.

Volkssturm. People's Militia, or home guard.

V-1. A heavy bomb, contained in a jet-powered missile, made to burst at a predetermined time (when a certain amount of fuel has been used or when the bomb runs out of fuel and explodes on impact).

V-2. A rocket propelled by fuel providing thrust. Loaded with a heavy bomb triggered by impact and faster than a plane. There was little defense against it other than barrage balloons anchored by cable to the ground.

WAC. Women's Army Corps, successor to the WAAC, or Women's Army Auxiliary Corps, started in May 1942.

Wehrmacht. The German army.

Index

Numbers listed in italics at the end of index entries indicate illustrations.

343